The Role of the
UNITED STATES
in a
CHANGING WORLD

Choices for the 21st Century

The Role of the United States in a Changing World: Choices for the 21st Century is a project of the Choices for the 21st Century Education Project of the Center for Foreign Policy Development, Brown University.

The Center for Foreign Policy Development is a nonprofit research organization at the Thomas J. Watson Jr. Institute for International Studies. The Center's mandate is to bring together scholars, practitioners, politicians, and the public in a search for policy choices that can lead to consensus on American national security and foreign policy. The Center is supported by private contributions, foundation grants, and Brown University.

Choices for the 21st Century Education Project was established to help citizens—student or adult—think constructively about foreign policy issues, increase public interest in foreign policy issues, improve participatory citizenship skills, and encourage public judgment on policy priorities.

Directing Staff, Center for Foreign Policy Development

Director:	Mark Garrison
Research Director:	Richard Smoke
Associate Director:	Alan Sherr
Assistant Director:	Deana Arsenian
Project Director:	Susan Graseck

Choices for the 21st Century Project
Center for Foreign Policy Development
Box 1948, Brown University
Providence, RI 02912

The Role of the
UNITED STATES
in a
CHANGING WORLD

Choices for the 21st Century

Written by Mark Lindeman and William Rose
with Mark Malkasian

DPG

The Dushkin Publishing Group, Inc.

About the Authors:

Mark Lindeman is a Jacob K. Javits Fellow in the Political Science department at Columbia University. He is a visiting research associate at the Center for Foreign Policy Development at Brown University and the author of *The United States and the Soviet Union: Choices for the 21st Century* (Guilford, CT: The Dushkin Publishing Group, 1990).

William Rose is associate professor of Government at Connecticut College, where he directs the International Relations major. He is a visiting research associate at the Center for Foreign Policy Development at Brown University and vice president of the Northeast International Studies Association. He is the author of *U.S. Unilateral Arms Control Initiatives: When Do They Work?* (Westport, CT: Greenwood Press, 1988).

Printed in the United States of America

Library of Congress Catalog Card Number 92-61523

International Standard Book Number (ISBN) 1-56134-110-X

First Edition, First Printing

Preface

The landmarks of international politics are being transformed at a dizzying rate. Many debates (and textbooks) from just a few years ago now seem trapped in obsolete assumptions. The Cold War rivalry between the United States and the Soviet Union, long a central axis of world politics, has abruptly dissolved. Russia no longer appears to be a plausible global rival despite its continuing nuclear strength. The superpowers' nuclear arms race, once of grave concern in the United States and many other countries, has fallen from most people's minds. Many Americans are now more concerned with other problems and issues, both abroad and at home. The central assumptions and purposes of U.S. foreign policy are now the subject of a great debate, both among citizens and in the expert community.

The Role of the United States in a Changing World: Choices for the 21st Century addresses these central questions head-on. Instead of treating each foreign policy issue separately, this book relates them to a single question: What role should the United States play in the post–Cold War era? By itself, such a broad question could be more overwhelming—or incoherent—than helpful. But the book provides college students of all levels with a framework they can use to confront the question constructively.

The book presents four alternative Futures, or long-term goals, for U.S. foreign policy. As students examine each Future, they will consider its historical roots and fundamental beliefs, economic costs, and near-term policy implications. They will weigh arguments, pro and con, concerning the Future's feasibility and impact upon the rest of the world. The Futures are neither predictions nor comprehensive prescriptions for U.S. policy. They work best as a springboard for helping students examine what constitutes a sound and stable foreign policy. After evaluating the Futures, students are asked to design a plausible Future of their own.

Future 1, *Standing Up for Human Rights and Democracy*, calls for the United States consistently to support democratic governments and movements, while opposing—at times with military force—brutal and aggressive tyrants. This Future holds that dictatorships pose the greatest threat to peace; therefore, promoting democracy, despite the costs, best serves U.S. interests and values. Future 2, *Charting a Stable Course*, calls for the United States to promote peace and stability in various regions through alliances and diplomatic initiatives. It argues that the United States may at times have to support stable but undemocratic governments, and encourages a central U.S. role in global politics. In Future 3, *Cooperating Globally,* the United States would collaborate with other nations to address global problems and promote common interests. This Future calls for the United States to accept limits on its sovereignty—for instance, its ability to intervene unilaterally in other countries—in order to foster cooperation. Future 4, *Building U.S. Economic Strength,* calls for profound reductions in military spending and the gradual elimination of U.S. troop deployments overseas. It argues that these moves may reduce U.S. influence abroad, but also will reduce the risk of war—and permit a massive shift of resources to solving the United States' social and economic problems.

Additional chapters examine the history of U.S. foreign policy, challenges facing the United States, the relationship between values and interests in U.S. foreign policy-making, analytical methods for addressing competing claims about how the world works, and the use of the Futures framework to help understand specific policy debates. Parts of these chapters are especially appropriate for students with little background in foreign policy studies. Other parts raise challenging issues for any audience. Each chapter is organized to focus student inquiry and provoke discussion and research. The text provides a questionnaire to promote considered judgments on beliefs, values, and policy priorities. Then it provides guidance to students developing a Future 5, and it presents a selected bibliography of useful resources, and a ballot that invites students to make their views known. An Instructor's Resource Guide offers suggestions for adapting the Futures to various class settings.

The Role of the United States in a Changing World is intended for all levels of college classes in international relations, U.S. foreign policy, and other courses treating these issues. This material does not assume any specific background in the topic matter, but encourages students to apply and build on their present knowledge. These materials can be used as units spanning several class sessions or as the framework for an entire course. They can be used to conclude a course or unit on related issues, or to introduce students at the beginning of the course to key issues that they will consider in more detail later.

Acknowledgments

Many people, at the Center for Foreign Policy Development and elsewhere, have worked over the years to formulate and apply a Futures framework to a variety of foreign policy issues. Here we can acknowledge only a handful of the Choices for the 21st Century Education Project's continuing collaborators. The Center's director, Mark Garrison, has given unwavering support to the Choices Education Project. Research director Richard Smoke has made important contributions at every stage.

Every member of the Choices Education Project has played a crucial role in the book's completion. Susan Graseck, project director, has provided guidance, encouragement, a healthy sense of perspective, and concrete suggestions. She is also a delight to work with. Mark Malkasian, curriculum coordinator and contributing author, wrote the historical chapter and weighed in on many difficult questions throughout the work. Project assistant Ashley Tucker carefully parsed the text for errors and weaknesses, and cheerfully tracked down missing facts. Research assistant Stephanie Marrone gave valuable comments on the treatment of international economics, and research assistant Richard Chang helped track down a variety of statistics and visual aids used in the text. Staff assistant Anne Campau Prout provided much-needed logistical support.

These Futures were first presented early in 1991 in a mini-unit for high school students. Karl Berger was the principal author of the high school text, and gave his time to help us improve the present one. Brown University professors Jo-Anne Hart and Mike Spagat helped refine the framework for the high school text, as did Mark Garrison and Richard Smoke. Center research associates Susan Eckert, Mark Kramer, and Stephen Shenfield gave useful guidance in their areas of expertise. Thomas Weiss, associate director of the Thomas J. Watson Jr. Institute for International Studies at Brown, also advised in developing the high school text.

The present text adapts the earlier presentation of the Futures, but is otherwise new. It was extensively reviewed by Mark Garrison, Richard Smoke, and Stephen Shenfield. Jo-Anne Hart and research associate Michael Song offered expert advice on several topics. Center editorial associate Lorraine Walsh provided her usual exhaustive commentary, greatly improving the finished product.

This text was made possible with support from the Ettinger Fund and an anonymous member of the Rockefeller family, and with institutional support from the Center for Foreign Policy Development.

Several instructors offered to test a prototype of the present text in their classes. Our thanks to William Anderson, Western Illinois University; Kevin Cassidy, Fairfield University; Richard Friman, Marquette University; Roger Hamburg, Indiana University at South Bend; Donald King, Dordt College; Eric Mlyn, University of North Carolina at Chapel Hill; Stephen Schwark, Sagamon State University; and Eugene Wittkopf, Louisiana State University. Thanks also to Bill Rose's students at Connecticut College, who warmed to the task of critiquing a professor's work in progress. Other important comments came from the following outside readers: Don Bakker, Nauset Regional High School; Michael Burlingame, Connecticut College; Alex Hybel, Connecticut College; Timothy Lomperis, Duke University; Stephen Schmidt, Connecticut College; and Steven Van Evera, Massachusetts Institute of Technology.

John Holland and Irv Rockwood at The Dushkin Publishing Group helped us to craft a readable text, and copy editor Robert Mill rooted out many lingering infelicities. We thank them for their professionalism and patience.

Our wives, Lucy Miller and Susan Rose, endured the late nights and weekends that were devoted to writing and refining various drafts. Lucy weighed in occasionally on questions of style, usually after 11 P.M. Sue prevented Michael Rose (18 months) from dissecting daddy's computer. Lucy and Sue also graciously refrained from sabotaging our modem connections. Now that this year-long project is completed, they'll be glad to get their spouses back into the swing of family life. Our many thanks for their emotional support, tolerance, humor, and friendship.

Mark Lindeman and Bill Rose
for the Choices Education Project

Contents

Introduction

There are periods of history when profound changes occur all of a sudden. . . . We are now in one of those periods, which obliges the United States to rethink its role in the world, just as it was forced to do by the cataclysmic changes that followed the end of the Second World War.

—Stanley Hoffmann, "What Should We Do in
the World?" *Atlantic* (October 1989)

How involved America should be in world politics and what values it should seek to foster—and at what cost and risk—are questions that remain open, unanswered, and largely unaddressed.

—Robert Jervis, "The Future of World Politics:
Will It Resemble the Past?" *International Security* (Winter 1991/92)

Today, the United States finds itself in a world that has fundamentally changed. For more than 40 years the United States and Soviet Union were the foremost powers and rivals in international affairs. Now the Soviet Union no longer exists, and its former republics seek U.S. aid. In all the decades of Cold War, few Americans had stopped to consider what would come next if the Cold War ended. Now the question must be confronted. What role will the United States play in the new world that is emerging?

The events and debates of the recent past point in contradictory directions. In the 1991 Gulf War, more U.S. troops went into combat roles than at any time since the Vietnam War. Yet with the Cold War's end, the United States was moving to make deep reductions in the defense budget—with considerable debate over what to cut and what to do with any savings. The Gulf War presented a paradox: although it involved broad international military and financial cooperation against Iraqi aggression, the United States largely determined the form of cooperation. In the future, will the United States be stronger than ever, or will it have to defer to other countries' preferences?

Some American observers see new opportunities and new dangers around the world. In the former Soviet Union, Eastern Europe, and elsewhere, democracy seems to be on the rise, although some new

1

governments are democratic in name only. With U.S. and Soviet/Russian cooperation, many regions have found or moved toward peaceful resolutions of disputes. Yet peace faces many challenges in the former Soviet bloc, where long-suppressed tensions have surfaced. Human rights abuses, poverty, and pollution threaten people around the globe, and Americans continue to learn about emerging ecological hazards like ozone depletion and possible global warming. At the same time, as the U.S. economy stumbles, many Americans are pressing for a new focus on economic and social problems at home. As a new era of world history begins, we find ourselves, as a nation, in need of redefining our long-term goals.

To gain a sense of a new role for the United States in this changed world, we must look deeply into the shared values that bind us together and define us as Americans. We also must examine our assumptions about how the world works and figure out ways to test our ideas. In sum, we must consider who we are as a nation and how the United States fits into an evolving international system.

Several basic purposes inform any effective foreign policy: to defend against outside attack or harm, to further national interests through geopolitical power and economic strength, and to defend or promote national values. However, many contradictory policies may fulfill these broad goals, and choosing among competing options requires value judgments. The responsibility of determining the general direction for U.S. foreign policy belongs to all Americans. Experts can clarify the goals and trade-offs the nation must consider, and lay out specific policy choices along with their costs and risks. But experts have no special insight into which goals should have priority and which risks are worth taking. These are decisions of national scope, which all Americans must make together.

The Four Futures

To bring this subject into clearer focus, the Choices for the 21st Century Education Project has produced a framework of four alternative images, or Futures, of the United States in the year 2005. A wide range of community groups, students, and scholars have used these Futures (and earlier versions of them) to focus their discussions. The Futures make contrasting assumptions about the nature of global affairs, especially with regard to the United States: the threats it faces, what its priorities should be, and the role it should play in the world. Based on these assumptions, each Future presents a goal for 2005, together with the policies that the United States would have to follow to attain it. These Futures are not predictions of what will actually happen, and they do not present every possible policy or important issue. They do, however, highlight plausible options for the future of the United States.

One goal of this text is to help you apply the methods of political science in order to form considered judgments on policy issues. You should critically assess contending assumptions and policy proposals, carefully examining historical evidence and other relevant facts. Look for ways to test your own ideas against the facts, and then ask whether those ideas can be made more specific or more accurate. When you finish, you may have a new sense of how complex these issues are. But you also should have found many of your own answers, and have a clearer sense of which questions are most important.

What Follows

The following chapter presents a history of U.S. foreign policy that focuses on three previous periods in which the United States debated and then decided to adopt a new role in the world. As you read the chapter, you should consider what arguments were being made for and against various policies, what values were at stake, and—more speculatively—how different decisions might have led to different outcomes. Some attention is paid to the role of public opinion in these decisions. However, the emphasis is more on the arguments than on why certain positions prevailed. Obviously, many aspects of the governmental process and domestic politics enter into foreign policy formation, but they are not the focus of this text.

Chapter 2 presents the four Futures themselves. Keep in mind that you may disagree with some details of a Future while still supporting its general direction. As you read each Future, be sure to consider both its strengths and its weaknesses. Your role is not that of a judge pronouncing "thumbs up" or "thumbs down" on each Future, but of a critical and creative thinker attempting to find the best answers to key analytical and policy questions.

Chapters 3 through 5 delve into central issues in more depth than the Futures alone permit. Chapter 3 focuses on threats and challenges facing the United States, along with some of its options for responding. Chapter 4 emphasizes the value trade-offs with which U.S. policymakers must come to terms, such as inevitable conflicts between U.S. ideals and self-interest. Chapter 5 illustrates some analytical tools that we can use to sort out more narrowly factual issues about the ends and means of policy, such as the questions, "Are democracies peaceful?" and "Do economic sanctions work?" Together, these three chapters present a wide range of issues and arguments, without prescribing policy conclusions, that should enter into informed judgments about the U.S. role in the world.

Chapter 6 returns to the Futures and explores their uses and limits for understanding current or prospective policy debates. Following this chapter is a matrix demonstrating differences among the Futures on several key issues. Chapter 7 asks your opinions on a wide range of threats, beliefs, and policies, as well as the Futures themselves. Necessarily the questionnaire takes the form of multiple choice, but many readers find that the questions resist simple answers. Indeed, the questionnaire should help you decide which questions have simple answers and which ones do not. Chapter 8 challenges you to form your own "Future Five," and provides some ground rules for making your Future as sound as possible. At the end of the book is a brief ballot that you can use to add your voice to a nationwide poll on this important subject.

CHAPTER 1

Critical Junctures in the History of U.S. Foreign Policy

n his farewell address of 1796, President George Washington responded to the question that again frames discussion of U.S. foreign policy: what role should the United States play in the world?

Washington conceived of the United States as a unique experiment—founded on democratic principles, safeguarded by the rule of law, and free from the sordid dealings of European politics. In his address, Washington warned Americans to "steer clear of permanent alliances, with any portion of the foreign world." He particularly feared treaties that would entangle the United States in European disputes and inject the rivalries of the Old World into U.S. domestic politics.

But Washington was also a realist. He recognized that the United States needed international trade in order to prosper. Future U.S. leaders, Washington maintained, should seek to extend the young republic's commercial relations while carefully avoiding political connections. The first president advised his successors to follow a policy that would allow the United States to develop arrangements that were "temporary, and liable to be from time to time abandoned or varied, as experience and circumstances shall dictate; constantly keeping in view that 'tis folly in one nation to look for disinterested favors from another."

Americans followed Washington's advice. The thought that governed U.S. policy for most of the nineteenth century was stated in the Monroe Doctrine of 1823, which declared a political divide between Europe and the New World. The United States avoided interfering in events in Europe, and demanded that European countries not establish new colonies in the Western Hemisphere. U.S. isolation from events overseas permitted the young nation to expand across the continent and take advantage of the bountiful resources within its borders.

Over the past two centuries, the United States has changed beyond George Washington's imagining. Events have compelled Americans to rethink the U.S. role in the world on a number of occasions. Over time, changes in the American scene—unmatched economic growth, ever-widening global power, waves of immigration, and startling social transformations—have inevitably left Americans wrestling with conflicting foreign policy ideas derived from various aspects of the American experience. Many Americans pride themselves on their idealism—their love of freedom, liberty, justice, and other noble ideals. At the same time, many applaud the clear-eyed pragmatism that helped make the United States a world power. Basic American political values affirm that human beings are capable of progress, but many Americans have little hope for much of the world outside U.S. borders. Such contrasts naturally enter into the foreign policy debate. Many Americans believe that the United States must play an active role in international politics, while others seek to keep it isolated from the turmoil and chaos of distant nations. One element within the American tradition holds that every country has the right to run its own affairs without outside interference; a contrary current of thought contends that the United States sometimes has the right and a duty to intervene around the world.

The complexities of American political thought are highlighted by the decision-making during three critical junctures in U.S. foreign policy: the debate over the fate of the Philippines and Cuba following the Spanish-American War; the debate over the United States' entry into World War I and role in the postwar world; and, following World War II, the debate over the global role of the United States. These were times of fundamental choice. In each case, when beliefs and values clashed, philosophical tensions were heightened.

The United States Looks Outward

The late 1800s marked a turning point for the position of the United States internationally. The nineteenth century had witnessed the country's explosive growth from a weak, isolated republic to the world's leading economic power. As the country changed, so did expectations about U.S. foreign policy.

Following the Civil War, the United States tentatively increased its involvement in international affairs. In 1867 it purchased Alaska from the Russians, and in the 1890s established a presence in the Pacific by acquiring Samoa and Hawaii. The most crucial foreign policy issue of the era, however, developed from the United States' confrontation with Spain over the island of Cuba. A great debate over U.S. imperialism followed.

Entering the Spanish-American War

In 1895 Cubans began to struggle for independence from Spain, which had ruled Cuba since the sixteenth century. The rebellion came at a time of fundamental change in the United States. Spurred by explosive industrial growth, millions of Americans poured into big cities. At the same time, millions of immigrants from Europe settled in urban centers. Mass-circulation newspapers, pioneered by William Randolph Hearst and Joseph Pulitzer, sprang up. Public schools provided free education for all. In Washington, policymakers struggled to keep up with the pace of change. More Americans were able to participate in political debates with the advent of mass literacy and the availability of newspapers.

The changes at home also spurred a rethinking of U.S. policy abroad. The United States' growing economy prompted it to develop commercial ties with virtually every region of the world. Many politicians and other leaders pressed for a stronger U.S. presence in international affairs to match the country's economic prowess. They were largely motivated by unabashed pragmatism, believing that U.S. foreign policy should plainly serve the commercial interests of the country. One such advocate was Captain Alfred Thayer Mahan, a U.S. naval officer. In 1890 he wrote a historical study entitled *The Influence of Sea Power Upon History*. According to Mahan, sea power was the key to protecting access to distant markets and hence national economic strength, and it helped provide military security. He called for a stronger navy, a canal across the Isthmus of Panama, U.S. dominance of the Caribbean, and control of Samoa and Hawaii. Mahan's view was adopted by many of the country's most influential policymakers. *Military Strategist*

Although such strategic issues were important in the debate over Cuba, the arguments of Mahan and a few Washington insiders had little impact on the U.S. public. For most Americans in the late 1890s, Cuba's struggle with Spain was an emotional issue. Most Americans resented the colonial powers of Europe in general, and Spain was especially reviled. Not only did the Spanish rule Cuba and Puerto Rico with a heavy hand, but many Americans saw the Spanish monarchy as backward and corrupt. These sentiments deepened when a Spanish army of 200,000 men set out to crush the Cuban rebellion in 1896. The Spanish attacked villages where support for the revolt was strong, and herded hundreds of thousands of peasants into fortified towns. They also burned fields of crops and slaughtered thousands of farm animals in hopes of starving out the rebels. The sensationalist newspapers of Hearst and Pulitzer inflamed the public with details of Spanish brutality at a time when photographs were just beginning to be a regular feature of the daily press. Pulitzer's *New York World* wrote: "Blood on the roadsides, blood in the fields, blood on the doorsteps, blood, blood, blood." When the U.S. battleship *Maine* exploded mysteriously in Havana Harbor in February 1898, the press rushed to blame the Spanish. Although President William McKinley had previously urged caution, he too became convinced that the United States should intervene in Cuba. In April 1898 he asked Congress to declare war.

Grant Hamilton, Judge, 1898.

The Spanish Brute Adds Mutilation to Murder

In 1898 cartoons depicting Spanish brutality in Cuba were common. This cartoon portrays Spain as a bloodthirsty, inhuman creature standing over the graves of sailors from the battleship *Maine*.

By the time the nation went to war, there was little opposition to fighting against Spain. The conflict itself proved equally one-sided, with the U.S. Navy playing a decisive role. On May 1, U.S. ships destroyed the Spanish fleet in the Philippines' Manila Bay to prevent it from joining the war in Cuba. In July, the United States crippled the Spanish fleet in Cuba. Without naval support, the Spanish forces on the island were soon forced to surrender. Called a "splendid little war" by Secretary of State John M. Hay, the fighting lasted only four months.

U.S. Policy Toward the Spanish Colonies

When the war ended, a national debate ensued. The United States, which had emphasized for the past century that it was itself a breakaway colony, now found itself in control of former Spanish colonial possessions. Americans had to decide what would happen to the Spanish colonial possessions of Cuba, Puerto Rico, the Philippines, and Guam. By the summer of 1898, President McKinley expressed his support for annexation of the Spanish possessions. Opinion was most divided on the fate of the Philippines. The islands themselves were of dubious value to the United States. Although Senator Albert Beveridge of Indiana spoke of the Philippines as "a base at the door of all the East," most Americans saw little advantage in possessing a poor country halfway around the world.

To generate public support for annexation, McKinley conducted a whistle-stop tour of the Midwest before the November elections of 1898. In his speeches, the president appealed to a sense of American duty and honor. "As I look into your earnest faces," he told a crowd in Indiana, "I know that you would have this nation help the oppressed people who have by the war been brought within the sphere of our influence." Duty and honor aside, annexation was supported by a new generation of strategically minded U.S. policymakers. Leaders like Senator Henry Cabot Lodge of Massachusetts and Theodore Roosevelt, then assistant secretary of the Navy, feared that if the United States did not annex the Philippines, Germany or Japan would. Although they had no desire to impose U.S. rule over the entire archipelago, Lodge, Roosevelt, and others saw the Philippines as a prime site for a naval base in the Far East. In the age of coal-powered ships, these bases were vital for naval and commercial vessels that needed to refuel when patrolling or shipping in distant seas. Roosevelt, in particular, believed that when the United States' economic interests were at stake, it could not remain isolated from international power struggles.

Opponents to annexation were not convinced. After the war, most Americans wanted U.S. troops to come home as soon as possible. An imperial role in the Philippines struck many Americans as contrary to the very ideals for which, they believed, the U.S. had fought. When it authorized McKinley to enter the war in April 1898, Congress had passed an amendment requiring the United States to grant Cuba self-government once the fighting was over. The public's distaste for Old World imperialism was even stronger. Less altruistically, many Americans also feared that the populations of annexed territories would eventually gain U.S. citizenship and hence political power.

In December 1898 Spain signed a treaty turning over Cuba, Puerto Rico, Guam, and the Philippines to the United States. McKinley and his allies had achieved a clear military and diplomatic victory abroad. To cement this victory on the home front, McKinley took his whistle-stop campaign to the South, lobbying hard for Senate ratification of the treaty. McKinley convinced many Americans that the United States could adopt a role of global stewardship without the evils of European imperialism. Most American religious journals spoke of rule over the Philippines as Americans' duty to bring Christianity and civilization to a backward part of the globe. At the same time, Senate opponents of the treaty argued that the Constitution forbade the United States from acquiring territory for purposes other than eventual statehood. Nevertheless, with public opinion favoring the treaty, William Jennings Bryan—leader of the opposition Democratic Party and an early opponent of annexation—concluded that rejecting the treaty would be a political mistake. The treaty narrowly received the required two-thirds majority for ratification in February 1899.

At the time, few Americans understood the complexities of establishing U.S. rule in the Philippines. Like the Cubans, the Filipinos had already been fighting for their independence from the Spanish when the United States entered the conflict. The leader of the Filipino forces, Emilio Aguinaldo, declared his country an independent republic in June 1898, two months before the U.S. Army forced the Spanish to surrender control of Manila. At this point, there was little reason for discord between the U.S. troops and the Filipino guerrillas. Both groups were happy to see the Spanish go and looked forward to rebuilding the islands.

By February 1899, however, Americans and Filipinos were at war. The shooting began two days before the Senate treaty vote when an American soldier fired on a Filipino patrol that refused orders to halt. Within hours, fighting had spread to much of the area around Manila.

Since the arrival of U.S. troops on the islands, the two sides had misunderstood one another and held incompatible goals for the post-Spanish Philippines. McKinley and other U.S. leaders assumed that the United States would annex the Philippines, taking on a dominant political role that would gradually advance Philippine society. Meanwhile, Aguinaldo had battled against colonialism since 1895 and felt that he had earned the right to govern an independent nation.

With the onset of the fighting between the Americans and Filipinos, McKinley dispatched additional troops to the islands, and by November

Detroit News, 1898.

How Some Apprehensive People Picture Uncle Sam After the War

Many people were concerned about what the implications of colonial rule would be for the United States. This cartoon depicts Uncle Sam struggling with unruly children. Other cartoons of this genre presented Uncle Sam as a figure of authority looking after young children.

The White Man's Burden

Take up the White Man's Burden—
  Send forth the best ye breed—
Go, bind your sons to exile
  To serve your captives' need;
To wait in heavy harness,
  On fluttered folk and wild—
Your new-caught, sullen peoples,
  Half-devil and half-child.

* * *

Take up the White Man's burden—
  No tawdry rule of kings,
But toil of serf and sweeper—
  The tale of common things.
The ports ye shall not enter,
  The roads ye shall not tread,
Go make them with your living,
  And mark them with your dead.

—Rudyard Kipling,
The Five Nations (1903)

1899 Aguinaldo's regular army had been shattered. But rather than concede defeat, Aguinaldo adopted guerrilla tactics, hoping gradually to wear down U.S. resolve. Americans were in fact unprepared to fight an enemy who had no uniforms or well-defined territories. The war dragged on until the middle of 1902. In the process, 4,200 Americans and 100,000 to 200,000 Filipinos were killed by war and disease. A U.S. force of 70,000 built bridges, cleared roads, and opened schools, but they also burned crops, tortured prisoners, shot civilians, and forcibly relocated villagers. Ultimately, the bloodiest part of the struggle took place after an attack on a U.S. garrison claimed 48 American lives. U.S. forces then crushed the resistance by destroying many villages from which the guerrillas drew support. In the words of one commander, the region was turned into a "howling wilderness."

The Literary Digest, 1898.

Civilization Begins at Home

News of the final stage of the war shocked newspaper audiences back in the United States. Many Americans had little idea why U.S. troops were fighting so far from home. The brutality of the last months of the war prompted congressional investigations into army tactics and the courts-martial of a number of U.S. officers. Anti-imperialist newspapers were quick to publish the most lurid accounts of army abuses, and many citizens were troubled by the essays of prominent Anti-Imperialist League members, such as the philosopher William James and the author Mark Twain. Finally the United States repressed the rebellion and established order in the Philippines. Stories of war atrocities soon faded from the news and public outrage diminished.

In Cuba, resistance to U.S. rule was also strong, although not violent. To protect U.S. business and security interests on the island, the United States granted Cuba only limited independence. Senator Orville Platt inserted an amendment into the new Cuban constitution. Known as the Platt Amendment, it gave Washington the right to oversee the Cuban economy, veto international commitments, and forcibly intervene whenever necessary "for the protection of life, property, and individual liberty." News of the proposed amendment sparked demonstrations and protests in Cuba, but the McKinley administration insisted that the Platt Amendment was the price Cubans would have to pay for ending U.S. occupation of the island. The amendment passed the Cuban assembly by one vote.

In the following decade, the United States consolidated its position as a strong regional power. U.S. troops intervened repeatedly in the countries of Central America and the Caribbean to protect U.S. interests. Meanwhile, U.S. technology overcame tremendous obstacles in building the Panama Canal. By the early 1900s, U.S. dominance over Latin America was unquestioned. Moreover, the United States had emerged as a force to be reckoned with in the Pacific and the Far East. And as many U.S. policymakers often noted, all of this had been accomplished with the United States acting unilaterally and remaining detached from the squabbles of Europe.

Questions to Consider

1. Why was the aftermath of the Spanish-American War considered a watershed in U.S. foreign policy?

2. What were the major options for the United States in deciding the fate of the former Spanish possessions? What beliefs and values supported the competing choices?

3. What was the outcome of this debate? What values were most strongly reflected in the path chosen, and which were compromised? How do you explain the outcome?

World War I Challenges Isolationism

When war broke out in Europe in August 1914, the overwhelming majority of Americans agreed that the United States should stay out of the conflict. American public opinion had always looked dimly on the ambitions of the great imperial powers of Europe. War was viewed as the inevitable result of the continent's complex web of alliances and secret treaties. Although many Americans feared the rising strength of Germany, they wanted no part in the fighting overseas.

President Woodrow Wilson led the effort to keep the United States detached from the war. Wilson feared that taking sides would not only drag the United States into the European conflagration, but also aggravate tensions among ethnic groups at home. "The United States must be neutral in fact as well as in name during these days that are to try men's souls," he told the nation. "We must be impartial in thought as well as in action." To emphasize his point, Wilson had 60,000 copies of his statement on neutrality printed in four languages and displayed in post offices nationwide.

In less than three years, however, Wilson came before Congress to ask for a declaration of war against Germany. The president's transformation from a proponent of neutrality to an advocate of war parallels the shift in public opinion between August 1914 and April 1917. As president, Wilson expressed the views held by most Americans of his time. Deeply held moral principles were the bedrock of his personal outlook, and he saw no need to compromise those values in his foreign policy. At the core of Wilson's convictions was the belief that the United States had a special mission in the world: American values—democracy, freedom, and justice—were the right of all humankind.

Wilson based his "democratic" theory of international relations on a set of principles: peace, self-determination, the rights of small nations, the superiority of public opinion over diplomatic machinations, and an emphasis on international cooperation to counter narrow national interest. In 1914 these principles led Wilson and the country to turn away from the conflict in Europe. Yet in 1917 the United States went to war to promote these same ideals. During the interval, a broad array of forces had pushed Wilson and the country to take sides against Germany.

The Road to War

The cultural affinity between the United States and Great Britain is one important reason the United States sided with Britain against Germany. The two countries shared a common language and democratic traditions. Furthermore, British trade was vital to the American economy. To help protect its "special relationship" with the United States, the British cut the transatlantic cable that brought news from Germany directly to the United States. From the early stages of the war, the British controlled the flow of information that the United States received about Europe.

Germany's military strategy also turned American opinion against Germany. In 1914 Great Britain had the most powerful navy in the world.

The British intended to starve Germany into submission by blockading shipments of food to Germany. To this end, the British mined the North Sea to prevent merchant vessels, including ships of neutral nations, from reaching Germany and her neighbors. To counter British naval might, Germany relied on its fleet of submarines, or U-boats (*Unterseeboote*). In February 1915 the Germans declared the waters around the British Isles a war zone. Neutral ships were advised not to enter the area. Berlin also took out advertisements in U.S. newspapers, warning Americans not to travel on British ships. U.S. leaders differed on how to respond to the German threat to American citizens. Secretary of State William Jennings Bryan hoped to make it illegal for Americans to sail on British ships. Wilson, however, insisted that under international law Americans had the right to travel on any ship. The president pledged that Germany would be held accountable for the loss of American lives.

On May 7, 1915, a German U-boat torpedoed the British luxury liner *Lusitania* off the coast of Ireland. The attack killed 1,198 people, including 128 Americans. Although the ship had been flying a U.S. flag, it was carrying 4,200 cases of small-arms ammunition and 1,250 artillery shells. Few Americans knew of the ship's cargo. Instead, the country was outraged that the liner was sunk without warning. In September the Germans promised not to attack unarmed liners, after two more Americans died in the sinking of a British ship. Nevertheless, the attacks had done irreparable damage to the German image in the United States.

The *Lusitania* sinking prompted Wilson to take a tentative step on the road to war. Publicly, the president continued to oppose U.S. involvement, arguing that the country was "too proud to fight." Nevertheless, in the summer of 1915 Wilson launched a low-key campaign to improve U.S. military preparedness. His hope was to build a volunteer army, but by January 1916 he was forced to recognize that the popular response was lukewarm. Wilson decided to take his appeal to the people. In a nationwide speaking tour, he warned that "the world is on fire" and lamented "how difficult it [had] been to maintain peace." Crowds of up to one million turned out to hear the president, and support broadened for a stronger national defense.

Wilson was far from beating the drums for war. In the 1916 presidential race Wilson campaigned under the slogan "He kept us out of war." The Republican candidate, Charles Evans Hughes, also took a cautious position on U.S. involvement overseas. After a narrow electoral victory, Wilson renewed his efforts to achieve a peace settlement in Europe. On January 22, 1917, he called on the warring countries to accept his plan for "peace without victory." Nine days later, Germany smashed the president's hopes for peace by announcing a resumption of unlimited submarine warfare. Germany decided that its U-boats could force Great Britain to surrender before the United States could aid the Allies. Wilson felt he had no choice but to sever relations with Germany. In a further blow to Germany, the British intercepted a note written by

Oscar Edward Cesare, *The Sun*, 1915.

Out of the Depths

This cartoon shows the British luxury liner *Lusitania* being forked out of the water by Death, wearing a German (Prussian) helmet.

the German foreign minister, Arthur Zimmermann, to the German ambassador in Mexico. The note revealed Zimmermann's plan to draw Mexico into the war against the United States in return for German help in regaining the states of Texas, New Mexico, and Arizona. The day after receiving the dispatch, Wilson ordered the arming of U.S. merchant ships.

Even as the United States headed toward war, Americans showed little desire to enter the conflict. Wilson, too, was ambivalent. The president was much more interested in crafting peace than waging war.

As early as May 1916 he proposed the formation of an international body to uphold his cherished values, and advised Americans that a substantial U.S. role in the postwar world was inevitable. He offered a peace plan based on the equal rights of nations, the liberty of all people to determine their own government, freedom of the seas, and global limits on armaments. Ultimately, Wilson maintained that war against the Central Powers was the only way to achieve these objectives. After German U-boats sank three U.S. merchant ships in March 1917, Wilson asked Congress for a declaration of war. On April 2 he proclaimed that "the world must be made safe for democracy. Its peace must be planted upon the firm foundations of political liberty."

The United States at War

Although the resolution for war easily passed Congress, the United States remained in many ways a divided nation. Speaking to the Senate on April 4, 1917, Senator George Norris of Nebraska expressed the common belief that arms manufacturers, stockbrokers, and bond dealers stood to profit enormously by the entry of the United States into the conflict. He maintained that financial interests and the munitions industry were behind efforts to control the press "in the greatest propaganda that the world has ever known, to manufacture sentiment in favor of war."

Once the United States declared war, those who continued to oppose the war came under intense political pressure to conform. Some even faced challenges to their patriotism. Theodore Roosevelt, for example, charged that by questioning U.S. participation in the war, Wisconsin senator Robert LaFollette, Jr., was "loyally and efficiently serving one country—Germany." Nevertheless, despite a public backlash against all things German, few Americans were enthusiastic about fighting in Europe. In the first six weeks after the U.S. declaration of war, only 73,000 men volunteered. The president had called for an army of one million. Without sufficient volunteers, Congress was compelled to institute a draft.

At the same time, Wilson created a Committee on Public Information headed by a journalist, George Creel, to build public support for the war. The committee succeeded in injecting the Wilson administration's view of the war into the American press. New laws, including the Sedition Act of 1918, allowed the government to jail war critics.

Wilson's Peace Plans and the Return to Isolationism

Despite continued opposition at home, more than one and a quarter million U.S. troops reached France between June 1917 and the fall of

1918, and were decisive in forcing Germany to agree to an armistice in November 1918. Even before the conflict was decided, Wilson was drafting a plan for the peace. In January 1918 he announced a proposal to reshape international relations. Wilson's Fourteen Points restated his principles of self-determination, open diplomacy, freedom of the seas, free trade, and arms control. His proposal envisioned an association of nations that would guarantee the political independence and territorial integrity of all countries.

The Germans sued for peace on the basis of the Fourteen Points. At the Peace Conference in Paris, Wilson sought fair treatment of Germany and rights for oppressed nations in the face of French, British, and Italian interests. He also made sure that a global association of nations was included in the peace settlement. When Wilson returned to the United States in July 1919, he was greeted by cheering crowds and an escort of warships. He assumed that even his adversaries in the Senate would approve the Versailles Treaty worked out in Paris.

Wilson proved badly mistaken. He had failed to consult with leading Senate Republicans in developing his Fourteen Points, nor did he invite any of his political rivals to accompany him to Paris. More importantly, he had disregarded Americans' long-standing distaste for international entanglements. Senate Republicans, led by Henry Cabot Lodge, objected most strongly to the formula for the League of Nations. Under Article 10 of the treaty, League members would be required to come to the defense of any member under attack. The United States could be compelled to fight to preserve the borders of a French colony in Africa or protect British imperial interests in India.

Wilson might have been able to overcome objections to the treaty through negotiation and compromise with its opponents, but he had no intention of giving in on his basic principles, and his relations with his critics verged on mutual contempt. Rather than negotiate with the Senate, Wilson sought to rally public opinion behind the treaty. In September 1919 he traveled 8,000 miles by rail, giving 40 speeches in 29 cities during the course of a three-week speaking tour. Wilson emphasized that the United States had a moral obligation to take an active international role by joining the League of Nations. The president's oratorical power, however, was silenced by a debilitating stroke. Partially paralyzed, Wilson was unable to shape the Senate debate on the treaty and refused to consider amendments. In March 1920 the treaty was defeated in the Senate by a vote of 38 for and 53 against.

After this rejection of Wilson's vision, the country returned to its prewar isolationism. Americans in 1920 elected a prominent opponent of the League of Nations, Republican Warren G. Harding, largely on his pledge to return the country to "normalcy." But whereas before 1914 isolationism had been accepted almost instinctively by the vast majority

John T. McCutcheon, *The Tribune* (Chicago), 1918.

Interrupting the Ceremony

of Americans, the policy was supported with a more urgent, often defensive fervor during the interwar years (1918 to 1941). The establishment of communism in the Soviet Union, the rise of fascism in Europe, and the economic chaos of the Depression led many Americans to consider the outside world more dangerous than ever, and they were determined not to become involved in foreign conflicts. In the mid-1930s Congress passed a series of laws to prevent the United States from becoming embroiled in another war. For example, Americans were prohibited from shipping arms to nations at war. Some members of Congress suggested that the Constitution be amended to require a popular vote before Congress could declare war.

Questions to Consider

1. What foreign policy values did President Woodrow Wilson represent?
2. How did these values keep the United States out of war in 1914 and cause it to declare war in 1917?
3. After the war, what view of the U.S. role in the world competed with Wilson's? What beliefs and values supported it?
4. What was the outcome of the debate, and how do you explain it?
5. How did the U.S. Senate's rejection of participation in the League of Nations affect U.S. foreign policy during the interwar years?

The United States Assumes Superpower Status

Few observers could have guessed that a country so determinedly isolationist in 1940 would by 1950 take a leading role in the struggle against Soviet and communist expansion. And just after World War II, few Americans expected, or were ready to support, a dominant global role for the United States in the post–World War II era.

When World War II began, the debate in the United States was eerily reminiscent of World War I. Although most Americans empathized with Great Britain against Hitler's Germany and its allies, they nonetheless opposed direct U.S. involvement. Instead, the country went along with President Franklin D. Roosevelt's cautiously pro-British policy. In early 1941 Roosevelt won approval of the Lend-Lease program, which provided $7 billion in aid to Great Britain. The president insisted that Lend-Lease would keep the United States out of the war, a claim bitterly contested by isolationists. But events in Asia, not Europe, eventually brought the United States into the war. When Japan attacked Pearl Harbor on December 7, 1941, the United States immediately responded to the call to arms. In the next four years, the nation purposefully focused its enormous resources on the goal of defeating Germany, Japan, and Italy. Even fears of the Soviet Union were put aside in the name of a common alliance against fascism.

The Debate Begins Over the U.S. Role in the World

When the fighting finally ended in 1945, the United States stood unrivaled as the strongest nation on earth. Not only did the country escape having to fight the war on its own soil, but the United States possessed the only atomic weapons and the most advanced military. U.S. industry had surged forward during the war years, producing much of the equipment necessary for Allied victory. To many Americans, however, peace represented an opportunity to withdraw again from the center stage of world affairs. With the surrender of Japan in August 1945, President Harry S. Truman faced strong public pressure to bring U.S. troops home and demobilize the country's military force of 12 million men and women. Truman moved quickly to return soldiers to civilian life. By 1947 the military had been cut to 1.4 million people.

Even as the military demobilization proceeded, many U.S. policy-makers feared that another war was looming. Despite huge losses, the Soviet Union emerged from World War II as the world's second most powerful country. In helping to defeat Nazi Germany, the Soviet army swept over Eastern Europe. After the war the Soviets remained in Eastern Europe and took steps to control the states in the region.

Experts disagree on why the Soviet Union sought to control Eastern Europe. Some say the Soviets were mainly after a protective layer of small states that could serve as a buffer between the USSR and the West. Nature provides no natural defenses in the region; an unbroken plain stretches from France all the way across Central Europe and deep into Russia. Early in the nineteenth century Napoleon invaded Russia and destroyed much of the capital. Twice in the twentieth century Germany invaded, forcing Russia to surrender extensive territories in World War I and causing 20 million Soviet deaths in World War II. Thus, the argument goes, the Soviet dictator Joseph Stalin wanted to ensure that invading forces would not reach Russia again. By controlling the states near his border, he established a barrier against new attacks from the west.

Other experts disagree, claiming that Soviet efforts to control the region reflected aggressive Soviet intentions, or at least paranoia on Stalin's part. Even if Soviet actions were primarily defensive, however, from the perspective of Western Europe and the United States they appeared ominous, since they increased the Soviet Union's ability to invade Western Europe. In February 1946 Stalin predicted a future conflict between communism and capitalism and called on his people to make additional sacrifices, further increasing suspicion of his intentions. The Soviet armed forces remained formidable, maintaining an army of three to four million in 1947.

Stalin sought more territorial gains while resisting integration in the international economy. In early 1946 he announced that Soviet troops would continue to occupy northern Iran, despite a prior pledge to pull out after the war. Stalin also demanded that Turkey grant the Soviets partial control of vital sea lanes and give the Soviet Union part of its territory. U.S. and British pressure, backed by the presence of a U.S. aircraft carrier, forced Stalin to give in. Later in 1946 the Soviets rejected a one-billion-dollar loan from the United States and refused to join the U.S.-supported International Monetary Fund and the World Bank.

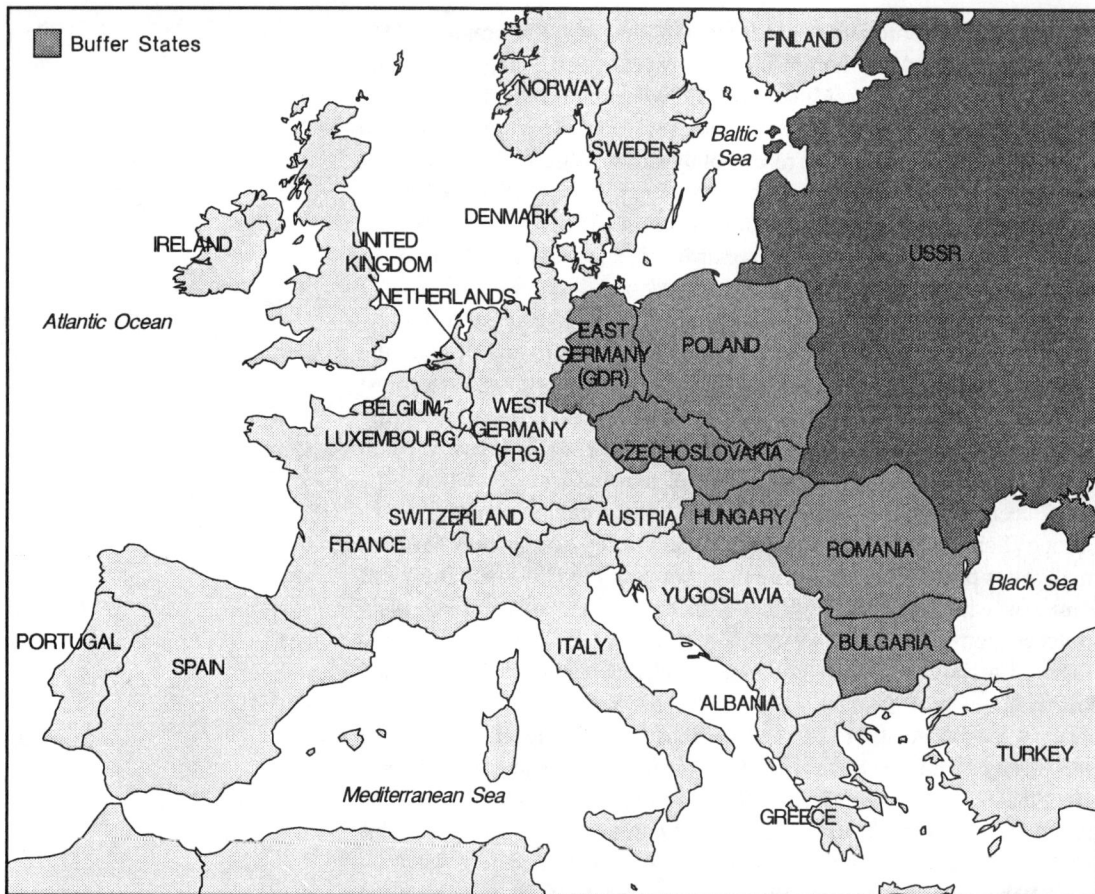

The Soviet Union's Buffer States After World War II

Some experts argue that Stalin wanted to control the states near his borders as a protection against an attack from the West. Others argue that Soviet actions in Eastern Europe reflected aggressive Soviet intentions toward Western Europe.

In March 1946 Sir Winston Churchill argued that the Soviets were dividing the world into two camps. In a speech delivered in Fulton, Missouri, the former British prime minister said: "From Stettin in the Baltic to Trieste in the Adriatic, an iron curtain has descended across the Continent. Behind that line lie all the capitals of the ancient states of Central and Eastern Europe. Warsaw, Berlin, Prague, Vienna, Budapest, Belgrade, Bucharest, and Sofia, all these famous cities and the populations around them lie in what I must call the Soviet sphere."

Churchill's "iron curtain" metaphor jolted many Americans. U.S. leaders were especially concerned: they realized that Britain was no longer strong enough to counter Soviet adventures. World War II had cost Britain one-fourth of its net worth. After the war ended, the British continued to spend billions to maintain troops in the Middle East, Greece, and Turkey, and to provide humanitarian relief in Germany. Less than two weeks before Churchill's speech, the British had informed Truman that they would have to reduce their presence in Greece and Turkey. After dominating the international scene for two centuries, the British empire was in retreat. An enormous power vacuum was opening up in global politics, and Churchill felt that the Soviets were moving quickly to exploit his country's weakness.

Regardless of the danger, the United States was hardly prepared to fight another war. At a meeting of the Allies in Yalta in 1945, President Roosevelt had told Churchill and Stalin that the American people would not permit U.S. troops to remain in Europe for more than two years after the war. U.S. foreign policy lacked a solid foundation from 1945 to 1947, while Americans reconsidered their country's role in the world.

U.S. Policy Toward the Soviet Union: Containment or Cooperation?

Among those who contributed most to the debate over the United States' relationship with the Soviet Union was George F. Kennan. One of the few Soviet specialists trained in the United States during the 1930s, Kennan had served at the U.S. embassy in Moscow during World War II. As early as 1944 he advised the U.S. ambassador to the Soviet Union, Averell Harriman, that postwar Europe would be divided into U.S. and Soviet spheres. Conflict, he believed, would inevitably result. In February 1946 Kennan put down his thoughts in a long memorandum to the State Department. The memorandum was circulated widely among U.S. policymakers; it provided the intellectual moorings for many who mistrusted the Soviet Union. Kennan believed that the Soviet system was based on a paranoid hostility toward the outside world. According to his view, cooperation between the United States and the Soviet Union was impossible. Instead, Americans should work to contain the expansion of Soviet power throughout the world. Moreover, only the United States was strong enough to balance Soviet power.

Kennan's argument was put to the test in Europe and the Mediterranean. The Soviet Union and its allies aided communist parties in the war-ravaged West European countries. France and Italy already had strong communist parties, and major labor strikes might have brought the communists to power or at least into coalition governments. Meanwhile, Turkey faced communist guerrillas and pressures from the Soviet Union to concede part of its territory, and Soviet allies provided weapons and other aid to armed revolutionaries in Greece. Many Europeans and Americans feared that the Soviet Union might dominate all of Europe through a combination of military force and political influence. Kennan and his allies favored strong U.S. action to oppose communism. Yet the national mood showed little interest in intervention. In the elections of 1946 Republicans gained control of the House and Senate largely by promising tax cuts. Even politicians who stressed their willingness to stand up to communism shied away from committing U.S. troops or financial aid.

Within the Truman administration as well, U.S. foreign policy was not settled. Most, like Secretary of State James F. Byrnes, favored a "get tough" policy toward the Soviets. Others, particularly Secretary of Commerce Henry Wallace, wanted a more conciliatory policy. In a speech delivered in September 1946, Wallace riposted: " 'Getting tough' never brought anything real and lasting—whether for schoolyard bullies or businessmen or world powers. The tougher we get, the tougher the Russians will get." Also, in a 1946 letter to *The New Republic*, Wallace argued that the U.S. monopoly on the atom bomb and its efforts to build military bases overseas seemed to the Soviets like aggressive moves threatening the Soviet Union. In his view, the United States' ideological support for democracy in Eastern Europe only deepened Soviet suspicions. The Soviets feared that the United States was trying to surround the Soviet Union with unfriendly neighbors, who might eventually attempt to destroy it. Wallace believed that the United States should focus on removing "any reasonable Russian grounds for fear, suspicion and distrust"—not on building up against the Soviet threat. Byrnes objected that Wallace's expression of such views undermined U.S. foreign policy. Truman concurred and dismissed Wallace from the cabinet.

The Pillars of the United States' Containment Policy

By early 1947 President Truman was convinced that the United States had no choice but to assume a more active role internationally. He and his advisers feared that West European countries would soon run out of money to pay for U.S. goods, thus sending the world economy into a downward spiral. The situation in Greece and Turkey was also becoming more worrisome.

Truman believed that by themselves these dangerous regional problems would little impress Americans. Moreover, public opinion was unsympathetic toward the idea of the United States seeking to balance Soviet power. If they were to support an active foreign policy, the public had to believe that basic values, such as freedom, were threatened. Thus the Republican chairman of the Senate Foreign Relations Committee warned Truman that he must "scare the hell out of the American people" if he wanted Congress to pass a bill aiding Greece and Turkey. Truman therefore presented his concerns in the context of a global challenge from Soviet communism. He met with the most likely opponents of his policy, congressional Republicans, and called on them to help "free peoples" oppose "totalitarian regimes." The president formally announced what came to be known as the Truman Doctrine (see sidebar on p. 24) on March 12, 1947, when he requested and received economic and military aid from Congress for Greece and Turkey. This doctrine became a pillar of the United States' emerging postwar strategy of containing the Soviet Union and communism.

Another pillar of containment was the Marshall Plan, developed from a proposal unveiled in July by the new secretary of state, George C. Marshall. The Marshall Plan was a massive economic assistance program designed to rebuild Europe. Even the Soviets were invited to participate, although they did not accept. The Plan became the centerpiece of a national debate in 1947 and 1948. Across the country, hundreds of town hall meetings were called to discuss the future of U.S. foreign policy. Congress debated the Marshall Plan for 10 months.

Roy Justus, *The Minneapolis Star,* 1947.

Step on it, Doc!

On one side of the issue were proponents of U.S. global leadership, including the White House, the State Department, and the War Department (soon to be renamed the Department of Defense). They believed that rebuilding Europe would not only provide markets for U.S. exports, but would also strengthen the European public's support for democratic institutions. Without substantial U.S. assistance, they feared, Western Europe would be vulnerable to radical movements and communist takeovers.

The Truman Doctrine

At the present moment in world history nearly every nation must choose between alternative ways of life. The choice is too often not a free one.

One way of life is based upon the will of the majority, and is distinguished by free institutions, representative government, free elections, guarantees of individual liberty, freedom of speech and religion, and freedom from political oppression.

The second way of life is based upon the will of a minority forcibly imposed upon the majority. It relies upon terror and oppression, a controlled press and radio, fixed elections, and the suppression of personal freedoms.

I believe that it must be the policy of the United States to support free peoples who are resisting attempted subjugation by armed minorities or by outside pressures. . . .

Should we fail to aid Greece and Turkey in this fateful hour, the effect will be far reaching to the West as well as to the East. . . .

The free peoples of the world look to us for support in maintaining their freedoms.

If we falter in our leadership, we may endanger the peace of the world—and we shall surely endanger the welfare of this Nation.

—President Truman
to a joint session of Congress,
March 12, 1947

This internationalist position was opposed by several distinct currents of thought. Speaking from a traditionally conservative viewpoint, Senator Robert Taft of Ohio feared that taking on new international responsibilities would inflate the budget and give the military too much power. Much closer to the Truman administration's thinking was Walter Lippmann, a respected political commentator and advocate of hard-nosed realism in foreign affairs. Lippmann shared Truman's deep mistrust of Moscow but felt that the realities of the postwar world compelled the United States to avoid confrontation with the Soviet Union while maintaining its commitment to promote democracy. Meanwhile, Henry Wallace voiced the opinions of many liberals, arguing that Truman's policies would "give guns to people when they want plows" and "divide Europe into two warring camps."

Wallace also forwarded an alternative, cooperative version of internationalism. He recalled the international good will that prevailed at the Yalta Conference in 1945, when the Soviets agreed to support the U.S. vision for the United Nations. At the time, President Roosevelt saw the United Nations as "a universal organization in which all peace-loving nations will fully have a chance to join." Roosevelt predicted that the United Nations would replace "the system of unilateral action, the exclusive alliances, the spheres of influence, the balances of power" and other mechanisms of conventional foreign policy. Wallace believed that this original conception of the United Nations was applicable. In the 1948 presidential campaign he took his message to the people as the Progressive Party candidate, but lost overwhelmingly.

To a large extent, criticisms of Truman's policies were undercut by hostile Soviet actions. In 1948 the Soviets sponsored a coup to topple the government in Czechoslovakia and imposed a blockade of West Berlin to force the Allies out of the city. Americans were wary of becoming entangled in international affairs. But in the face of threatening Soviet behavior and vulnerable Western European countries, they were even more worried about repeating the mistakes of the past two decades: the reluctance of Western democracies to stand up to the Nazis during the 1930s, and the decline of international trade that contributed to the Great Depression.

In April 1948 the Marshall Plan became law. Over the next four years, the United States devoted 12 billion dollars (equivalent to 64 billion dollars in 1991 dollars) to European recovery, mostly in the form of grants that did not have to be repaid. Equally important was the establishment of the North Atlantic Treaty Organization (NATO) in 1949, comprising the United States, Canada, Iceland, and many Western European countries. The United States pledged to come to the defense of any NATO country under attack—the first time the United States had made such a commitment in peacetime. NATO cemented the U.S.

commitment to European security and clearly drew a line that Moscow could not overlook. Although President Roosevelt had said U.S. troops would be out of Europe within two years after the war, Truman committed them to stay. NATO thus became the third pillar of the U.S. containment policy.

Containment Becomes Global

The Truman Doctrine, the Marshall Plan, and NATO—the three pillars of containment—thrust the United States into a new era of international involvement. Initially the United States focused on containing Soviet expansion in Europe, but by the end of the 1940s U.S. policymakers began to see a global threat. Two events in 1949 left a particularly deep impression on Washington. In September the Soviets successfully tested their first atomic bomb, ending the U.S. monopoly on the weapon. The Soviet Union was now becoming a potent adversary in nuclear capability, as well as ideology. The next month, communists led by Mao Zedong claimed control of mainland China and declared their allegiance to the expansion of communism worldwide. With the growing strength of the Soviet bloc, U.S. policymakers were forced to reassess U.S. military strength. They concluded that the country needed to build up its defenses—both nuclear and conventional—to meet its international commitments. The beginning of the Korean War in June 1950, when communist North Korea attacked non-communist South Korea, strongly reinforced this viewpoint and set off a massive U.S. military buildup.

During the Korean War, U.S. troops fought to protect South Korea from communist domination and to demonstrate U.S. credibility as a defender of the non-communist world. A secondary reason was to stand up for the UN principle of nonaggression. The United States led the UN operation to restore the peace, and small contingents of troops from additional countries joined the United States and South Korea to fight the North Koreans (and later the communist Chinese). Most Americans considered Korea largely a stage for the much larger struggle between the United States and the Soviet Union. For the next four decades, this Cold War perspective would frame nearly every U.S. foreign policy question.

The Cold War spurred the United States to develop regional security pacts throughout the globe. U.S. troops and nuclear weapons were sent to protect Europe. U.S. aid and favorable trade agreements helped Japan to rebuild its economy and achieve political stability. Ultimately, the United States created defense alliances with more than 50 countries and maintained more than half a million troops overseas.

Questions to Consider

1. In the 1945–48 debate over the U.S. role in the postwar world, what were the major options? What beliefs and values supported each?
2. Which positions won and lost, and why did this outcome occur?
3. Why did the Cold War occur? To what extent are the Soviet Union and the United States responsible? How much of the conflict was due to the postwar geopolitical situation, in which each super-power's efforts to increase its security and power necessarily undermined the security and interests of the other?
4. When and why did the United States' containment policy become global?

From Vietnam to the Cold War's End: Historical Context for the Future

The United States' Cold War policies continued for almost 40 years after the Korean War began, but important variations occurred within this period. Highly influential events and policies include the following: the Vietnam War and its aftermath, President Richard M. Nixon's détente and President Jimmy Carter's human rights policy, and a renewal of the Cold War and finally its decline during the administration of President Ronald Reagan.

The Trauma of Vietnam

The involvement of the United States in Vietnam grew out of U.S. Cold War policies. Policymakers feared that a victory of the communist North Vietnamese over South Vietnam would lead to other communist takeovers throughout Southeast Asia—the so-called "domino effect." During the 1950s the United States supplied South Vietnam with substantial military aid. In November 1961 President John F. Kennedy committed the first 7,000 U.S. troops, officially designating them as advisers. President Lyndon B. Johnson gradually moved to broaden U.S. involvement and met little opposition at home. When North Vietnamese gunboats attacked U.S. destroyers in the Gulf of Tonkin in August 1964, Johnson sought congressional authorization "to take all necessary measures to repel any armed attack against the forces of the United States and to prevent further aggression." The resolution was opposed by only two senators.

In the beginning, few people questioned the U.S. entry into the war. Most Americans accepted the need to oppose communism throughout the globe. In fact, President Johnson faced his strongest criticism from those who claimed he was not pursuing the war vigorously enough. Senator Barry Goldwater of Arizona, the Republican presidential candidate in 1964, suggested using whatever was necessary to win—including nuclear weapons. In February 1965, Johnson did order the bombing of North Vietnam, with non-nuclear weapons. At the same time, the United States increased the number of soldiers fighting in South Vietnam. Over the next three years, troop levels rose to nearly 500,000.

The watershed event of the war was the North Vietnamese offensive in early 1968. From a military point of view, the Tet (or Vietnamese New Year) offensive was a communist failure. By the end of February 1968, the Tet offensive had been largely crushed. In terms of U.S. public opinion, however, the communists achieved a major victory. The U.S. military had warned the Johnson administration that the North Vietnamese were planning an attack in early 1968, but the message was not shared with the public. Instead, the White House maintained that the communist forces were nearly exhausted. Only days before the Tet offensive, Johnson had reported in his State of the Union address that the United States was making progress in the war. Tet suggested to many Americans that the communists were far from defeated, and public opposition to the war intensified.

Bill Mauldin, *The Sun-Times* (Chicago), 1966.

The Strategists

National Security Council meeting, March 27, 1968. President Lyndon B. Johnson confers with Generals Creighton Abrams and Earl Wheeler.

In Washington as well, many of the country's top leaders gave up on winning the war after Tet. On March 31, 1968, Johnson changed the course of U.S. policy in a televised address to the nation. The president announced a freeze in the number of U.S. troops in Vietnam, a limit to the bombing of North Vietnam, and a proposal to begin negotiations with Hanoi. Finally, Johnson also said that he would not be a candidate for president.

Nearly five more years passed before the United States withdrew from Vietnam. Richard M. Nixon won the presidency in 1968 while pledging to achieve "peace with honor." But Americans indicated less and less interest in fighting the Cold War in Southeast Asia. By early 1970 a majority of Americans wanted U.S. troops to come home regardless of what happened to South Vietnam. When the South Vietnamese government finally fell to the communists in 1975, few Americans were willing to renew the struggle against communism in Southeast Asia. Public opinion had undergone a dramatic transition, focusing much of the country's attention on problems at home.

The Vietnam War had demonstrated the limits of U.S. Cold War policy. By the 1970s, U.S. leaders and the general public were adjusting their thinking to a new set of global realities. During the previous two decades, other countries had been catching up with the United States. With U.S. help, Europe and Japan had emerged as economic competitors. Meanwhile, the Soviet Union had largely closed the gap in nuclear weapons.

Détente and Human Rights

During the 1970s and 1980s, Americans elected presidents with sharply different ideas about the U.S. role in the world. At the same time, the public sent congressional representatives to Washington who often contradicted the foreign policy of the White House. President Richard Nixon, for example, believed that hard-headed bargaining could bring about a lasting détente, or reduction in tensions, with the Soviet Union and China in 1972. His strategy involved enmeshing the Soviets in the global economy, to encourage Soviet cooperation with Western countries. Nixon also wanted the power to respond forcefully to Soviet actions in the Third World. But congressional concern for human rights limited Nixon's policy. In 1974 Congress passed amendments that restricted U.S.-Soviet trade because of Soviet human rights abuses. At the same time, memories of Vietnam heightened public suspicion of U.S. intervention in the Third World. Congress accordingly restricted Nixon's efforts to counter perceived Soviet threats in Angola and elsewhere.

Jimmy Carter was elected president in 1976, at a time when public distrust of the foreign policy establishment was peaking. President Carter emphasized universal concerns, such as human rights and global interdependence. He attempted to deal with the causes of regional conflict by promoting local reform in Central America, the Middle East, and elsewhere. In 1977 he led the campaign to return the Panama Canal to Panama. Like Nixon, Carter found that his policies often clashed with public sentiments. In the late 1970s, communist advances in distant Third World countries, a communist revolution in neighboring Nicaragua, and especially the Soviet invasion of Afghanistan led many Americans to believe that Moscow was gaining influence at the expense of the United States. Some observers also warned of an ominous buildup in Soviet weaponry.

Cold War II

Ronald Reagan's campaign promises to stand up to the Soviet Union and to restore U.S. power and influence resonated with the public that elected him president in 1980. During his tenure, Reagan significantly increased the U.S. defense budget. Anti-communism dominated his view of the world, prompting him to frame Third World conflicts as part of the larger U.S.–Soviet struggle. Reagan viewed the pro-Soviet Sandinista regime in Nicaragua as a threat to U.S. security. He sought not only to contain communism in Central America, but also to overthrow the Sandinista government by aiding the Contra guerrilla forces.

Reagan, like his predecessors, faced congressional opposition to some of his policies, especially in Central America. Some members of Congress were upset by reported human rights violations by the Contras, and many feared that supporting the Contras would eventually lead to the deployment of U.S. troops into another quagmire like Vietnam. Public opinion polls also showed consistent opposition to Contra aid. By the late 1980s, U.S. support for the Contras had largely fizzled.

The Cold War Ends

The impetus for the most important changes in U.S. foreign policy during the Reagan administration came from within the Soviet Union itself—namely, the rise to power of Mikhail Gorbachev in 1985. The new Soviet leader recognized that his country was in a steep economic decline that threatened its superpower status. Radical changes at home were needed to reverse the decline, as well as drastically changed relations with the outside world. An end to the arms race with the United States was essential, and an infusion of Western investment highly desirable. Gorbachev made many concessions on arms control and Moscow's overseas involvements to gain U.S. cooperation. In 1987, for example,

The August 1991 coup was opposed by many people. Boris Yeltsin, standing on a tank, rallied the citizens of Moscow to stand firm against the coup's leaders.

this new spirit of compromise led the two superpowers to agree to eliminate all their intermediate-range nuclear missiles.

Gorbachev's policies of reform did nothing to halt the Soviet decline or to increase satisfaction with the system. In 1988 national groups in the non-Russian republics of the Soviet Union increasingly took to the streets to voice their dissatisfaction with the Soviet system. Protest movements spread to the Soviet satellites in Eastern Europe the following year. Gorbachev did not intervene as communist regimes fell throughout the region. When the Berlin Wall came down in December 1989, many Americans saw the event as the conclusion of the Cold War.

As new governments in the former Soviet bloc struggled to implement political and economic reforms, the Soviet Union itself continued to founder. Gorbachev's drastic steps created more and more disruptions in the system, but they failed to create a new system. He vacillated between democracy and authoritarianism while trying to hold the Soviet Union together. In August 1991 hard-line communists staged a coup in an attempt to roll back the reforms and preserve central power. After three days, however, the coup collapsed, further strengthening the hand of the authorities in the republics. One by one, the republics of the USSR declared their independence from Moscow. In December 1991 Russian president Boris Yeltsin and the heads of several other republics formed the Commonwealth of Independent States (CIS), a loose confederation designed to help coordinate aspects of their economic, political, and military policies. By the end of the year, every republic except Georgia had joined the CIS, and the Soviet Union officially came to an end. With CIS approval, Russia took over the Soviet seat on the UN Security Council.

The lowering of the hammer-and-sickle flag that had flown over the Kremlin for more than seven decades capped one of the most eventful years since the end of World War II. The defeat (but not removal) of Iraqi dictator Saddam Hussein in the Persian Gulf War, the failure of a hard-line coup in the Soviet Union, and a stubborn recession at home left many Americans benumbed by the rush of events. Yet most people in the former Soviet Union face much worse economic hardships in 1992 and beyond than they did under communism, as do citizens in many East European countries. Moreover, with the end of the communist repression, ethnic conflict has been rekindled. Yugoslavia, for instance, disintegrated into violent civil war as some ethnic groups sought independence from the Serbian-dominated federation. Tens of thousands have been killed and over a million people have been forced to flee their homes. Meanwhile, the Middle East remains unstable and potentially explosive.

Questions to Consider

1. How did the U.S. experience in Vietnam alter American ideas about their role in the world?
2. How did the growth of Soviet military power in the 1960s and 1970s influence the course of U.S. foreign policy?
3. Why did the Cold War end? What are the consequences of its end, and what do they mean for the future?

Into the Future

As the 1990s continue to unfold, the United States is stepping cautiously into a new era of international relations. The assumptions of the Cold War are no longer relevant, but a new consensus has not yet emerged. As with the other historical junctures explored in this chapter, the United States has reached an important crossroads. In the coming chapters, you will have an opportunity to consider some of the central issues that will influence the role of the United States in the world in the next century.

CHAPTER 2

Four Futures:
A Framework for Discussion

As in the past, changes in the international environment and in national interests are again prompting Americans to reassess the role of the United States in the world. In the following four alternative images of the United States in the year 2005, Americans have reached very different conclusions about the nature of global affairs, the threats facing the United States, its national goals, and consequently the role it should play in the post–Cold War era. Together these four images or Futures represent a broad range of possible directions in which the United States can head over the next 10 years.

Each of the four Futures presents a goal for the year 2005, together with the policies the United States would have to follow to attain it. The year 2005 has been selected because it allows you to focus on long-term goals without being overly concerned with contemporary issues. Additionally, it is far enough into the future to permit important gradual changes, yet close enough to the present to allow plausible projections.

The specific goals and policies embedded in the Futures should be understood as competing manifestations of broad foreign policy goals that every country has in some form. As you read the Futures, you should be aware of these purposes:

(1) *The defense of the country* against outside attack or harm. Harm could mean physical devastation in a nuclear attack, terrorist strikes against a country or its citizens abroad, or a painful economic embargo. These are clear-cut instances of hostile acts. Some harms are less direct, but nonetheless important, such as attacks on a close ally or aggression in a resource-rich region that disrupts the international economy. Also, some harms are not created by hostile acts: for instance, global warming and other ecological hazards are not desired by anyone, yet some observers think they are among the greatest threats to the United States and the world.

(2) *The furthering of its interests* by maintaining or increasing its geopolitical power and its economic strength. "Power" is defined as the military, economic, and political resources that can be used to get other countries to act in ways that make your country safe and strong, and to keep other countries from acting in ways that may threaten or weaken

your own. Power takes many shapes: Can a country defend itself? Can it send troops to invade or defend other countries? Does it keep its promises and carry out its threats? Does it give economic aid, and can it threaten economic sanctions such as embargoes? Conversely, can it endure economic sanctions itself? Does it have powerful allies, and good relations with neutral countries? Among these aspects of power, economic strength stands out because it can mean a better life for the country's citizens. Economic strength is affected both by domestic policies, such as amounts and priorities of government spending, and by foreign policy decisions about trade, economic aid, and much else.

Notice that these first two goals are closely related. It makes sense to distinguish between self-defense and the active expansion of power, but the distinction may not go very far. Sometimes the same military forces can be used to defend a country, to help protect its allies and trade routes, to intervene in a conflict around the world, or to conquer an enemy. Also, state leaders have many times justified massive arms buildups, and even attacks on other countries, as self-defense. Given the many uncertainties of military power and war, these claims are often sincere, or at least plausible.

(3) *The advancement of national values.* Every country has certain values that it would like, ideally, to see prevail in the world around it. For the United States, these values include respect for human rights, governmental accountability to the people, and peaceful resolution of disputes. These values can be viewed as broad, long-term policy interests: if they thrive around the world, the United States—and other countries—may be safer and better off.

Each of the Futures will emphasize different elements of these general goals and integrate them so as to present you with real choices—but not the only choices. Scholars and politicians can not always be neatly categorized as supporters of one or another Future. Each Future contains quotes from various people that address distinctive themes of that Future, although these people may not support the Future as a whole. Nor should you simply adopt one of the Futures as your own.

When you read the Futures, immerse yourself in them one at a time. As you consider the beliefs about the international environment that support a Future, picture in action these images of how the world works. Assuming the world does work this way, what are the implications for both the ends and means of U.S. foreign policy? Likewise, when you read about the values that guide the Future, think about how they influence the general role of the United States in the world, as well as more immediate policy questions.

Each Future is an exercise in *advocacy*, and most of the evidence presented supports the Future's main features. However, each Future also contains some amount of self-criticism, and often substantial criticism of other Futures. As you read, notice how the Futures present competing arguments and how evidence is sometimes used selectively to support conflicting conclusions. Being attentive to these issues helps set the stage for *analysis*, which you will be doing in subsequent chapters as you try to make sense of all these arguments and facts. Also, when you read the Futures, think about whether each one addresses your own concerns. You may discover that you like one of these Futures, aspects from several, or none at all. Be sure to keep track of the issues that you feel you need to learn more about before making informed judgments. Some of these questions will be raised in Chapters 3 through 5, and many will require additional research or reflection. Eventually, you will develop your own future, a Future 5, that addresses what you think are the most important issues facing the United States today. By clarifying your assumptions and the priority of your values—through individual reading, classroom activities, and discussions that continue outside of class—you will be able to make a thoughtful contribution to the debate on the course of U.S. foreign policy.

THE FOUR FUTURES AT A GLANCE

FUTURE 1: Standing Up for Human Rights and Democracy

It is the year 2005. Over the past 10 years, Americans came to realize that, as the home of freedom and democracy, the United States plays a special role in the world. During this time, the United States followed a principled foreign policy. It supported the governments of the world that had both a good human rights record and the backing of their people, and opposed those that didn't. The United States especially supported struggling nations that were taking their first steps toward democracy. At times, the United States may have used economic sanctions or even military force to stop tyrannical governments from killing their own people or attacking neighboring democracies. Now these tyrants are causing much less trouble. In 2005 the world is becoming a safer and more humane place for all peoples.

FUTURE 2: Charting a Stable Course

It is the year 2005. Over the past 10 years, Americans came to understand that as the world's only superpower, the United States is looked upon by the nations of the world as an important source of stability and security. During this time, the United States carefully maintained strong alliances to make our competitive world a more stable place. This helped prevent aggressive countries from threatening peaceful nations and the international economy. As a result, the United States remains the world's superpower, and is richer from doing business with its many allies. The United States sometimes had to support stable but undemocratic governments, and occasionally sent some of its troops to fight again, but this has been a small price to pay for global stability. In 2005 the United States is defending its interests by making the world more secure.

FUTURE 3: Cooperating Globally

It is the year 2005. Over the past 10 years, Americans came to understand that they live in an interdependent world. During this time, the United States addressed problems around the world not on its own but in cooperation with many other nations. Instead of trying to police the world single-handedly, for example, the United States does not use military force abroad unless the UN Security Council authorizes the operation in advance. In collaboration with other countries, the United States now spends much more money to restore the environment, help poorer countries, and protect the peace. This has been hard work, but it makes the United States more secure and prosperous in the long run. In 2005 we are working together to address the common threats that concern us all.

FUTURE 4: Building U.S. Economic Strength

It is the year 2005. Over the past 10 years, Americans came to realize that having the world's strongest economy is far more important than having our troops spread across the world. During this time, the United States gradually brought its troops home and cut its military spending by about two-thirds. It used the hundreds of billions of dollars saved to strengthen its economy, reduce its dependence on foreign oil, and address other pressing national problems. The United States is still capable of defending North America, and maintains a small strike force for rapid action when Americans abroad are seriously threatened, but is no longer a military giant. In today's world, U.S. security and world leadership depend on economic—not military—strength. And in 2005, the United States is rapidly growing stronger.

35

Standing Up for Human Rights and Democracy

It is the year 2005. Over the past decade, Americans came to realize that the United States has a special responsibility to stand up for human rights and democracy across the globe. People around the world were already demanding pluralism and individual rights, as the fall of the Berlin Wall in November 1989 made dramatically clear. The democratic and human rights revolutions in Eastern Europe, in the former Soviet Union, and in other parts of the world needed and deserved our support. So did people around the world who continued to suffer under oppression.

The end of the Cold War, followed by the U.S.-led victory in the Persian Gulf War and the disintegration of the Soviet empire, left it clear that the United States was the most powerful country on earth. We sadly realized, however, that although the Gulf War was over, many countries, including Iraq, were in the hands of despotic leaders who terrorized their own populations and threatened neighboring countries. We came to recognize an essential link between dictatorship and aggression: oppressive governments too often threatened the peace, unrestrained by democratic opposition or even freely expressed minority opinions. Thus Americans understood that the United States had moral and practical reasons for supporting human rights and democracy, and they decided to act boldly.

Over the past 10 years, the United States has followed a principled foreign policy—helping governments of the world that have a good human rights record and their people's support, and opposing those that do not. It provided moral and political backing, economic assistance, and military protection for countries that were taking their first steps towards democracy. To stop tyrannical governments from abusing their citizens, the United States used political pressures, economic sanctions, and in extreme cases even military force. Above all, it did whatever was necessary to deny aggressor states the fruits of conquest. Now that tyrants know that the United States means business, they are causing much less trouble.

Standing up for human rights and democracy has not been cost-free, but the United States could afford the expenses, and the outcome was well worth it. By 2005, the world has become noticeably safer and more humane. The era of the dictator-aggressor is ending.

Future 1 Is Based on These Beliefs

1. The principal threat to U.S. security and global peace is posed by dictatorial countries. Unchecked by public opinion or a democratically elected legislature, dictatorships like Hitler's Germany and Saddam Hussein's Iraq are free to start wars that suit the dictators at their peoples' expense. These countries, as well as their neighboring countries, are at the mercy of their leaders' whims and misjudgments. Moreover, to make their people forget about domestic problems, dictators sometimes cause dangerous international crises in an attempt to rally the population around nationalist themes. This was the major reason Argentina invaded the British-held Falkland Islands in 1982. Dictatorial powers also enabled Panama's Noriega to trade in drugs despite international disapproval, and Libya's Qaddafi to sponsor terrorist attacks.

2. Democratic states, in contrast, are more peaceful and law-abiding. The people—those who carry the burdens of war or other outrageous acts—constrain their governments from starting unnecessary wars or violating additional international norms. The institutional checks and balances structured into democratic states also make it less likely that they will rashly begin wars. Peaceful democratic states like Canada and Switzerland are examples. Although democratic states became involved in the two world wars, they were always the victim of aggression by a dictatorship or were coming to the aid of an ally under attack by a dictatorship. Furthermore, no truly democratic state has ever attacked another democratic state.

3. U.S. interests in security and peace are served when fellow democracies are protected and when aggressive dictatorships are converted into democracies. The advantages of preserving and promoting democracy are illustrated by World War II. Without the United States' support of Great Britain during the war, the United States might not now have democratic allies in Europe. Germany, Italy, and Japan were all repressive dictatorships when they started the war. Once defeated and committed to democracy, however, they became peaceful, law-abiding states with excellent human rights records. More recently, Argentina became a peaceful democracy after its defeat by the British in the Falklands War.

4. U.S. security interests are best served when most power is held by democratic countries. Powerful democracies are a force for good and pose no threat to humane, peaceful states. Thus Canada and Mexico do not expect to be attacked by the United States simply

A steadfast concern for peace can never be maintained except by a partnership of democratic nations. No autocratic government could be trusted to keep faith with it or to observe its covenants.

—Woodrow Wilson to Congress in asking for a declaration of war against Germany in April 1917

The main thing is that the Western countries are pluralistic democracies. Their governments are under the control of legal public institutions, and this practically rules out the pursuance of an aggressive foreign policy. In the system of Western states . . . the problem of war has essentially been removed.

—Andrei Kozyrev, "Building a Bridge—Along or Across a River: The Parameters of Our Security," *New Times*, Moscow (October 23–29, 1990)

America will increasingly have to acknowledge that elected tyrants— like [the Republic of Georgia's recently deposed president] Mr. Gamsakhurdia—are scarcely better than unelected ones, and it will have to choose its allies not by choosing between dictators and democrats, or between friends and foes in a cold war, but between so-called democrats and genuine democrats.

—Thomas Friedman,
New York Times
(January 12, 1992)

Democracy is more than just a procedure for electing officials—it is a way of life and a set of traditions and institutions. Most importantly, it requires an independent judiciary that can enforce rights, protect the opposition and insure that not only are elections democratic but that daily life is democratic as well.

—Michael Sandel,
New York Times
(January 12, 1992)

because it is more powerful, and they feel no need to form an alliance to try to balance U.S. power. In Europe, likewise, democratic Germany has no desire to acquire nuclear weapons to match the nuclear capabilities of democratic Britain and France. Yet democracies must be powerful to deter aggression by dictators who care little about the wishes and lives of their own people, let alone world opinion. To these tyrants, it must be made perfectly clear that any aggression on their part will be met with overwhelming force—so that after the war their countries will be greatly weakened and their governments will be destroyed. Faced with resolute, strong democracies, dictatorships will start fewer wars. Also, with fewer opportunities for aggression that might rally their populations around patriotic themes, dictators will face increasing domestic pressure for political change.

5. Although the United States still faces threats from aggression-prone dictatorships, none is as strong or as threatening as was the Soviet Union. In the post–Cold War era, with the downfall of the Soviet communist party and the disintegration of the USSR, the United States is sufficiently strong to give priority to promoting human rights and democracy. During the Cold War, when the United States' top priority was countering Soviet power, it often supported anti-communist dictators as the lesser of two evils. Such compromises may sometimes be unavoidable, as when the United States supported the Soviet Union itself against Nazi Germany. However, the habit of aiding dictators is dubious at best, and now it has less justification than ever.

6. Democracy and dictatorship are ideal types; few countries are entirely peace-loving and democratic, or aggressive and repressive. South Africa, under apartheid law, had a democratically elected government. Yet the government limited the political and economic rights of the black majority in a dictatorial fashion. Other governments, although supported by the majority of the population, repress minority rights. In 1990 Kuwait had many repressive domestic policies, but it was less aggressive and therefore less dangerous than Iraq. The United States must recognize these gradations on the spectrum from vibrant democracies to menacing despotisms. It should reserve its warmest support for true democracies, and intervene forcefully against the most militant countries.

Future 1 Is Based on These Values

1. Democracy is the best form of government. Majority rule, with respect for the rights of minorities, most justly represents the will of the entire population. Full-fledged democracies, with institu-

tionalized checks and balances, serve to protect the rights of citizens at home, and they act abroad in ways consistent with the basic values and interests of their citizens.

2. Human rights are important and at least some are universal. Clearly, government-sponsored genocide or torture are repulsive and deserve our condemnation—whether or not the government was elected or is supported by a majority of the population. Violations of other human rights that we hold dear, as in denying the freedoms of speech, assembly, and religion, should not escape our scrutiny.

3. U.S. foreign policy should uphold these principles as much as possible, even if we must accept some material costs and risks. For example, although U.S. economic sanctions against the South African government cost U.S. companies some profits, actively opposing apartheid was the moral and appropriate policy. This would have been true even if the sanctions had not contributed to subsequent reforms.

4. The United States has a special obligation to promote democracy and respect for human rights around the world, unilaterally if necessary. The United States is widely considered the world's standard-bearer of freedom, justice, and democracy—despite several post–World War II cases in which anti-communism was put above respect for elections and national self-determination. The end of the Cold War removes any justification for such actions that go against these values. Furthermore, the great strength of the United States adds to its obligation to promote human rights and democracy. Consistent U.S. leadership in these moral causes provides Americans with a sense of national pride, and it adds prestige to their image in the eyes of others.

Human rights are by definition universal, which means that by definition the world should care about them. Just as a responsible free world must condemn their suppression, it must respond when democracy is fledgling and fragile.

—Thomas Oliphant,
Boston Globe (August 23, 1991)

Let every nation know, whether it wishes us well or ill, that we shall pay any price, bear any burden, meet any hardship, support any friend, oppose any foe to assure the survival and the success of liberty.

—John F. Kennedy, inauguration
speech (January 6, 1961)

What Should the United States Do in the 1990s to Head Toward Future 1?

Here are some political, military, and economic policies that the United States can follow in the 1990s to help bring about this Future. The historical examples illustrate that such policies can work—and therefore that Future 1 is feasible. Future 1 supporters do not have to endorse every policy listed, however.

1. The United States will give political and moral support only to governments that treat their citizens properly, and that are democratically elected or have evident popular support.

2. The United States will apply political pressure to dictatorships such as Iraq, North Korea, and Cuba—making it clear that the

United States will no longer tolerate their oppressive and aggressive behaviors. It will push China to allow its own citizens more freedom. It will even pressure long-time allies (such as Turkey and Israel) to end their occasional human rights abuses, such as imprisoning suspects indefinitely without charge and beating or torturing detainees.

3. The United States will end alliances with and stop arms transfers to undemocratic governments and to those with poor human rights records. This policy means moving U.S. military bases from countries like Saudi Arabia and Turkey unless they improve their human rights policies. The United States and its allies—those countries that respect the principles of democracy and human rights—are now so much more powerful than the forces of tyranny that we need not continue military relations with countries that violate our values.

4. The United States will protect its democratic allies and encourage other democracies to join in this mutual protection. Thus, for example, the United States will invite Eastern European democracies to join an expanded North Atlantic Treaty Organization (NATO). Other East European countries, such as Romania and Bulgaria, will be invited only if they adopt more democratic policies, such as guaranteed respect for minority rights. The United States will continue to deploy its military troops and supply armaments to its democratic allies that are threatened by hostile governments.

   History shows that alliances among democratic states serve causes of peace and freedom, and that their absence creates insecurity. In 1914, for example, the lack of an explicit alliance between the democracies of Britain and France led the German Kaiser to attack France. Had he known about Britain's eventual support for France, he probably would not have ordered the attack. And prior to World War II, the United States' refusal to ally with Britain and France allowed Germany's Hitler to be aggressive in Europe. In contrast, a U.S.–led NATO prevented the Soviet empire from invading Western Europe. Moreover, NATO's perseverance eventually exhausted the Soviet Union and led to its retreat from Eastern Europe.

5. The United States will give greater amounts of economic aid, as well as trade and investment incentives, to emerging democracies such as those in Eastern Europe and Africa. Such aid will help these new regimes to rebuild, will increase their legitimacy and therefore the durability of democracy, and will encourage other countries to democratize.

6. The United States will use economic sanctions against countries that have poor human rights records, especially if they are aggressive or otherwise threaten their neighbors. For example, until China permits freedom of speech and assembly, the United States will not grant it Most Favored Nation trade status. Furthermore, if China continues to export weapons to tyrants in the

Middle East or unsafeguarded nuclear technology to countries like Pakistan and Iran, the United States will urge its allies to punish China economically.

The United States has the world's biggest economy and thus exerts enormous economic influence. U.S. sanctions against South Africa helped force the government to move away from apartheid, and sanctions in the 1980s against the Pinochet regime of Chile pressured the country to become democratic.

7. The United States will arm and support freedom fighters who try to make their countries more humane and democratic. Obvious historical examples are U.S. support for French and Norwegian resistance fighters under Nazi occupation during World War II. Clear contemporary examples are harder to find, because although the democratic ends may have been commendable, the means sometimes involved gross violations of human rights. The efforts by the Nicaraguan Contras to overthrow the Sandinista government in the 1980s are an example of this grey area.

8. The United States will use military force, if necessary, to prevent dictators from building or using nuclear and other weapons of mass destruction, from supporting terrorism or drug trafficking that threaten American lives, or from mass murders of their own people. If a dictatorship starts a war with a democracy, the United States will fight until the aggressor surrenders unconditionally; this will help ensure that a democratic government replaces the dictatorship. We may stop short of total conquest if the aggressor possesses nuclear weapons, but the attacker must clearly suffer more than the victim.

How Much Will Future 1 Cost the United States?

This future will have some short-term costs. Maintaining the world's strongest military is obviously expensive, although with the decline in the Soviet threat the U.S. military budget can be trimmed a bit. Some economic aid programs will not cost very much in relation to the total U.S. economy, although others—such as efforts to rebuild the economies of the larger democratic republics in the former Soviet Union—will be expensive. The United States may also lose some important trading partners among undemocratic developing countries, such as Saudi Arabia and China, should it decide to stop selling them weapons and other goods or stop buying their products. In order to fund the costly economic and military policies, the United States may have to raise taxes, cut domestic spending, or borrow more money and thus increase the budget deficit. If its West European and Japanese allies join in these efforts to stand up for democracy, the costs to the United States will be reduced.

While supporting fragile democracies and stopping the world's bullies may be expensive, doing nothing may be far more costly in the long term. For example, the withdrawal of U.S. economic support for Germany in the late 1920s contributed to the collapse of the German economy, consequent social unrest and political polarization, and in 1933 the election of Adolf Hitler. Hitler then abolished the remnants of freedom and democracy and started Germany on its path of genocide and aggression. The United States did not confront Germany until 1941, when it was far more powerful and defeating it entailed enormous costs.

As the policies that promote democracy succeed, and the most dangerous governments fall from power and are replaced by humane and peace-loving ones, the United States will gradually reduce its spending on these efforts. Furthermore, the new democratic governments will want to improve economic ties with the United States. And as these new democracies take root and their economies grow strong, their citizens will have more money to purchase U.S. products.

Charting a Stable Course

I t is the year 2005. Over the past decade, Americans came to understand that the United States has a responsibility to itself and to other countries of the world to be a major source of security and stability.

As we entered the 1990s, we saw that although U.S.–Soviet relations had improved, the world had grown dangerously unstable. The instability of the post–Cold War era was first brought home when Iraq, a poor country with an enormous army, invaded its oil-rich but militarily weak and unaligned neighbor Kuwait. Iraq thus threatened to dominate the world's oil supplies and to devastate the international economy. The United States had no choice but to use its troops to protect both its interests and the economic and military stability of the world.

After the Persian Gulf War, the United States learned that it could prevent such dangerous conflicts by better using its influence to deter potential aggressors and to preserve a stable international economy. It also realized that ethnic conflict in the region of the former Soviet empire threatened to upset the regional balance of power and to escalate to wide-scale war. As a result, the United States took action.

Over the past 10 years, the United States maintained strong political, military, and economic alliances that made our competitive world a more stable place. Together with its allies, the United States helped prevent regional wars that would have shocked the world's economy or upset the global balance of power. With regional balances of power the risk of war was smaller, and fewer states felt compelled to acquire nuclear weapons to protect themselves. The United States has also remained the world's superpower, and it is richer from doing business with its many allies.

This international role sometimes required the United States to support stable but undemocratic or repressive governments, and occasionally it sent its troops to fight again. Maintaining the world's strongest military has not been cheap, although the United States shared the burdens of expense and risk with its allies. By 2005, however, we have seen that these are small prices to pay for making countries of the world more secure—a goal that serves U.S. national interests.

The world order of the future will revert to that which existed before 1939, and most notably after World War I: It will be marked by power politics, national rivalries, and ethnic tensions.

—James Schlesinger, "New Instabilities, New Priorities," *Foreign Policy* (Winter 1991–92)

43

Future 2 Is Based on These Beliefs

The end of the Cold War does not mean the end of political, ideological, diplomatic, economic, technological, or even military rivalry among nations. It does not mean the end of the struggle for power and influence. It very probably does mean increased instability, unpredictability, and violence in international affairs.

—Samuel Huntington, "No Exit: The Errors of Endism" *The National Interest* (Fall 1989)

As any Latin American will quickly point out, even a truly democratic superpower is capable of intervening in the affairs of its smaller neighbors.

—Samuel Huntington, "No Exit: The Errors of Endism," *The National Interest* (Fall 1989)

It would be foolish to claim . . . that the United States after 1991 can return to the role it played in world affairs before 1941. For as the history of the 1930s suggests, the absence of imminent threat is no guarantee that threats do not exist.

—John Gaddis, "Toward the Post-Cold War World," *Foreign Affairs* (Spring 1991)

1. In the twenty-first century, the major threats to U.S. security and prosperity will arise from imbalances of power and instability. Countries with too much power may be tempted to engage in aggressive actions that threaten U.S. economic, political, and military interests. Regional imbalances of power can provoke insecure states to begin a military buildup, possibly including nuclear weapons, to protect themselves. An insecure state may even initiate a war, trying to prevent another country from striking a crippling first blow. Political and economic instability also exacerbates these risks of war.

2. The root cause of these threats is the anarchic international system, in which no supreme authority protects states from attack or guarantees their vital interests. In this insecure, competitive environment, states that want to survive must acquire power and use it in whatever way seems necessary to protect themselves. Their strategies may include strengthening and modernizing armed forces, forming alliances, transferring arms to an ally, or going to war. Anarchy and power politics will likely persist, moreover, because states are reluctant to surrender their ability to act unilaterally to some supranational authority. For instance, even at the height of United Nations (UN) cooperation during the 1990–91 Persian Gulf crisis, none of the permanent members of the UN Security Council said that they would surrender their veto on important questions of peace and security.

3. Despite international anarchy, order and peace can be preserved through stable balances of power. Countries go to war either when they believe they cannot preserve their current standing peacefully, or when they believe they can gain power by overwhelming an adversary. Arms races are dangerous when they lead to uncertainty about, or rapid shifts in, the balance of power. A stable balance reduces incentives to attack, whether for national gain or out of fear. Because the United States is the world's leading military power, its support may be needed to maintain workable defensive coalitions. Yet any attempt to impose its will upon the world is likely to be resisted effectively by other countries. One historical precedent is how the states of Europe eventually put a stop to Napoleon's efforts to conquer the region and establish democratic republics. France's ideological crusade harmed its national interests.

4. Power politics work the same for dictatorships and democracies. Any state can go to war to advance or defend its interests, if it sees fit. Democratic governments are vulnerable to the consequences of power imbalances, and they can misjudge the likely benefits and risks of both war and peace. Therefore, even if a world of democracies were possible, it would not assure peace. Nor is it practical to rule out cooperation with dictators to

preserve a balance of power. In World War II, the United States and its allies needed to make common cause with the totalitarian Soviet Union against the greater threat of Nazi Germany. Likewise, it was necessary in 1990 and 1991 to side with undemocratic Saudi Arabia and Kuwait against Iraq, the aggressor and strongest state in the region.

5. It is especially important for the United States to help preserve the balance of power in Europe and the Middle East. Any country that dominates all of Europe will become the world's strongest economic and military power; any that dominates the Middle East will jeopardize the world economy. In either case, U.S. security and economic interests would be threatened despite the geographical distance.

   U.S. military commitments are a prerequisite for balances of power and hence for peace in these regions of vital interest. The United States' economic leverage, though significant, may not be sufficient to keep and restore stability. As the 1990–91 Persian Gulf War demonstrated, even the economic sanctions that ruined Iraq's economy failed to coerce Saddam Hussein to pull out of Kuwait or to stop his nuclear weapons program. U.S. military power was required to achieve these results.

6. The danger of nuclear weapons falling into the hands of irresponsible national leaders or terrorist organizations is a fast-growing threat to the United States' physical security. Therefore, the United States should continue its efforts to prevent nuclear proliferation. It is especially important for the United States to work for regional stability, thus reducing the incentives for countries to acquire nuclear weapons.

Future 2 Is Based on These Values

1. Americans value their country's protection from military attack, coercion, and economic collapse most highly. With these vital interests secured, Americans may enjoy their freedoms and way of life. Whenever vital interests come into conflict with secondary national interests or ideological objectives, the vital interests must dominate.

2. Americans value human rights, democracy, and national self-determination, both for themselves and for others. Yet we must recognize that not all peoples of the world hold these values as highly as do Americans, that some people define human rights and democracy differently, and that some countries are multinational empires with national groups that do not have self-determination. These complexities invite caution. For example, interfering in other countries' affairs for ideological reasons may

As the previous dominant conflict (a.k.a. Cold War) is declining, many lesser ones (with a heavy growth potential) are jostling to take the Cold War's place. Here is an abbreviated checklist: the disintegration of the Soviet Union, Iraqi ambitions, Libyan mischief, economic catastrophe in Eastern Europe, Yugoslavia's explosion, Arab-Israeli war, nuclear and poison gas proliferation, Islamic fundamentalism, the collapse of the marvelous Western economy that stretches from Frankfurt via New York to Tokyo. Take your pick and try to imagine any crisis management minus the United States.

—Josef Joffe, "Entangled Forever," *The National Interest* (Fall 1990)

There is now another greatly enhanced element in fostering international stability: discouraging or preventing the further spread of nuclear weapons. . . . Under the Nuclear Non-Proliferation Treaty, the United States has large responsibilities—in brief, to provide protection for the non-nuclear weapons states. Its force posture should remain overtly such that all are convinced that the United States can fulfill those responsibilities.

—James Schlesinger, "New Instabilities, New Priorities," *Foreign Policy* (Winter 1991-92)

[Future] U.S. policy will have to strike a more deliberate balance among global needs for continued American commitment, the desirability of some devolution of U.S. regional security responsibilities and the imperatives of America's domestic renewal. . . . More emphasis will have to be placed on cooperation with genuine partners, including shared decision-making in world security issues.

—Zbigniew Brzezinski,
"Selective Global Containment,"
Foreign Affairs (Fall 1991)

cause resentment and instability. At the very least, therefore, the U.S. desire for stability requires that it does not attempt to coerce other countries to adopt American values. If regional stability is not threatened, however, the United States may promote democracy and respect for individual and group rights by example and other nonconfrontational means.

3. Americans value their country's vital role in alliances that help maintain a stable balance of power, peace, and prosperity. They realize that their allies will share in deciding policy, as they will also share in the costs and risks of maintaining stability.

What Should the United States Do in the 1990s to Head Toward Future 2?

Here are some political, military, and economic policies that the United States can follow in the 1990s to help bring about this Future. The historical examples show that such policies can work, and therefore that Future 2 is feasible. Future 2 supporters do not have to endorse every policy listed.

1. The United States will maintain alliances with West European countries and Japan, thus decreasing the risk of war in these important regions and stabilizing the global balance of power. The United States will also keep its alliance with South Korea, even though that country is not totally democratic; such an alliance in 1950 would have prevented the Korean War. Providing security for these countries will ease incentives for them (and therefore their neighbors) to acquire nuclear weapons. The United States will back its security guarantees to these countries by deploying military forces within them or nearby.

2. The United States will work to form alliances in the Middle East. The United States' long-time support for Israel may be converted into a formal alliance as part of a regional settlement: the United States and other countries may guarantee Israeli security, if Israel gives up the occupied territories. Such a settlement should bring more stability to the Middle East, encouraging Israel to limit or phase out its nuclear program. In order to prevent any country in the region from achieving hegemony over Persian Gulf oil, moreover, the United States will help maintain a balance of power in the Gulf. It may form alliances with countries like Saudi Arabia and Kuwait (even though they are not democratic), or participate in a regional collective security arrangement that will defend against any country's aggression.

3. The United States will encourage burden sharing among its allies. The risks and expenses of maintaining stability must be divided

more fairly, especially since the United States can no longer afford to shoulder most of the effort. Since its allies will be making fair contributions to these efforts, the United States must also share the responsibility and right to make decisions for the alliance.

4. The United States will support, in coalition with its allies, humanitarian aid and economic reforms in the struggling countries of the former Soviet empire, in order to prevent dangerous instabilities.

5. The United States will encourage peace settlements that will enhance regional stability, such as the Middle East settlement referred to above. Such settlements should include balanced and verifiable arms control agreements and confidence- and security-building measures among the parties. For the same reason, the United States will also support peaceful settlements within countries such as Cambodia, Angola, and Nicaragua.

6. The United States will have an arms transfer policy designed to preserve balances of power in unstable regions. If a balance already exists in a region, the United States will support multilateral limits on arms transfers to maintain the balance. If a regional balance does not exist, it will support only those arms transfers that are necessary to achieve or maintain a balance. The United States will sell, or in some cases give, weapons to its allies in unstable regions if these transfers promote a military balance. It will trade weapons freely with its allies in stable regions such as Western Europe.

7. The United States will do more business with countries like China, even though their governments have different standards of human rights than the United States does—as long as they agree not to cause trouble in regions vital to U.S. interests. With this business, for instance, China will feel less economic need to sell weapons to dangerous countries and groups—thus enhancing regional stability. Furthermore, the U.S. economy will benefit from access to China's huge market.

8. The United States will covertly arm and aid rebel groups trying to overthrow their governments or to declare their nation's independence—if it seems that the revolution will likely make the whole region more balanced and stable, and if the new government serves U.S. interests.

America—even with a diminished military presence abroad—will remain the principal source of nuclear deterrence and the ultimate guarantor of the proposition that any disruptor of security will be faced by a dominant coalition. At the same time America will be able to focus more on the imperatives of its domestic renewal, thereby buttressing its long-term capacity to sustain a policy of continued, but also more selective and proportionate, global commitment.

—Zbigniew Brzezinski, "Selective Global Containment," *Foreign Affairs* (Fall 1991)

Over the next decade, the most serious source of instability in world politics will probably be the political, economic, and social fragmentation that is already developing where communism has collapsed. . . . We in the West are not focusing as carefully as we should on the problems of reconstruction and reintegration in that part of the world. But should fragmentationist forces prevail there, the resulting anarchy—and mass emigration away from anarchy—could destabilize any number of power balances.

—John Gaddis, "Toward the Post-Cold War World," *Foreign Affairs* (Summer 1991)

How Much Will Future 2 Cost the United States?

The United States will have to have the world's strongest military in order to remain the world's superpower and balancer, so it may need to keep its defense spending moderately high. The United States will be working with its allies, however, and this will certainly be less expensive than being the world's only policeman. Maintaining troops overseas will also be less expensive if U.S. allies agree to share the burdens more equitably. To encourage burden sharing, the United States will agree to give up its dominance in alliance decision-making and instead rely on genuine consultations. If the nations of the world agree to reduce their numbers of weapons and troops, moreover, the United States will spend proportionately less. Thus, with thoughtful alliance management and arms control policies, the United States could reduce its military budget.

The U.S. arms transfer policy will have mixed economic results, depending on whether the United States sells or gives the weapons to its allies. Obviously, selling them will help the United States' balance of payments, and giving them away will strain the federal budget. An indirect effect of arms transfers, however, is that the U.S. military will get more for its money, because of the increased efficiency of weapons development and production. Regional arms control agreements will also have mixed economic effects. If the agreement reduces the need to give weapons to an ally, then the United States will save money. If that ally had previously purchased U.S. weapons, however, the arms control agreement may harm the United States' balance of payments.

Cooperating Globally

It is the year 2005. Over the past decade, Americans came to understand that they live in an interdependent world in which their interests are intertwined with the interests of other countries. A crisis in the Middle East may disrupt the flow of oil to industrialized countries and cause a deep recession. If markets are depressed in developed nations, countries like Brazil will profit less from exports to them. To achieve economic growth, the Brazilians would then have to depend more on the resources of the Amazon basin, cutting down tropical rain forests to clear land for crops, cattle, and development. Rain forest destruction would in turn contribute to global warming and the extinction of plant and animal species. These and many other interconnected global threats are clearly beyond the capacity of the United States to handle alone. Americans finally realized that the only way to prevent and solve many problems facing the world is for all nations to confront them together.

Over the past 10 years, the United States collaborated with many other countries and accepted some limits on its own actions. Instead of trying single-handedly to police the world, for example, the United States gives military and financial support to the efforts of the United Nations to keep or restore the peace. The United States does not use military force abroad unless the UN Security Council supports the operation in advance. It also supports the efforts of international organizations to mediate regional disputes, in order to strengthen alternatives to war for resolving conflict.

The United States is following the UN's lead to set up regional arms control and disarmament regimes, to establish zones free of nuclear weapons, and to regulate the transfer of armaments (including U.S. weapons). It is doing its part to improve the economic and ecological conditions in Eastern Europe, the former Soviet Union, and the developing world, both for humanitarian reasons and to reduce pressures for disruptive mass migrations. The United States also supports UN sanctions against all countries that harbor or aid terrorists, and cooperates with international organizations to stop the spread of diseases and to solve the problem of illegal drugs.

These multinational efforts cost money, but the United States is sharing the burden with other countries. Because the UN has assumed primary responsibility for peace and security, moreover, the United

Our economy is increasingly and inextricably intertwined with the rest of the world. We cannot hide from nuclear conflict even if it occurs far away for reasons that do not concern us. If the Earth's air and water are fouled or its climate is changed, we cannot find sanctuary. Like it or not, our only hope for a secure future is to work with other nations to reduce threats to the common security.

A pragmatic vision of the post-Cold War world involves multiple international organizations dedicated to solving particular problems. These would have overlapping membership and substantial power for well-defined purposes. The United States would make cooperative problem solving a central theme of its diplomatic efforts. It would play a lead role in some efforts and a supporting role in others.

—Alice Rivlin, "New World, New Dangers," *Washington Post* (April 10, 1990)

States has reduced its military spending. While some of the savings are being put to use at home, most of the money saved helps to fund the U.S. share of the international efforts to provide for global military, economic, and ecological security. By 2005, because of this cooperation, the United States and other countries are well on their way to being more secure and having a decent quality of life for themselves and for future generations.

Future 3 Is Based on These Beliefs

1. The threats facing the United States in the twenty-first century will be global in scope: they include dangers accompanying the disintegration of some multinational countries, the spread of weapons of mass destruction and ballistic missiles, aggressive actions by militarized or fanatical states, terrorism, poverty and social upheavals, wars, the breakdown of economic collaboration, environmental catastrophes, AIDS, and drug trafficking. As the Cold War and its dangers disappeared, it gave way immediately to the threats posed by the discovery of a hole in the ozone layer, Iraq's aggression against Kuwait, and the disintegration of Yugoslavia.

2. Interdependence characterizes the global system, so that U.S. interests are linked to the interests of others. Economic interdependence, for instance, means that countries of the world rise or fall together. Economic protectionism by some countries spreads to others, so that trade declines and all economies suffer. Economic collaboration and mutual assistance, in contrast, benefit all countries. To help struggling countries become stronger economically, moreover, will eventually benefit the United States. These countries can then provide more valuable goods, export markets, and investment opportunities for U.S. citizens and companies.

   Military interdependence means that one country cannot be truly secure if its military forces are seen as a threat that makes another country so insecure that the latter responds with a counterthreat. Instead, to avoid expensive and dangerous arms races, countries can cooperate to create mutual or collective security arrangements, where countries are protected in ways that do not undermine the security of others. And environmental hazards offer striking examples of ecological interdependence. For instance, chlorofluorocarbons (CFCs) released into the atmosphere by any country destroy the high-altitude ozone layer that protects the entire Earth from being exposed to dangerous levels of ultraviolet radiation.

3. States are not the world's only important units; we also have transnational and subnational groups and organizations. Some transnational actors try to benefit all. These include private organizations, such as Amnesty International, which defends human rights, and intergovernmental organizations, such as the United Nations, that work on global problems. Other transnational actors, such as international terrorist organizations, are destructive. Multinational corporations can have both positive and negative effects: economic development on the one hand, exploitation and ecological damage on the other. Subnational actors include farmers in Columbia and Peru whose livelihood depends on growing coca leaves for cocaine traffickers, in part because U.S. trade barriers prevent them from exporting certain legal crops to the United States; farmers in Japan who pressure their government to maintain barriers to free trade, as well as other farmers who produce for the export market and desire free trade; and local industries that release pollution into the atmosphere and water.

4. Traditional instruments of state power, such as military force and covert operations, have little relevance in solving most problems of interdependence. The United States is not about to threaten Brazil with a naval blockade to coerce the Brazilian government to halt rain forest destruction. Nor will it drop herbicides on European farms to prevent them from growing state-subsidized crops (and thereby gaining an unfair advantage on the world market). More subtle policy instruments are obviously required. Some will be new and stronger international institutions used to coordinate state policies. Other measures will be at the national and local level. These lower-level measures are useful, for example, to regulate pollution.

5. Conflict is inevitable, but war is not. In the post–Cold War era, countries and groups will still have conflicts and be concerned about protecting their interests. However, because of strengthened institutions to keep the peace and to resolve conflicts, countries will rely less on violence and national military power to settle their conflicts. Just as post–World War II West European states have avoided war among themselves for almost half a century, countries of the world will rely more on international and regional institutions to offer credible alternatives to war and other forms of organized mass violence.

6. Cooperation is both desirable and possible. By their nature, threats resulting from interdependence cannot be solved by one country alone, not even by the United States. Therefore, international organizations such as the UN have a responsibility to help address these threats. To serve its interests in an interdependent world, the United States—as a respected and powerful country— must support international efforts to confront interdependence problems. As the successful UN operations to reverse Iraq's

There are conflicts which cannot be resolved unilaterally. The war in Afghanistan and between Iran and Iraq are examples of this. These two long-term situations were to bring not only the United States, but the Soviet Union and the rest of the world, a new sense of realism: if the UN did not exist, a new international situation would be needed to resolve conflicts; therefore, it was better to improve the existing organization than to build a new one.

—Indar Jit Rikhye, "Speaking with Indar Jit Rikhye About Peacekeeping," *United States Institute of Peace Journal* (June 1991)

The post-Cold War era . . . provides . . . the opportunity to strive for truly collective security and an international rule of law, in which self-help by the use of military force for resolving conflicts among nations loses its legitimacy. The U.N. charter and the instruments available under it can gain increasing credibility through increasing use and thus provide the framework for an evolving rule of law.

—Carl Kaysen, Robert McNamara, and George Rathjens, "Nuclear Weapons After the Cold War," *Foreign Affairs* (Fall 1991)

invasion of Kuwait illustrated, the end of the Cold War has made real cooperation more feasible.

7. To bring about collaboration through an international institution, either countries with veto power must agree on their basic interests, or the voting formula should shift from consensus (where any country with a veto can prevent agreement) toward something resembling majority rule. Thus, for cooperation to work, all countries (including the United States) will have to accept some compromises and unfavorable decisions.

Future 3 Is Based on These Values

1. Americans are not only citizens of a great country, but also citizens of an interdependent world. Since we feel responsibilities both toward our own people and toward all of humankind, we wish to divide the "peace dividend" between rebuilding our own economy and helping to solve global problems. We should encourage others to adopt this global ethic, which will help to create a sense of world community—a prerequisite for building and sustaining effective international institutions to manage our common problems.

2. Human rights are important, but only those rights that are recognized by the members of the UN should be enforced globally. Agreement is already apparent or close, for example, on prohibiting genocide and torture. The UN and other international organizations have also been offering their services to hold and monitor fair elections. The United States will work with other countries to uphold the rights endorsed by the UN, even at the costs of annoying governments that violate human rights and experiencing some economic losses from imposing trade sanctions.

   Where agreement is lacking, such as on banning the death penalty or removing all restrictions on publications or religious practices, the rights are not universal but relative—important to some governments but not to others. We have no inherent privilege to intervene elsewhere on behalf of these relative rights, and others have no license to impose their standards upon us.

3. Peaceful change is an important American value. The United States would prefer a world where conflict is managed cooperatively, without organized mass violence. This value leads it to want to strengthen international legal and peacekeeping institutions, even if this means it will not get its way on every issue.

4. Americans also value fairness, and recognize that payment for cooperative efforts should be assessed by a country's ability to

pay, not simply by its proportion of the world's population. Since the United States comprises 5 percent of the world's population and generates about a quarter of the world's gross national product, its contributions should be much closer to its proportion of the world's wealth—perhaps 20 percent of the costs. This means that others will pay for the remaining 80 percent, and the United States will clearly not be the world's policeman and banker.

5. Without first seeking and acquiring international approval, no country—including the United States—has the right to unilaterally pressure another country to behave in a certain way, to deploy military forces in other countries, or to start wars around the world. Of course the United States will retain the right to defend itself, but it will rely on international efforts to defend its citizens and interests abroad.

What Should the United States Do in the 1990s to Head Toward Future 3?

Here are some political, military, and economic policies that the United States can follow in the 1990s to help bring about this Future. The historical examples show that such policies can work—and therefore that Future 3 is feasible. Future 3 supporters do not have to support every policy listed.

1. The United States will accept UN Security Council jurisdiction on decisions to use military force. That is, it will agree not to send troops to fight abroad unless the 15-member Security Council (with all five of its permanent members, including the United States) decides that it should. UN approval of U.S.-led operations countering Iraq's aggression against Kuwait added legitimacy to the effort and helped to hold the coalition together. The United States carried the burden of that battle, however. In the future, no more than 20 percent of the UN force will be composed of U.S. troops.

2. The United States will work to establish a permanent UN standby force, capable of rapid deployment to crisis areas. This will express the UN commitment to the principle of peacekeeping, and having it ready should expand the options available to help prevent wars or to restore the peace. At the same time that this force is established, the United States will gradually reduce the number of its troops abroad, with the goal of eventually having no independent U.S. forces outside of North America.

3. To promote the concept of mutual security, the United States will support international efforts to reach global and regional arms

The Security Council [has] primary responsibility for the maintenance of international peace and security. . . . [It] may decide what measures not involving the use of armed force are to be employed to give effect to its decisions, and it may call upon the members of the United Nations to apply such measures. . . . Should the Security Council consider that [these] measures . . . would be inadequate or have proved to be inadequate, it may take such action by air, sea, or land forces as may be necessary to maintain or restore international peace and security.

Nothing in the present Charter shall impair the inherent right of individual or collective self-defense if an armed attack occurs against a Member of the United Nations, until the Security Council has taken the measures necessary to maintain international peace and security. Measures taken by Members in the exercise of this right of self-defense shall be immediately reported to the Security Council and shall not in any way affect the authority and responsibility of the Security Council.

—UN Charter, Articles 24, 41, 42, and 51

If at the request of Kuwait a peacekeeping force had been deployed on its border with Iraq in August 1990, the Gulf War might have been avoided.

—Bruce Russett and James Sutterlin, "The U.N. in a New World Order," *Foreign Affairs* (Spring 1991)

control and disarmament agreements, and to establish confidence- and security-building measures (CSBMs). Successes along these lines in Europe (such as the Conventional Forces in Europe talks and the expanded set of CSBMs agreed upon in 1990 in Vienna) helped lessen fears among the parties and encouraged more cooperative interactions. To reassure participants in future agreements, the United States will support the principle of UN inspection to verify compliance. To encourage other countries to follow, the United States will permit UN inspection of all arms control agreements to which it is a party—even agreements (such as the Biological Weapons Convention) that do not require inspection.

4. The United States will report to the UN all arms transfers and respect international agreements to embargo arms transfers. This will lend strength to the idea that international organizations should regulate the transfer of armaments.

5. The United States will support international efforts to restrain the spread of nuclear weapons. One way is to help promote mutual and collective security arrangements, so countries will have less incentive to acquire or keep nuclear weapons. Another is to encourage additional nuclear weapons–free zones to help prevent regional nuclear arms races. Such a zone in Latin America, for example, has dampened the nuclear competition between Argentina and Brazil. Finally, if the UN Security Council agrees, the United States will support economic or military actions against rogue nuclear countries.

6. The United States will support international boycotts and embargoes against countries that refuse to respect the rights of other countries, try to acquire weapons of mass destruction, support terrorism, engage in illegal drug trafficking, deny human rights, break agreements to protect the environment, or otherwise violate international law. Since the U.S. economy is so large and exerts so much international influence, the United States has a special responsibility to cooperate on such efforts. Thus, for example, the South African government felt greater pressure to end apartheid when the United States enacted sanctions in 1986; by 1992 South Africa was well on its way toward reversing apartheid. The United States will cooperate in these international efforts, even at the risk of irritating some governments and losing some benefits from trade.

7. The United States will help strengthen alternatives to war for resolving international conflicts. In the late 1980s and early 1990s, UN mediation led to the removal of Soviet troops from Afghanistan. It also helped bring to a close a number of civil wars that engaged other countries in conflict (such as in Angola, Cambodia, and Namibia). Also in the late 1980s, a multilateral mediation effort led by Costa Rica's president Oscar Arias helped to resolve the conflict in Central America between Nicaragua and several of its neighbors, paving the way for democracy in

The United States correctly wants to avoid the role of world policeman. The way to steer a middle path between bearing too much and too little of the international burden is to renew the American commitment to multilateral institutions that fell into abeyance in the 1980s. The use of multilateral institutions, while sometimes constraining, also helps share the burden that the American people do not want to bear alone.

—Joseph S. Nye, Jr., "What New World Order?" Foreign Affairs (Spring 1992)

Nicaragua. The United States will consistently support such efforts.

For mediation to work, however, the parties to a conflict must agree to participate in the process and then agree to accept the recommendations of the mediator. Since both preconditions are often missing, the United States will encourage countries that cannot reach agreement through negotiations or mediation to accept the compulsory jurisdiction and binding decisions of international institutions. In the hopes of strengthening such institutions, the United States will start by accepting the jurisdiction of the International Court of Justice in disputes between itself and other countries that accept its jurisdiction.

8. The United States will support the economic, political, and social development of peoples throughout the world. If suffering people see no hope for improving their lot, they will view calls for law, stability, and arms control as mechanisms to sustain an unacceptable status quo. Therefore the United States must help poor and oppressed peoples of the world redress their grievances and improve their situation. When assistance is useful, the United States will supply aid, often through multilateral institutions like the World Bank and the UN Environmental Program. It will increase its contributions to match the percentage of gross national product agreed upon by the UN. If other countries' governments are an obstacle to needed improvements, the United States will work with the UN to compel these governments to institute more humane policies.

What is at stake (in the Persian Gulf War) is more than one small country, it is a big idea: a new world order where diverse nations are drawn together in a common cause to achieve the universal aspirations of mankind—peace and security, freedom and the rule of law.

—George Bush,
State of the Union Address
(January 30, 1991)

How Much Will Future 3 Cost the United States?

With the Cold War long over and the permanent UN rapid-deployment peacekeeping force becoming established, the United States will no longer need to remain the world's military superpower and will therefore cut back on its military spending. While some of the savings are being put to use at home, enough of the money saved will be spent on international collaboration to pay for a 20 percent contribution to these efforts.

Building U.S. Economic Strength

The United States has never been less threatened by foreign forces than it is today. But the unfortunate corollary is that never since the Great Depression has the threat to domestic well-being been greater. By winning the cold war, however, we have earned about a decade of freedom to reorient our foreign policy and concentrate our resources, energy and attention on dealing with the domestic crisis.

—William G. Hyland, "Downgrade Foreign Policy," *New York Times* (May 20, 1991)

It is the year 2005. Over the past decade, Americans came to understand that having the world's strongest economy is far more important and less risky than having troops spread across the world.

For several decades after World War II, the United States was a military superpower and the leader of the international economic order. Even before the Cold War ended, however, the United States' relative economic position was declining. While it was spending its wealth and intellectual resources defending distant countries like West Germany and Japan, which could easily afford to defend themselves, those countries were pulling ahead of the United States economically and technologically. Unburdened by military spending, they were becoming the world's economic leaders. The United States, in contrast, was so bogged down militarily around the world that it could not afford to deal with the greatest threats facing it in the 1990s: its weakening economy, its lack of economic competitiveness, a huge national debt, an aging infrastructure, crime, drugs, AIDS, pollution, and homelessness. It was clear that if the United States did not change with the times, it would lose its international standing and its prized way of life.

In the post–Cold War political environment of the past 10 years, the United States gradually brought its troops home and cut its military spending by about two-thirds. It used the hundreds of billions of dollars saved to strengthen its economy, improve its energy self-sufficiency, and address other pressing national problems. The United States is still capable of defending North America, and maintains a small force to strike quickly when Americans abroad are seriously threatened, but it is no longer a military giant. It has reduced the risk of fighting costly wars for dubious interests and values. In today's world, U.S. security and world leadership depend on economic—not military—strength. In 2005 the United States is rapidly growing stronger. If it ever needs to build up its military power again, it will have the strong economic base required. The country's economic, social, and political successes show the world what a vibrant democracy can accomplish.

Future 4 Is Based on These Beliefs

1. In the twenty-first century, the major threats to U.S. interests will be intensified economic competition from advanced countries and a domestic economy too weak to deal with immediate threats to Americans at home. The United States' lack of economic competitiveness, if allowed to continue, will undermine the basis of its power and influence. With inadequate funds to spend on domestic problems, moreover, U.S. citizens will face the insecurities of homelessness, poor nutrition and health, an inadequate education system, crime, and pollution.

2. The root cause of the United States' economic weaknesses is "imperial overstretch." The country has been spending far more on military defense than was objectively required, and hence not enough on domestic needs. It has also been stationing troops abroad to defend countries like Japan and Germany, which for several decades have had enough money to defend themselves. Unburdened with high military expenditures, these countries have channeled their financial and intellectual resources to pull ahead of the United States in key areas of technology. If the trend continues, they will become the world's economic superpowers, with all the economic and political leverage that entails.

3. The international system is anarchic, with no supreme authority to protect individual states from aggression by other states. Therefore it is a competitive system, where states must watch out for themselves as they seek to survive, retain their sovereignty, and prosper. States require power to achieve these aims, and, when necessary, they will engage in power politics to protect and further their national interests. Although states are interconnected with one another, they are not uniformly interdependent on all issues. Thus, U.S. security and prosperity does not necessarily depend on the security and prosperity of all countries. If the United States becomes energy independent, for example, it will not rely on imported oil and therefore will not need to be concerned about future wars in the Persian Gulf.

4. Power is the primary means to achieve various foreign policy ends. Power has both military and economic components, and what counts is relative capability—as one country gains power, other countries lose comparative standing. Because war is always possible in an anarchic environment, states must be attentive to their relative position in the system and therefore their relative military and economic power. If military power becomes less important, economic power becomes proportionally more so.

5. With the end of the Cold War and its attendant risks of confrontation with the Soviet Union, economic strength has become more essential to U.S. security than military strength. As long as the United States maintains a nuclear arsenal, the threat of a devastat-

Although the United States is at present still in a class of its own . . . it cannot avoid confronting the two great tests which challenge the longevity of every major power that occupies the "number one" position in world affairs: whether it can preserve a reasonable balance between the nation's perceived defense requirements and the means it possesses to maintain those commitments; and whether . . . it can preserve the technological and economic base of its power from relative erosion in the face of ever-shifting patterns of global production. The United States now runs the risk . . . of . . . "imperial overstretch": . . . the sum total of the United States' global interests and obligations is nowadays far larger than the country's power to defend them all simultaneously.

—Paul Kennedy, *The Rise and Fall of the Great Powers* (1987)

What is lost in the self-congratulations of many Americans over the collapse of communism is that the time of the American empire has also run out.

—Earl Ravenal, "The Case for Adjustment," *Foreign Policy* (Winter 1990-91)

Since the collapse of the Soviet empire, American officials have been scrambling for alternative rationales for U.S. intervention-ism. . . . Two have emerged as leading candidates: preserving international "stability," and leading a worldwide movement for democracy. These two objectives would seem to be inconsistent if not fundamentally incompatible, but both have two features in common: Each would entangle the United States in a morass of regional, local, and even internecine conflicts throughout the world; and more often than not, each would involve the United States in conflicts that have little or no relevance to America's own vital security interests.

—Ted Galen Carpenter, "The New World Disorder," *Foreign Policy* (Fall 1991)

The powerful state may, and the United States does, think of itself as acting for the sake of peace, justice and the well-being of the world. But these terms will be defined to the liking of the powerful, which may conflict with the preferences and interests of others. In international politics, overwhelming power repels and leads others to try to balance against it. With benign intent, the United States has behaved, and until its power is brought into a semblance of balance, will continue to behave in ways that annoy and frighten others.

—Kenneth Waltz, "America as a Model for the World? A Foreign Policy Perspective," *PS* (December 1991)

ing U.S. retaliation will deter any country from attacking the United States. This change in military technology has permanently altered the calculations of state leaders, making it less important for the United States to maintain large military forces. The United States benefits from a balanced distribution of military power, in which no other country is able to threaten key U.S. trade relations. The United States does not have to station troops abroad or maintain overseas alliances to help keep the balance, due to the disintegration of the Soviet Union and the increased strength of West European democracies and Japan.

6. The United States' national interests do not require it to take a leading role in defending or promoting democracy abroad, and efforts to promote democracy rarely succeed anyway. Stationing U.S. troops overseas is also risky and costly. The U.S. alliance commitment to defend South Vietnam, for instance, led the United States to get involved in a war that did not affect its vital interests. The United States sacrificed billions of dollars and tens of thousands of lives in this war, fearing that a communist victory there would lead to a "domino effect" of communist takeovers throughout Southeast Asia and around the world. Yet, when South Vietnam finally was defeated, no significant dominoes fell. The United States' efforts to promote democratic and economic reforms in South Vietnam were also miserable failures. It has had similar difficulties engineering democracy in Grenada and Panama, although its military forces were victorious in these countries.

Alliances are mediocre peacekeeping arrangements, not just for the United States today but in general. In 1914, for example, Austria felt confident in attacking Serbia only because Austria was backed by its German ally. Because of alliance commitments, moreover, a small war in the Balkans spread to engage all of the allies and become a world war. And war would not have occurred in the Middle East in 1956 had there been no alliance among Britain, France, and Israel—the three countries that attacked Egypt.

Future 4 Is Based on These Values

1. The U.S. government must be concerned first and foremost with the safety and welfare of American citizens. Most U.S. military expenditures have not made Americans safer—indeed, at times Pentagon programs and troop deployments have increased the risk of war. U.S. foreign aid programs, dominated by military assistance, have often failed to serve either U.S. interests or humanitarian values.

2. Democracy and human rights are wonderful values, to be defended at home at all costs. Yet not all peoples of the world hold these values as highly as Americans do, and some define human rights and even democracy differently. The dilemma was illustrated by events in Algeria in late 1991 and 1992, when the Islamic Salvation Front won an overwhelming victory in one of the first free and fair elections since Algeria's independence in 1962. Yet, claiming that the precepts of the fundamentalist party are inherently anti-democratic, the military and its allies overturned the elections, saying that their takeover was necessary to retain other democratic freedoms. The paradox was expressed in a French political cartoon: A veiled Muslim woman casts her vote in that election, commenting to the election official that this is her first and last vote. Who are we to say who is right? Thus, while perhaps we can encourage the spread of our versions of democracy and human rights by example or by offering incentives, it would be presumptuous to force others to adopt them.

3. We value highly the right of all nations, including our own, to determine their own fate. This value ranks above our desire to see our versions of democracy and human rights spread abroad. A foreign policy corollary of national self-determination is the principle of non-intervention, which obviously conflicts with trying to coerce others to adopt our values. Our respect for national sovereignty also conflicts with the desires of some to strengthen international organizations, if this means that states lose their ability to act unilaterally.

4. National interests outweigh all of these grand principles. Thus, if international circumstances change radically, so that protecting our vital interests requires us to violate these values, then we should do so. For example, the United States will interfere in other countries' affairs if crucial U.S. interests are at stake. Likewise, if necessary to protect U.S. interests, the United States will surrender some sovereignty to international organizations.

5. The United States values its leadership in democratic ideals and high standards of living more than its military power or political influence over other countries. It cannot impose democratic ideals abroad, but it can serve as a dynamic example of democracy's benefits.

What Should the United States Do in the 1990s to Head Toward Future 4?

Here are some political, military, and economic policies that the United States can follow in the 1990s to help bring about this Future. The

What is desperately required is a psychological turn inward. . . . This turn will affect foreign policy. Taking on new commitments in the Middle East and Persian Gulf while maintaining most of the old ones in Europe and the Far East cannot be justified in the face of a disastrous domestic agenda: crime, drugs, education, urban crises, Federal budget deficits and a constant squeeze on the middle class, the backbone of our democracy.

—William G. Hyland,
"Downgrade Foreign Policy,"
New York Times (May 20, 1991)

historical examples show that such policies can work—and therefore that Future 4 is feasible. Future 4 supporters do not have to support every policy listed.

1. The United States will gradually phase out our permanent alliances around the world, except with Canada, Mexico, and the Caribbean nations. Of course, the United States will consider cooperating militarily with other countries if such a course of action ever seems essential to national security interests.

2. The United States will bring home, over time, all troops stationed abroad. U.S. armed forces will be redesigned to defend only North America. The United States will also maintain a small force that is able to respond quickly around the world when American lives are at stake, such as during a hostage crisis. This special force will be able to rescue or evacuate Americans from a hostile or uncooperative country, much as Israeli commandos rescued Israeli citizens at the Entebbe airport in 1976. The advantages of this policy outweigh marginal disadvantages, such as the decreased ability to defend other regions. U.S. influence will not greatly decline, since economic power is more important than military power.

3. The United States will encourage arms control agreements to reduce the size of other countries' nuclear and conventional arsenals. These countries will then have more funds available to serve the needs of their own people. The United States will oppose efforts to achieve total nuclear disarmament, however, because nuclear weapons provide the United States with inexpensive security.

4. The United States will gradually cut its military budget by about two-thirds. This will be possible when the United States ends most military commitments, brings its troops home, reduces the size of its conventional forces and nuclear arsenal, and closes many home-based military facilities. The United States' general macroeconomic health requires these changes, although local, microeconomic disadvantages will result: layoffs in the military and in defense industries, and tax losses in defense-dependent communities.

5. The United States will redirect the $200 billion cut from the U.S. annual military budget to improve both U.S. economic competitiveness and the lives of U.S. citizens.

6. The United States will become energy self-sufficient. To do this, it may intensify energy conservation measures, pump more oil from the ground and seabed, burn more coal, increase its reliance on nuclear energy, build more dams and tidal projects, use solar and wind power, and/or explore new energy sources (such as nuclear fusion or collecting and transmitting energy from satellites).

7. The United States will rely more on economic policy instruments. Once the U.S. economy is rebuilt, for example, the United States will have more leverage to get its way in negotiations over economic and environmental issues. The United States will also use economic incentives, and possibly sanctions, to encourage other countries to improve their human rights records, to become more democratic, or to undertake beneficial economic reforms.

8. The United States will be judicious and selective in the allocation of foreign aid. The biggest portion, military aid, will be eliminated. The top priority for U.S. economic aid will be those programs that will directly serve U.S. national interests. What is left over can serve humanitarian and ideological goals.

9. Because the United States values its sovereignty and the principle of national self-determination, it will generally not support efforts to strengthen international institutions that will reduce our freedom of action. The United States will support limited cooperation when it is clearly in the U.S. self-interest.

10. Non-intervention will be a principle of U.S. foreign policy, which means that the United States will not use violence or the threat of violence to influence politics within other countries. This does not prevent the United States from using moral suasion, or economic concessions and sanctions, to promote democracy, human rights, or development. The United States will not isolate itself from the rest of the world economically and politically. Americans still care about the welfare of other peoples, and will act to help them when it does not compromise U.S. national interests or values.

How Much Will Future 4 Cost the United States?

Future 4 will save the United States an enormous amount of money. Eventually it will allow the United States to cut its military budget by about two-thirds, which will free up $200 billion yearly. The United States will redirect almost all of these funds to strengthen its economy and to better address problems at home. This will still leave billions available to promote U.S. interests and values.

Some local communities will experience dislocations from the closing of military bases, the loss of military contracts and jobs, and lower tax revenues. Future 4 supporters will have to decide whether or not some of the "peace dividend" should be used to cushion these effects—by providing unemployment benefits, by retraining or relocating affected people, and by providing local aid for government services.

Since the failed coup in Moscow, U.S. hawks, citing new Soviet uncertainties and the world's almost limitless capacity for generating violence, have claimed that this is no time to cut military spending. Some liberals counter that our main interest is in aiding the Russians—either by using funds that would otherwise go to the military to facilitate the economic and democratic transition, or through a more ambitious aid program. Yet America, weighed down by deficits and by pressing domestic ills, cannot afford to listen to either group. In any event, no popular support exists for the tax increases or domestic spending reductions needed to finance high levels of Pentagon spending or a proposal to shift military funds to foreign aid.

We need to respond only to Soviet actions that would directly and concretely affect American security and prosperity, such as the fragmentation of the Soviet nuclear command or future troublemaking in our Caribbean backyard. And we should devote our real efforts to real interests, like reducing our dependency on unstable regions, like the Persian Gulf.

—Alan Tonelson, "Put America First," *New York Times* (September 7, 1991)

CHAPTER 3

Challenges Facing the United States

A s we contemplate the role of the United States in the post–Cold War world, we must sort through a wide array of foreign policy issues. In the process, we must keep in mind the three broad purposes that set the standard for any effective foreign policy: to defend the country against outside attack or harm, to further the country's interests by maintaining or increasing its geopolitical power and its economic strength, and to defend or promote national values. However, many policies may fulfill these broad purposes, and competing policies often present different priorities of values and contradictory beliefs about how the world works. For example, Americans may share a single purpose—such as defending the United States from harm—but propose drastically different approaches. One policymaker may want to promote democracy abroad, in the belief that democracies are peaceful in their relations with other democracies. Another may call for U.S. participation in alliances, believing that this will discourage aggression and prevent the rise of a country strong enough to threaten the United States. Further differences arise over the means to attain those goals. Should we promote democracy by example? Economic pressure? Military force?

Another difficulty arises in setting priorities. Foreign policy generally entails some difficult balancing of goals. For instance, the United States has endorsed respect for human rights around the world; it also has opposed pro-Soviet or anti-American political movements. When these two goals have come into conflict, the United States has often supported governments that violate human rights but are sympathetic to U.S. interests. To critics, aid to dictators flies in the face of the United States' deepest values. To supporters, such aid is sometimes the lesser of two evils, the best way of protecting the United States and its allies. The United States must balance these and other concerns.

This chapter explores the threats to U.S. safety and strength, and policies that may help to counter these threats. It also examines some of the positive U.S. interests that U.S. policy should support. Chapter 4 examines how value priorities affect policy preferences, and Chapter 5 presents some methods of sorting out the likely consequences of U.S. policy.

After the Cold War: New Issues in Europe

Despite isolationist themes in U.S. foreign policy, the United States has always paid attention to events abroad, and especially in Europe. This emphasis on Europe can be explained by the United States' distinctive strategic position. The United States enjoys an unusual degree of physical security, especially with respect to its neighbors. The adjoining countries, Canada and Mexico, pose no significant threat to it. Among countries in the Western Hemisphere, only Cuba under Fidel Castro has been consistently hostile. Even so, Cuba only posed a military threat for the short time that Soviet nuclear missiles were under construction there. The most significant threats have come from great powers elsewhere in the world—and most great powers have been European.

Skeptics have questioned whether the United States has vital interests at stake in Europe. The answer largely depends on one's definition of "vital." The threat posed by Germany in the two world wars was mostly indirect. Few believed that Germany would invade the United States. But if Germany (and its allies) had dominated Europe and Asia, the United States could have been cut off from allies and trading partners, a position that even isolationists were eager to avoid. Similarly, few analysts feared that the Soviet Union would launch a nuclear attack on the United States. Instead, they feared that by expanding its global influence and military power, the Soviet Union would gradually compel the United States to acquiesce in Soviet dominance of world affairs.

Europe continues to weigh heavy in the global balance because of its industrial development. Between them, the United States and Western Europe produce almost half of the world's industrial goods. The United States also trades extensively with West European countries. Also, Europe remains a center of global political influence. The imperial might of Great Britain and France earned these countries permanent seats on the United Nations' Security Council. Although these countries have given up their colonies, they still have clout in the regions they formerly controlled.

Renewal and Upheaval

For more than 40 years after World War II, the United States' preeminent concern about Europe was that the Soviet Union would dominate the region. Since the Soviet Union's abrupt collapse, this threat has been replaced by a broader—but less direct—danger: political chaos throughout Eastern Europe and Soviet lands. In the many states where socialist governments have fallen, new governments are struggling to

Atlantic
Ocean

Svalbard
(NORWAY)

Arctic

Franz Josef
Land
(RUSSIA)

U.K.

North
Sea

NORWAY

Oslo

SWEDEN

DEN.

Copenhagen

Stockholm

GERMANY
Berlin

Baltic Sea

FINLAND

Helsinki

Barents
Sea

Kara
Sea

Kaliningrad
(RUSSIA)

Riga

Tallinn

ESTONIA

POLAND
Warsaw

LITHUANIA
Vilnius

LATVIA

Final boundaries of Estonia, Latvia and
Lithuania with the former Soviet Union are
expected to be confirmed by agreement.

CZECH.

BYELARUS

HUNG.

Minsk

ROM.

MOLDOVA
Kishinev

Kiev

UKRAINE

Moscow

RUSSIA

Black
Sea

GEORGIA

TURKEY

Tbilisi

ARMENIA
Yerevan

AZERBAIJAN

SYRIA

Baku

Caspian
Sea

Aral
Sea

KAZAKHSTAN

Lake
Balkhash

Baghdad

IRAQ

Tehran

IRAN

TURKMENISTAN

Ashkhabad

UZBEKISTAN

Tashkent

Alma-
Ata

Bishkek

KYRGYZSTAN

KUWAIT

Kuwait

Dushanbe

TAJIKISTAN

SAUDI
ARABIA

AFGHANISTAN

Kabul

PAKISTAN

The States of the

Chukchi
Sea

Ocean

Bering
Sea

East Siberian
Sea

Laptev
Sea

States of the Former Soviet Union

Armenia
Azerbaijan
Byelarus
Estonia
Georgia
Kyrgyzstan
Latvia
Lithuania
Moldova
Russia
Tajikistan
Turkmenistan
Ukraine
Uzbekistan

Sea of
Okhotsk

Occupied by the Soviet Union
in 1945, administered by Russia,
claimed by Japan

RUSSIA

Lake
Baikal

Sea of
Japan

Tokyo ★

JAPAN

Ulaanbaatar ★

NORTH KOREA

P'yongyang
★

M O N G O L I A

Seoul
★

Beijing ★

SOUTH KOREA

Yellow
Sea

C H I N A

East China
Sea

| 0 | 400 | 800 kilometers |
| 0 | 400 | 800 miles |

Names and boundary representation
are not necessarily authoritative.

1671 2-91 STATE (INR/GE)

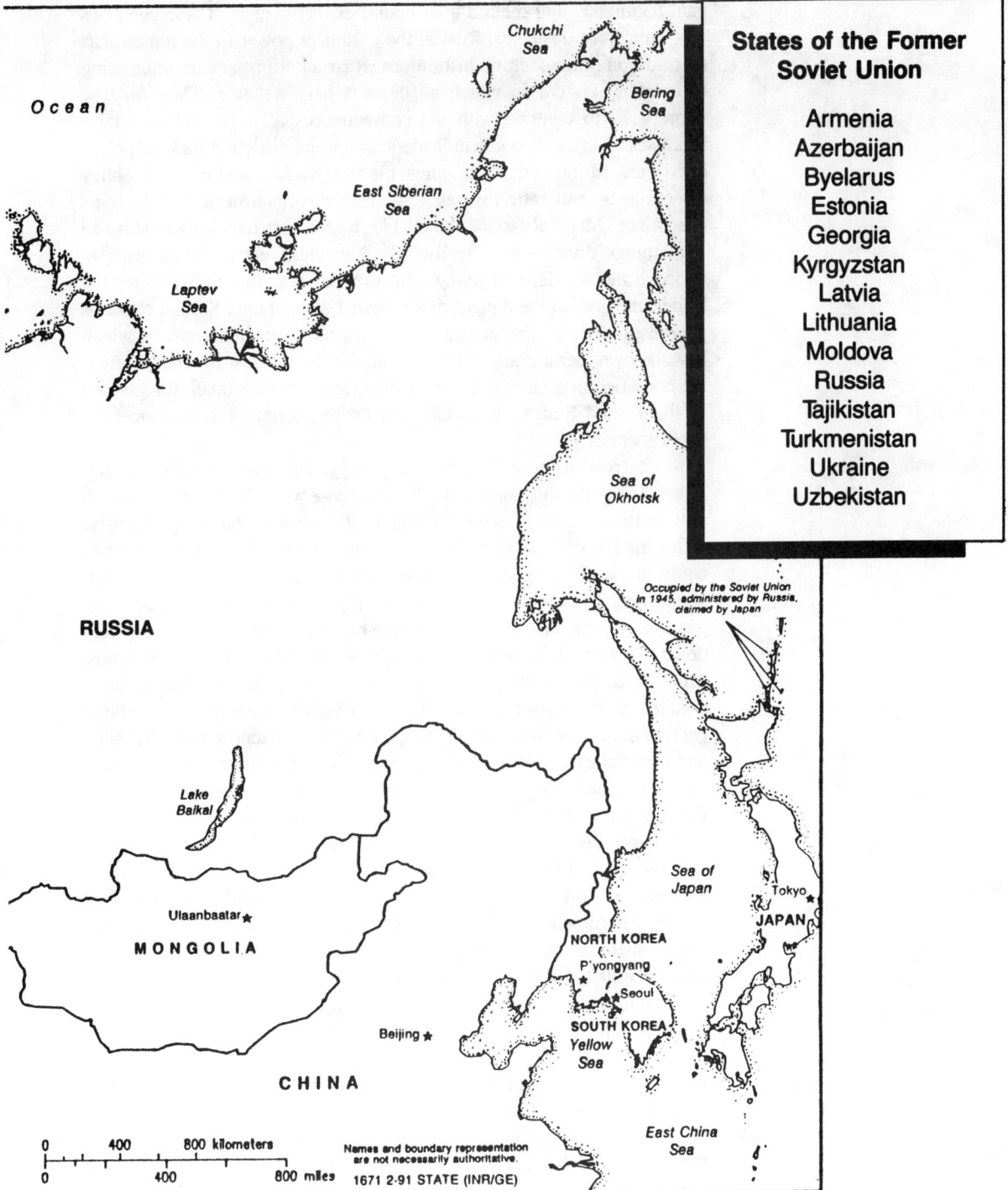

Former Soviet Union

Map courtesy of the State Department

gain legitimacy and rebuild their countries' economies. These countries face enormous obstacles. Russia, the dominant power in the region, has no tradition of democratic institutions. Russian reformers are attempting to create a system in which all citizens have a voice. They may be unprepared to contend with the consequences: divisive debates, false promises, distrust of political leaders, and great difficulty making policy decisions. Moreover, even when elected leaders settle on a policy direction, bureaucratic resistance or sheer disorganization can delay its enactment. Many Russians would like to see a strong leader who can "get things done"—specifically, who can enact economic reforms to improve the standard of living. But skeptics fear that the stronger the leader, the greater the danger of a renewed dictatorship. Similar tensions prevail in other ex-Soviet and East European countries, most of which have known democratic rule for only a few years in this century. Democratic government, however imperfect, is often taken for granted in the United States; in Russia and its neighbors, it is an uncertain experiment.

The road to economic recovery is perhaps even more uncertain. According to the most optimistic Western observers, these countries need only to lift the heavy hand of government control so that free enterprise and initiative can flourish. However, the former Soviet bloc countries confront bewildering complications. First of all, the region's governments, despite all their faults, provided important benefits. Workers were guaranteed jobs, and basic goods were heavily subsidized to keep prices down. These policies led to tremendous waste and inefficiency, and most economists give high priority to ending them. Yet to change these policies, Eastern governments must in effect rip down the few working parts of their economic system, subjecting their citizens to acute hardship and uncertainty in the near future. Next, these countries seek to rebuild their industrial base so that they may share in the prosperity of Western Europe. But vital productive resources—from factories to oil—have long been controlled by government bureaucracies, and there is no magic formula for distributing resources to responsible investors. In Russia, for instance, a group of former bureaucrats and speculators called the "mafia" dominate many cities' economies. While reformers seek fair and efficient distribution of government-controlled resources, they must recognize that some tasks require a large government role. Roads must be rebuilt; toxic waste dumps must be cleaned up; economic policies must be adjusted to limit inflation and stabilize weak currencies. To meet these and many other challenges, Eastern governments must grow stronger in some respects even as they give up much of their former authority.

To these predicaments, add the explosive factor of ethnic conflict. In the first half of the century, much of Eastern Europe was torn by violent national rivalries that cut across state borders. There is an important distinction between nations and states. A nation can be defined as "a

For many, this picture is a living symbol of the failed East European economies.

group of culturally and historically similar people who feel a communal bond and who feel they should govern themselves to at least some degree."[1] A state, or country, is a political entity that exercises power within its territory and is recognized by other states. All over the world, one can find states that contain several nations. Canada contains two dominant nations—one speaking French and the other English—who have often wrestled for political power. Likewise, many nations, or peoples, straddle state borders.

Both types of situations—multinational states and multistate nationalities—have created dangerous conflicts in the former Soviet bloc. Armenia and Azerbaijan, two formerly Soviet republics, have disputed the status of Nagorno-Karabakh, a part of Azerbaijan dominated by ethnic Armenians; several times fighting has broken out in this area. The South Ossetian region of Georgia, another former Soviet republic, has claimed independence from Georgia and seeks unification with the North Ossetian region of the Russian Federation. In the fighting between the Georgian government and the South Ossetians, hundreds have been killed and tens of thousands have fled for North Ossetia.

Disputes over boundaries and possible ethnic tensions also plague relations between Russia and Ukraine, arguably the two most powerful

---

1. John T. Rourke, *International Politics on the World Stage*, 3d ed. (Guilford, CT: The Dushkin Publishing Group, 1991), 583.

The Former Yugoslavia

states of the former Soviet Union. The dangers are evident in two conflicts that have involved large-scale military operations. First, ethnic Russians and Ukrainians living in the eastern part of Moldova, another former Soviet republic, have sought independence for the so-called Dniester Republic. These Slavic peoples refuse to remain a part of Moldova because the majority ethnic Romanians, who are not Slavic, are considering uniting with their brethren across the border. The Moldovan government sought to repress this independence drive, and during the summer of 1992 Russian-controlled units of the former Soviet army got involved in the battle to protect the Russian minority.

The dangers are also evident in the dismemberment of Yugoslavia, until recently a stable multinational state. Serbia, the largest Yugoslavian republic, dominated the Yugoslav army and Yugoslavian politics. When neighboring republics asserted their independence, the army responded forcefully, with the avowed intent of preserving unity and protecting ethnic Serbs in other republics. The country disintegrated into civil war. Elsewhere, long-established states face ethnic conflicts that had been suppressed under Soviet dominance. For instance, Hungary and Romania have exchanged harsh words about the status of the Hungarian minority in Romania. Considering the many cases of such tensions, it seems likely that sooner or later one of them will lead to a war that drags in neighboring states.

A Bosnian soldier occupies a firing position overlooking Sarajevo, the capital of Bosnia-Herzegovina, during its siege by Serbian troops.

U.S. Interests in Europe

Why are these problems considered a United States security issue? The United States' special interest in this region largely stems from its traditional interest in Europe. Policymakers fear, first of all, that violence in Eastern Europe may directly embroil West European states. The risk extends to the possibility of nuclear attacks. Russia, Ukraine, Byelarus, and Kazakhstan still possess nuclear arsenals. These arsenals are so large that even deep reductions may not eliminate the danger to other countries, and possibly to the United States. If a nuclear war is most likely to be started out of fear and desperation, then the political upheaval in former Soviet territory may increase the risk of war. The former republics may go to war with each other over territorial and ethnic disputes, or they may threaten neighboring countries in an attempt to extract economic concessions. Even if a nuclear war were initially confined within former Soviet borders, its ecological harm and social disruption would quickly spread. For that matter, a non-nuclear war in the east would impose huge costs of its own, especially if it spread widely.

The threat of war aside, the United States has a stake of some sort in the success of political and economic reforms throughout the former communist nations. Continuing economic weakness in Eastern Europe may create a flood of refugees to the West, disrupting West European societies and economies. By the same token, the United States stands to gain if Eastern Europe and the former Soviet republics can achieve political stability and economic success on a democratic basis. Regional peace and prosperity would likely allow the United States to reduce sharply its military strength in Europe. It would also foster mutually beneficial trade relations, and enable states of the region to repay their debts to U.S. and other Western banks.

But how far should the United States go in aiding these states? Their economic problems are so profound that U.S. aid may be only a drop in the bucket. Some observers think that monetary aid might actually delay reforms by strengthening inefficient central governments. Others believe that aid targeted to strengthen private enterprise will advance the reforms. The United States has supported most multinational aid efforts, and has sent some private advisers, but has limited its economic commitment to the region. Whatever the impact of U.S. aid, it has provoked controversy at home. Some observers argue that the United States is being too cautious, wasting an opportunity to promote lasting peace and security in Europe. Others argue that the United States should now focus its attention on problems at home.

The United States must also determine the future of its troops in Europe. In 1989, when the Berlin Wall fell, over 300,000 U.S. troops were stationed in Europe at an annual cost to the United States of $50 billion. Now that Soviet troops no longer threaten Western Europe, the U.S. forces will be reduced. Many believe that a smaller but substantial number of troops—perhaps 50,000—should remain as a guarantee to Europe that the United States will try to keep the peace in the region. Not all the threats to peace come from the east: Europeans well remember that Germany started World War II, and largely provoked World War I. While renewed German aggression may seem almost inconceivable, a continued U.S. presence would provide some reassurance that no European power would mount a major offensive. However, some observers do not believe that U.S. troops actually play an important peacekeeping role, or that the advantages justify the expenses.

The European Community:
A Rift in the Trans-Atlantic Alliance?

As the Soviet threat ceases to be a rationale for U.S.–West European cooperation, the traditional alliance will be tested by economic competition and political differences. Since the 1950s, the West European countries have cooperated with each other ever more closely in economic matters. Currently, this cooperation is focused in the European Community (EC), whose twelve members include most West European countries. The smaller European Free Trade Association, of six countries (most of whom were neutral between NATO and the Soviet bloc), has close ties to the EC.

In 1987 the EC states agreed to remove most barriers to trade within the EC by the end of 1992, creating an undivided market of over 300 million consumers. Ideally, this project entails not only eliminating taxes on trade, but agreeing on common standards for their products. Many states have imposed various product requirements, sometimes to discourage imports, sometimes for other reasons, such as safety or environmental policy. These differences may take many years to resolve, but the EC countries have made considerable progress. The EC also is moving toward a common currency, the "ecu" (European currency unit). At present, shifts in the value of the many European currencies make it difficult to settle on prices in contracts. A common currency should solve that problem.

In some ways, closer EC cooperation can benefit the United States. For instance, common standards benefit U.S. exporters as much as EC companies, since it is harder to produce to a wide range of standards. However, some U.S. observers worry that the EC will raise barriers against non-European imports, forming an economic "Fortress Europe." Others believe the United States has little to fear: the EC countries have little to gain from a trade war, and so far have not shown the unity of purpose to carry one out. Nonetheless, EC policies have already provoked sharp trade disputes. For instance, in 1988 the EC countries adopted beef standards under which U.S. beef was banned because of its high level of hormones. The Europeans insisted that they were acting out of health concerns, but the United States retaliated with tariffs on various EC food exports. The EC states are likely to adopt other environmental or social standards, such as restrictions on pollution or minimum wage guarantees, that differ greatly from U.S. policy. If these differences lead to higher production costs in the EC, then the EC is more likely to impose restrictions on trade with the United States and other countries.

The EC's role in the new, post–Cold War Europe is still unfolding. Most of the states in the former Soviet bloc have applied for some form of membership in the EC. The consequent debate in the EC hinges on two priorities: "deepening"—improving economic coordination and political cooperation among the present EC states—versus "widening"—bringing

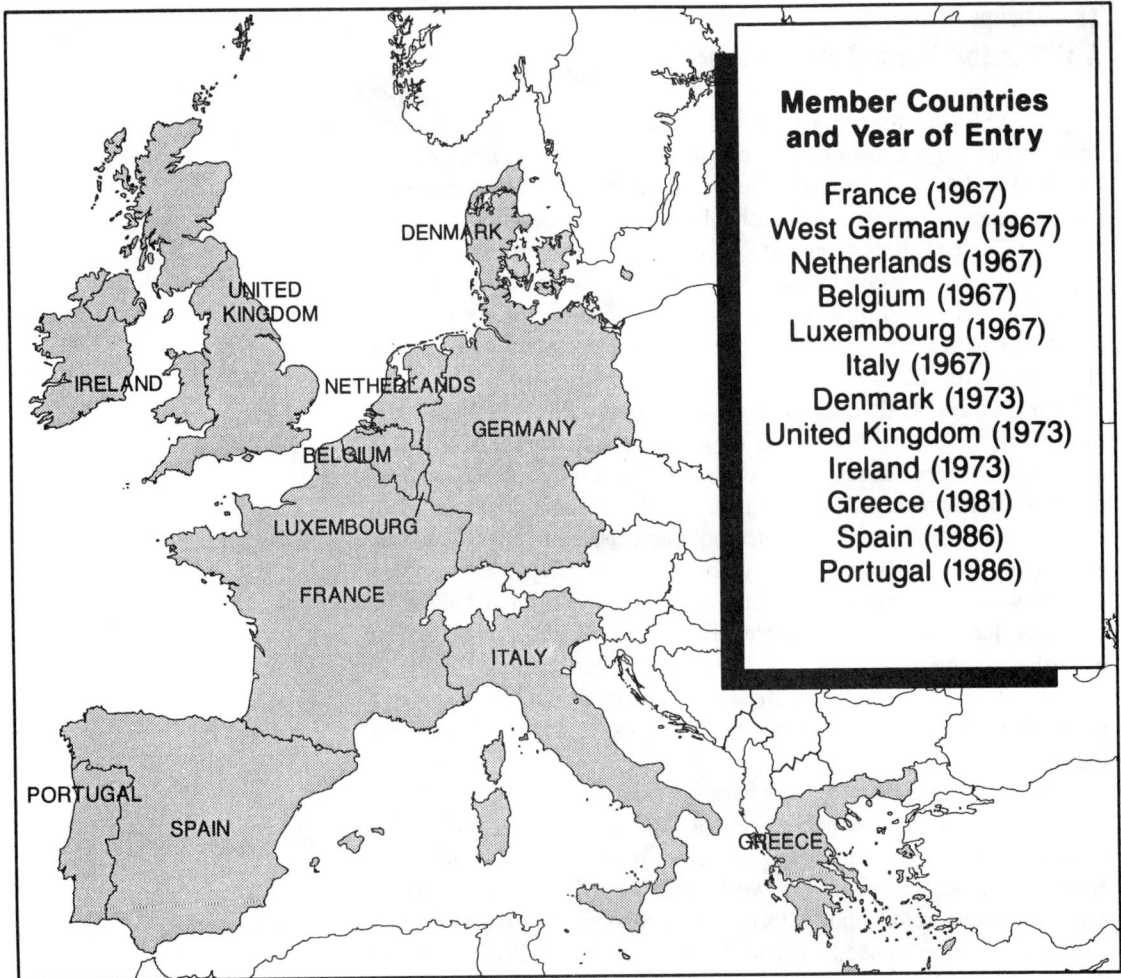

Member Countries and Year of Entry

France (1967)
West Germany (1967)
Netherlands (1967)
Belgium (1967)
Luxembourg (1967)
Italy (1967)
Denmark (1973)
United Kingdom (1973)
Ireland (1973)
Greece (1981)
Spain (1986)
Portugal (1986)

Membership of the European Community, 1992

The applications of Austria, Cyprus, Finland, Malta, Sweden, Switzerland, and Turkey to the European Community are still pending.

Eastern Europe and the former Soviet Union into the EC as quickly as possible. Those who emphasize deepening argue that the EC faces enough challenges without trying to integrate the much less developed economies of the Eastern countries. Advocates of widening reply that if the present opportunity for trans-European cooperation is squandered, the East may become a sinkhole of poverty and war. Whatever the balance between deepening and widening, the EC is bound to play a larger political role—one that leaves the United States with less influence in the region.

Questions to Consider

1. How important is it to the United States that there be peace and prosperity in the former Soviet bloc?
2. How large a role should the U.S. play there? Should it act as a leader, follow the lead of the West Europeans, or disengage itself?
3. Should U.S. troops remain in Europe? How many troops, and for what purpose?
4. How may U.S. relations with traditional West European allies change now that the common adversary is gone?

Small States and Non-State Actors: The New Threat?

In 1990, as the Cold War receded, U.S. policymakers began to discuss the "peace dividend," the money the country could save by sharply reducing military spending. Then, in August, Iraq invaded Kuwait, and soon it became obvious that the dividend would be delayed. Over the following months, the UN condemned the invasion and authorized military force to reverse it. The United States deployed over half a million soldiers and sailors in the Persian Gulf. In January 1991 the United States led a massive air assault on Iraqi forces in Kuwait and Iraq. The next month, U.S. ground forces led the attack that drove the Iraqis back through Kuwait and Iraq, forcing Iraq to surrender. To some observers, the Gulf crisis exemplified the greatest threats to U.S. security in the 1990s and proved the value of U.S. military strength to counter these threats. But others debate the wisdom of U.S. policy during the crisis, as well as the implications for present policy. A substantial fraction of all U.S. troops (including 29 percent of U.S. Army divisions) was stationed in the Middle East by February 1991; does this mean that deep troop reductions across the board would be a mistake? Some high-technology weapons systems performed well in the U.S. assault; should the United States now make a large investment in such systems? The policy debate goes well beyond military spending: how should U.S. diplomacy, economic aid, and every other aspect of foreign policy be structured to counter threats like that posed by Iraq? The threats must be clarified before these questions can be answered.

The Iraqi threat is unusual because, by traditional definitions, Iraq is not a global power capable of rivaling the United States. Apart from oil, the Iraqi economy is tiny compared to the United States'. Despite huge Iraqi military expenditures in the last decade, U.S. forces defeated Iraq while losing few American lives. Nor was Iraq's invasion of Kuwait

The Resurgence of Islam: What Does It Mean?

In 1979 the Iranian revolution, and the subsequent seizure of the U.S. embassy in Iran by radical students, jarred the U.S. public into awareness of the political power of Islamic fundamentalists. For decades the United States had backed the Shah of Iran, Muhammad Reza Shah Pahlavi, who cooperated with U.S. policy in the region and espoused economic and social development along Western lines. This social development did not extend to democracy. The Shah ruled as a dictator; his secret police, SAVAK, earned global notoriety for their brutality. However, the Shah did endorse a secular state in which religion would have little impact on policy. Both U.S. policymakers and the public were worried when the Shah fell and a radical Islamic leader, the Ayatollah Ruhollah Khomeini, came to power. Khomeini publicly expressed hostility toward the United States and his desire to spread a religious revolution throughout the region. Movements in other Arab countries embraced the same values. What is the Islamic resurgence all about, and how does it affect the United States?

Islam was founded by the prophet Muhammad, in what is now Saudi Arabia, during the early seventh century. Muslims consider Muhammad to be a successor to the Jewish prophets and Jesus. The Koran, or Quran, the sacred text of Islam, contains the word of God (Allah) as revealed to Muhammad. From the Koran and the sayings of Muhammad, a comprehensive social, political, and economic system was founded. As the Islamic community developed, however, it splintered into various sects. The two dominant groups today are Sunnis and Shi'ites. Sunnis, who represent the majority of Muslims worldwide, do not believe that their political and military leaders need to be religious leaders. Shi'ites believe that their leader should have both religious and political authority. Furthermore, Shi'ites, who have historically been an oppressed minority, view their lives as a constant struggle to restore the true faith and institute social changes under the guidance of their religious leader. The differences between the two communities have lessened with the Islamic resurgence that has been growing since the 1960s.

Many Muslims sense that Islamic regimes have failed to provide a just social order, yet they do not wish to emulate secular Western societies. They feel that Western concepts of government and social norms are not suited to their community or values. Resurgent Islam, Sunni or Shi'ite, seeks to integrate Islam into every aspect of daily life. Accordingly, its followers have sought to reform their society by modeling social behavior on Koranic precepts and the exam-

perceived as an extension of Soviet power, unlike the North Korean invasion of South Korea in June 1950 or the events leading to U.S. intervention in Vietnam. Iraq appears to be an independent regional power—but in a region very important to the United States. The most obvious threat posed by Iraq is that if it dominates the Middle East, it may control the price or quantity of oil provided to the United States and its allies. Observers debate the gravity of this threat, but it demands careful consideration. Iraq poses two other threats to the United States and U.S. allies: it supports terrorist attacks, and it seeks possession of nuclear weapons. None of these threats is unique to Iraq. Trade interference, terrorism, and nuclear proliferation are U.S. concerns in many ple of Muhammad and his companions, by replacing secular laws with Islamic law, and by modernizing without adopting Western values. Most Islamic countries are poor and their governments are unable to provide all of the needed social services. Islamic groups function mostly at the grass roots level, and, operating through mosques and other institutions, they have attempted to fulfill the social needs of their communities by offering health care, education, and soup kitchens for the poor. This has strengthened the appeal of the movement within poor communities and has attracted support from a segment of the student and middle-class population in Muslim countries.

What frightens many Westerners and Muslim secularists is politicized Islam—Islamic organizations that try to obtain political power in order to institute a state that is compatible with religious teachings. In January 1992 the Algerian general elections were canceled by the army when it appeared the Islamic Salvation Front, a fundamentalist party, would win. The near success of the Islamic Salvation Front in these elections shook many neighboring secular governments. Almost all Muslim countries follow, to some degree, the religious laws, and politicians use Islamic rhetoric to appeal to the people. But the increased demand from Islamic parties for

political representation has produced mixed responses. Jordan has allowed religious political representation in order to diffuse the appeal of religious organizations. Egypt and Tunisia have savagely repressed radical Islamic movements. Even Saudi Arabia, an orthodox Islamic state, faces radical religious opposition and has taken steps to silence it.

The United States and the West perceive politicized Islam as a threat. Anti-American feelings are strong in the Muslim world, especially among Shi'ites. The United States' past support of repressive regimes like that of the Shah of Iran, and its continuing support of Israel, are seen as an affront and a threat to the Islamic states. Contempt for Western values and lifestyles, such as materialism and the "sexual revolution," also play a role. These sentiments are not unique to Islam, but Muslim leaders like the Ayatollah Khomeini have used these feelings to gather support for their policies. Most Muslims, in fact, are not politically active, and those who are mostly want to remake their own countries, not oppose one overseas. Still, the Islamic resurgence manifests strongly held values that differ in many ways from American values, and create an inevitable tension in U.S.–Arab relations.

regions. Often regional threats are not even posed by countries, but rather by powerful non-state organizations, such as terrorist groups or the Colombian drug lords.

Access to Raw Materials and Trading Partners

Oil is the most obvious example of the dependence of the United States and its allies on imported materials. The United States imports about half of its oil. At the moment, only about 5 percent comes from the

WORLD PETROLEUM RESERVES (1989) AND MAJOR PETROLEUM IMPORTERS (1988)

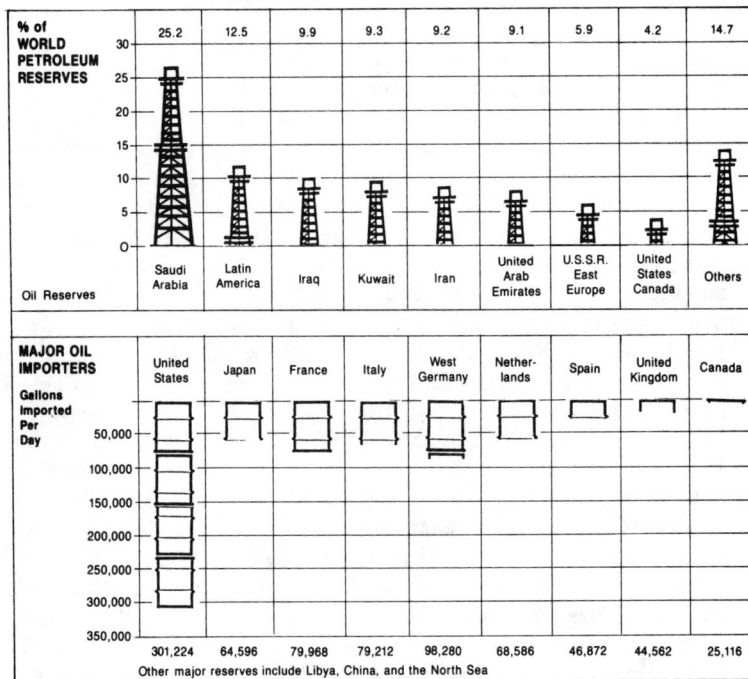

% of WORLD PETROLEUM RESERVES	Saudi Arabia	Latin America	Iraq	Kuwait	Iran	United Arab Emirates	U.S.S.R. East Europe	United States Canada	Others
	25.2	12.5	9.9	9.3	9.2	9.1	5.9	4.2	14.7

Oil Reserves

MAJOR OIL IMPORTERS — Gallons Imported Per Day	United States	Japan	France	Italy	West Germany	Nether-lands	Spain	United Kingdom	Canada
	301,224	64,596	79,968	79,212	98,280	68,586	46,872	44,562	25,116

Other major reserves include Libya, China, and the North Sea

Source: John Rourke, *International Politics on the World Stage*, 3rd ed. (Guilford, CT: The Dushkin Publishing Group, 1991), p. 246.

There is a wide gap in the world between where petroleum is located and produced and where it is consumed. The concentration of reserves in the Middle East and the massive import needs of the industrialized countries create a volatile political mixture, one that exploded in the 1990–91 Persian Gulf War.

Persian Gulf. Several U.S. allies are far more dependent on Gulf oil: Japan imports about 65 percent of its oil from the Gulf, and France about 40 percent. Some observers argue that these countries, rather than the United States, should have played the greatest role in countering Iraq. Yet U.S. policymakers felt that vital interests were at stake. The Persian Gulf states control over 60 percent of all known oil reserves. If for some reason the flow of Gulf oil was halted, other oil producers—including the United States, Russia, Mexico and Venezuela—would increase their production to narrow the gap, but they would not be able to close it. Huge disruptions in U.S. allies' economies would ensue. Because the U.S. economy has become closely tied to these other economies, its already weak banking system could be thrown into crisis. U.S. trade would suffer a harsh shock, or at worst collapse. For these reasons among others, the United States played a leading role in countering the Iraqi invasion of

Kuwait. Its allies did shoulder much of the economic expense of the war, but U.S. troops did most of the fighting.

In the months before the U.S.-led attack on Iraqi troops, the United States took a harder line toward Saddam Hussein than most of its allies did. Many in these countries (and some in the United States) felt that the United States was intervening not simply to defend access to oil, but to assert its continued leadership in world affairs. They believed the United States, in its desire to show a forceful reaction, overlooked less confrontational ways to assure access to oil. Many believed that the United Nations trade embargo and other sanctions against Iraq would eventually force Iraq to retreat from Kuwait. (See the discussion of economic sanctions in chapter 5.)

More importantly, these critics thought that the invasion posed little threat to the supply of oil. Iraq had long-standing claims on Kuwaiti territory. Also, Saddam Hussein had complained (with some justification) that Kuwait was exceeding its oil production quota, thus lowering the price and robbing Iraq of possible income. These motives suggested limited war goals: to annex at least part of Kuwait and to drive up the price of oil somewhat. Even if Iraq had broader goals, Iraq seemed—to these critics—too weak to dominate the region or choke off the supply of oil. At any rate, Iraq would not want to drive the price of oil too high. If it did, other countries could drill new sites to increase production, develop other energy sources, and reduce consumption by using energy more efficiently. These policies are expensive compared to buying cheap oil. However, if oil prices increased sharply, they would immediately look more attractive. After the war, critics pointed out that Iraq set Kuwaiti oil wells on fire only after the U.S. intervention. Arguably, U.S. policy may have actually increased the threat to oil supplies.

To supporters of the U.S. policy, the argument against Gulf intervention is as mistaken as the 1938 argument that Adolf Hitler would be content with a small piece of Czechoslovakia. They argue that Saddam Hussein was committed to gaining as much power as possible. After the invasion of Kuwait, Iraqi forces posed a direct threat to Saudi Arabia. Thus Iraq was, at the very least, bent on intimidating Saudi Arabia into abandoning its close cooperation with the United States. Sooner or later, U.S. troops would have to withdraw from Saudi Arabia, and the international sanctions against Iraq would collapse. Then Saddam Hussein would conquer Saudi Arabia outright, unless he felt he could achieve effective dominance without bothering to invade. Either way, he would control a large percentage of one of the most valuable commodities on earth. From there, he could either incite a global economic crisis, or bide his time and build his power. Iraq's resulting wealth could buy access to a dazzling array of weapons, possibly even nuclear and other weapons of mass destruction. On this reasoning, it was right for the United States to strike back at Iraq early: any delay would only have encouraged Saddam Hussein to plan further aggressions.

Costs and Troop Deployments in the Persian Gulf War

The Persian Gulf War cost the allied forces $61.1 billion overall.

Contribution:

Saudi Arabia	$16.84 billion
Kuwait	16.84 billion
Japan	10.01 billion
United States	7.46 billion
Germany	6.40 billion
United Arab Emirates	4.09 billion
Other countries	280 million

—Time (May 18, 1992)

There were approximately 700,000 allied troops.

Number of troops:

United States	425,000
Saudi Arabia	45,000
Egypt	30,000
Great Britain	25,000
Syria	17,000
France	15,000
Kuwait and other Arab countries	12,000
Other Muslim countries	8,000
Other countries	118,000

—Facts on File, Vol. 51, No. 2617 (January, 1991)

SELECTED COMMODITIES: NET U.S. IMPORTS AS A PERCENTAGE OF CONSUMPTION (1990)

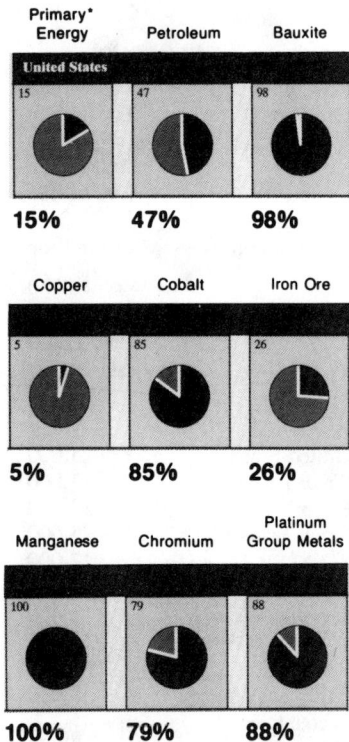

United States

Primary* Energy	Petroleum	Bauxite
15%	47%	98%

Copper	Cobalt	Iron Ore
5%	85%	26%

Manganese	Chromium	Platinum Group Metals
100%	79%	88%

*Primary energy includes coal, crude oil, natural gas liquids, and hydroelectric and nuclear electric power. It is often expressed in terms of barrels per day oil equivalent.

Source: U.S. Central Intelligence Agency, Handbook of Economic Statistics (Washington, DC: U.S. Government Printing Office, 1991), Figure 14.

Oil is the best known raw material that the United States and its allies must import, but not the only important one—and certainly not the only vital trade item. Gold remains a cornerstone of the international economy, and South Africa and Russia control over half of the world's known gold reserves. Cobalt is used to make high-strength metal alloys used in the manufacture of airplane engines. Zaire produces about three-quarters of the world supply of cobalt; Zaire and Zambia account for over half of U.S. cobalt imports. But the United States is as concerned about exporting its own products as it is about importing raw materials. U.S. exports account for 12 percent of its gross national product. Hence the United States finds it important to protect its access to key trade routes, such as the Panama Canal.

The United States tries to protect its trade interests in many ways. It maintains powerful military forces overseas, including a "Rapid Deployment Force" for quick action. In the Middle East, U.S. forces are backed by an implicit nuclear threat, under the Carter Doctrine of 1980, which states that the United States will use "any means necessary" to prevent an outside country from dominating the region. The United States gives aid to regional allies who defend U.S. interests. It also generally has worked to lower trade barriers: it has given "most favored nation" trade status to all but a few countries, and participates in many international trade organizations. And, of course, the United States works to make its exports desirable to other countries.

Regional Alliances: Benefits and Pitfalls

U.S. policymakers have realized that they cannot protect their access to Gulf oil through military power and threats alone. Accordingly, they have sought friends and allies in the Middle East. Israel has been the United States' closest friend in the region, although the countries are not formally allied. The United States provided crucial support for the creation of the state in 1948, and has given Israel large amounts of military and economic aid. In 1990 Israel received $3 billion in U.S. aid, the largest U.S. aid package to any country. Since the 1978 Camp David Accords between Israel and Egypt, the United States has also given aid to Egypt—$2.3 billion in 1990—and has sought close relations with Saudi Arabia. It thus hopes to reassure Arab states that the United States is not hostile, despite its support of Israel. Policymakers also hope to help Egypt and Saudi Arabia discourage other, more radical Arab countries from attacking Israel or challenging U.S. access to oil.

The informal U.S. alliance with Israel has conferred several advantages, but also some important costs. Aid to Israel has been fairly popular in the United States. American Jewish organizations have lobbied effectively for aid, and many Americans believe that in the aftermath of

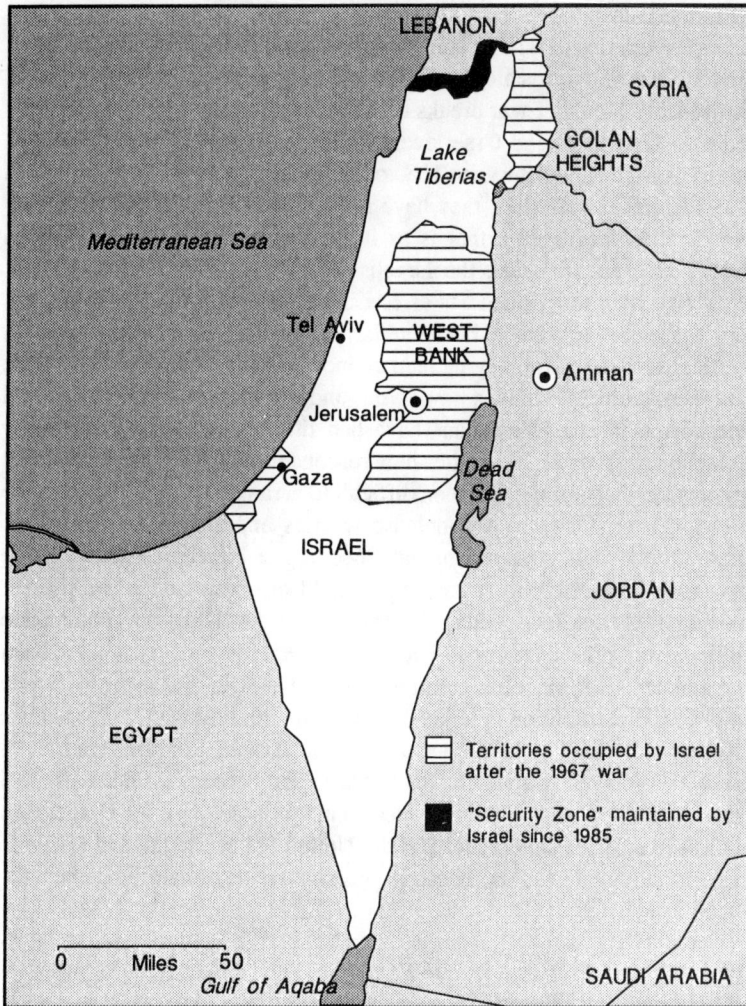

Israel and the Occupied Territories

Israel considers Jerusalem its capital. The United States believes the status of Jerusalem has to be determined in the peace talks, and has therefore established its embassy in Tel Aviv.

the Holocaust, Israel deserves special support as the only Jewish state. The two countries' intelligence services have often cooperated closely, and Israel has provided logistical support for various U.S. activities in the region. The costs of the relationship largely stem from Israel's bitter relations with the neighboring Arab states. Israel has battled Arab neighbors four times since 1948. In the 1948 and 1967 wars, Israel gained control of new territories, including the West Bank. These annexations improved Israel's defense posture, but have created perennial conflict with the Palestinian populations in the occupied territories. The United States' close ties to Israel place it in a precarious position. When Israeli actions offend Arab states, the United States takes some of the blame. Moreover, if another war breaks out in the region, the United States may be pressured to defend Israel even if U.S. leaders feel the Israelis have acted irresponsibly. Because U.S. policymakers place a great value on U.S.-Israeli cooperation, they have limited leverage over Israeli policy. Some observers believe that is as it should be. Others say that given heavy U.S. aid to Israel, the Israelis should be more accommodating.

Recently, the United States has increased its efforts to promote a lasting peace settlement between Israel and the Arab states. Such a settlement would probably include an independent state, or at least some autonomy, for Palestinians now living under Israeli rule in the occupied territories. These Palestinians have had little political power in either Israel or Arab states. No matter how reasonable a peace settlement seems to outside observers, it has been difficult to arrange. Israel is linked to the occupied territories by self-defense worries and ancient religious ties. Also, the Israeli government has encouraged Israelis to settle in the territories, precisely to strengthen its hold on these lands. The present influx of Soviet Jews makes it even harder for Israel to contemplate relinquishing the territories. The Arab states, for their part, have been hostile to Israel since its creation. Many have refused even to extend diplomatic recognition to Israel or to bargain directly with it. Peace talks were proceeding in 1992, but neither the Israelis nor the Arab states seemed prepared to make major concessions. Some U.S. observers feel that the United States should reduce its aid to Israel until Israel accepts a Palestinian state. Others feel that the United States should deal less with Egypt and Saudi Arabia, because these countries remain fundamentally hostile to Israel.

The Terrorist Threat

Terrorism is one of many phenomena easier to recognize than to define. Hijackings, kidnapping, bombings are all examples of terrorism, but it is surprisingly difficult to specify the common thread. Terrorism, essentially, is the use of force outside of combat, usually against civilians, to serve political ends through fear and intimidation. International terrorism became prominent in the late 1960s, as Arab groups attacked targets in the Middle East and Europe, and the Irish Republican Army (IRA) emerged in Great Britain. According to one governmental estimate, 40 percent of all terrorist attacks occur in Europe. For many years, U.S. citizens were rarely the target of attacks, except for a number of airplane hijackings. Then, in late 1979, Iranian militants seized the U.S. embassy in Tehran, holding its staff hostage for more than a year. The United States' inability to free the hostages shocked its people, contributing to Ronald Reagan's landslide victory over Jimmy Carter in the 1980 presidential election.

But worse was to come. In October 1983 Arab terrorists carried out a suicide truck-bombing of the U.S. Marine barracks in Beirut, Lebanon, killing 241 U.S. soldiers. In April 1986 an explosion in a West Berlin bar popular with American soldiers killed 1 U.S. citizen and wounded 60 others. The United States held Libya responsible and attacked the Libyan capital in retaliation. In December 1988 a bomb exploded on Pan American flight 103 over Lockerbie, Scotland, killing 189 Americans. These instances and several others demonstrated that the United States would not be immune to terrorist attacks.

So far, the United States has experienced no confirmed attacks on its own territory, but it is surely vulnerable to them. (Iraqi attacks were feared during the Gulf War, and intensive security measures were put into place around the United States.) Such attacks could take many forms. A few well-placed bombs could knock out electricity and communications networks throughout most of the eastern United States. If a nation managed to acquire a nuclear bomb, a major city might be threatened. Chemical or bacterial agents could poison a water supply, or be used for blackmail. A computer "virus" could infiltrate and wreck government, university, or industrial computers.

For many years, the Soviet Union provided training and encouragement to some terrorist groups in order to harass the United States and its allies. The United States claims to support only freedom fighters, not terrorists. However, in the 1980s several U.S.–funded rebel groups, such as the Nicaraguan Contras and Angola's UNITA, committed attacks on civilians hard to distinguish from terrorism. (Any war entails harm to noncombatants, but according to tradition and international law, that harm should be minimized. Guerrilla groups sometimes do focus their attacks on military targets, but some of the Contras' and UNITA's attacks were clearly directed at civilians.) Later, the United States and the Soviet Union cooperated to settle disputes involving several of their terrorist/ freedom fighter clients. Now Russian aid to terrorist groups is scarcely a concern. Instead, Russia and the other former republics themselves seem increasingly vulnerable to terrorist attack by alienated minorities, or perhaps each other.

International terrorism poses several dilemmas for the United States. U.S. leaders have declared that the United States will not deal with terrorists, yet on several occasions they have compromised this position in their efforts to gain the release of hostages. The best known instance is the 1986 "arms for hostages" scandal: the United States did not negotiate directly with the terrorists who held U.S. hostages in Lebanon, but illegally sold arms to the Iranian government, which was supposed to intercede for the hostages' freedom. In this case, "dealing" clearly failed, but U.S. leaders will be tempted to try again in the future.

The most obvious alternatives to "dealing"—launching dangerous

I'D LOVE TO DISCUSS JEFFERSONIAN IDEALS WITH SECRETARY BAKER. ...BUT JUST NOW I'VE GOT AN OFFICE FULL OF PEOPLE...

DANZIGER
The Christian Science Monitor
Los Angeles Times Syndicate

In 1992 President Alberto Fujimori of Peru suspended his country's constitution, claiming this step was necessary to fight the Shining Path guerrilla movement.

rescue attempts or simply ignoring the situation—have their own grave costs. Many believe the United States should retaliate against countries that sponsor terrorist acts, as it did when it bombed Libya in 1986. Critics reply that retaliation generally punishes the innocent and leaves the terrorists themselves unscathed. Again, the United States has compromised in several cases. It did not retaliate against Iran when Iran was considered the likely culprit in the Lockerbie bombing, perhaps because it feared provoking even more anti-American sentiment. And it removed Syria from its list of terrorist states after the Syrians helped gain the release of U.S. hostages in Lebanon, despite evidence of Syria's past support for terrorist activity. Many believe that such compromises are necessary, at least sometimes. Others believe that compromises only strengthen terrorist movements.

Apart from its direct impact, terrorism complicates other policy decisions for the United States:

- The threat of Arab terrorism puts additional pressure on the United States to bring about a peace settlement in the Middle East. Yet terrorist attacks on Israel strengthen many Israelis' resistance to negotiations. Critics of Israel say that its harsh treatment of Palestinians in the occupied territories and Lebanon also constitutes terrorism. In 1982 Israeli troops in Lebanon allowed their allies, the Christian Phalangists, to kill hundreds of Palestinian refugees in the Sabra and Shatila camps. More recently, the Israeli army has been criticized for its violent response to the Palestinian resistance movement, or intifada, in the West Bank. The army has harassed Palestinians, sometimes tortured them, and in a few cases killed them. Defenders of Israel argue that these abuses pale in comparison to the attacks on Israel, both military and terrorist.

- In Latin America, terrorism has impeded the United States' heavily publicized "war on drugs." In the late 1980s the United States encouraged Colombia to crack down on drug traffickers. The drug lords responded by murdering the justices of the Colombian Supreme Court, persuasively discouraging further cooperation with the United States. In the summer of 1991 the United States proposed to send aid and military advisers to Peru in its efforts to wipe out coca production. The Peruvian government, however, is opposed by a violent resistance movement called the Shining Path (Sendero Luminoso), and both sides have committed egregious attacks on civilians. Critics fear that advisers will get caught up in a civil war irrelevant to drug trafficking.

Nuclear Proliferation

At the moment, a handful of countries are known to possess nuclear weapons, and a few others are suspected to have them. The United States, Russia, the People's Republic of China, Great Britain, and France are all declared nuclear powers. (These are the five permanent members of the United Nations Security Council, who can veto any Security Council decision.) India, Israel, and South Africa are also believed to possess nuclear weapons. India's major rival, Pakistan, is considered close to nuclear capability. Israel set back Iraq's nuclear quest in 1981 by bombing an Iraqi nuclear reactor. Two South American rivals, Argentina and Brazil, have at times sought nuclear weapons, although neither country is expected to acquire them very soon. North Korea, Iran, Egypt, and Taiwan also have taken steps in the past towards acquiring nuclear arsenals.

The five declared nuclear powers and most of the world's non-nuclear countries have signed the Nuclear Non-Proliferation Treaty (NNPT). These countries participate in international programs designed to keep key technology and radioactive materials from being used in nuclear weapons. But India, Israel, Pakistan, Argentina, Brazil and Taiwan all have refused to sign the NNPT. Even some signatory states—notably Iraq—have secretly worked to develop nuclear weapons, or may have done so. Nevertheless, nuclear weapons have spread more slowly than many observers expected. The nuclear powers have cooperated fairly closely to keep nuclear capability to themselves. Non-nuclear states, for their part, have largely been content to seek protection from nuclear states or to buy powerful conventional weapons.

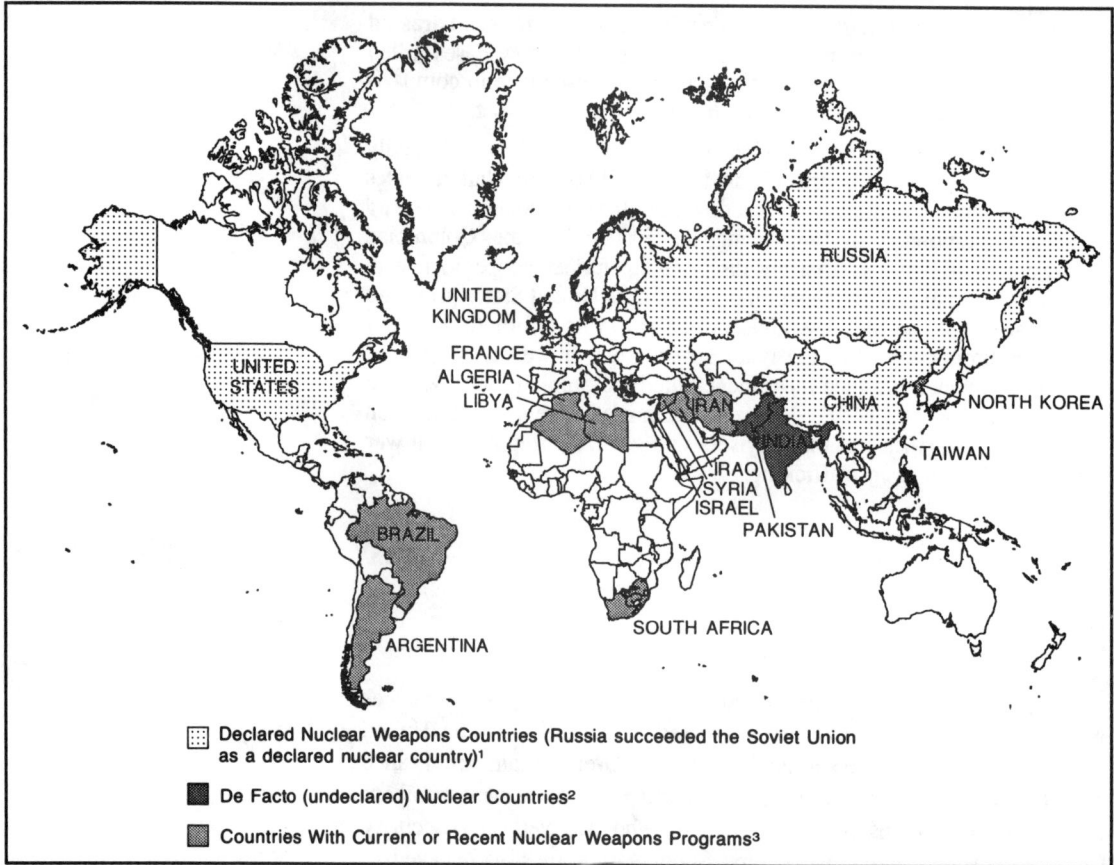

Declared Nuclear Weapons Countries (Russia succeeded the Soviet Union as a declared nuclear country)[1]

De Facto (undeclared) Nuclear Countries[2]

Countries With Current or Recent Nuclear Weapons Programs[3]

The Spread of Nuclear Weapons

[1]Ukraine, Byelarus, and Kazakhstan still have missiles armed with nuclear warheads but they have agreed to remove these weapons from their territory by the end of the decade. Russia continues to have tactical control of these and its own weapons. Russia has agreed to consult with other Commonwealth (CIS) leaders and secure the agreement of the leaders of Ukraine, Byelarus, and Kazakhstan before using its nuclear capability.

[2]Israel probably has 75–100 undeclared nuclear weapons. India probably has the essentials for 75–100 A-bombs and Pakistan probably has the material, and possibly the components, for 15–20 A-bombs. These countries have not joined the Non-Proliferation Treaty (NPT).

[3]South Africa was a de facto nuclear country until July 1991, when it signed the NPT and opened its facilities for inspection by the International Atomic Energy Agency (IAEA). Algeria, Brazil, and Argentina have attempted to develop nuclear programs. They have not joined the NPT but have accepted either IAEA inspections or NPT-style inspections of their facilities. The other countries in this category are all NPT members but have tried or are seeking to obtain nuclear capability.

The threat posed by a small nuclear arsenal is quite different from that posed by the five declared arsenals. Obviously, if a country has only a few weapons, it can hit only a few targets and has less margin for error. Also, the "near-nuclear nations" generally lack the rocket technology to attack over very long distances. (For this reason, many discussions of the Iraqi nuclear threat suggest that a nuclear bomb would have to be smuggled into the United States.) Small arsenals are relatively easy to destroy, because the missiles are few and not as well protected as the missiles in the declared arsenals. However, the vulnerability of small arsenals actually increases the overall risk of war: for instance, if Iraq were to acquire nuclear weapons, it might prefer to launch them against Israel before the Israeli Air Force could destroy them on the ground. Most observers believe that nuclear proliferation increases the risk of war, because of this pressure to "use or lose" a small nuclear force, and because some of the countries seeking a nuclear capability may use it for aggressive ends. Some observers counter that, at least in the long run, nuclear proliferation decreases the risk of war, because it can give countries the most effective insurance against attack.

Like opposition to terrorism and human rights violations, non-proliferation has sometimes taken second place in U.S. policy. During much of the 1980s the United States downplayed Pakistan's nuclear activity because Pakistan provided vital support for the Afghan resistance against Soviet occupation. The United States also muted its criticisms of Iraq's nuclear program, up until the Iraqi invasion of Kuwait. Then U.S. leaders cited the Iraqi program as a major argument for attacking Iraq. During the war, the United States tried (unsuccessfully) to destroy all of Iraqi nuclear capability. Some critics believed at the time that Iraq's progress toward a nuclear weapon was being overstated, and many were bothered by the sharp change in U.S. policy.

U.S. Arms Exports

Arms exports have been an important instrument of U.S. foreign policy in the Middle East and other regions. The United States has used weapons to promote a military balance in the region, to gain favor with some states, and to earn money. In 1991 the United States was the world's leading arms exporter, with more than $30 billion in proposed arms transfers—some $15 billion sold to Middle East states. In the Middle East, the United States has played a delicate balancing act of providing arms to both Israel and some of its Arab rivals. For instance, it sold AWACS radar planes to Saudi Arabia in 1986 despite Israeli fears that the planes could be used to coordinate an attack on Israel. The United States and Soviet Union were among 25 countries that sold weapons to both Iran and Iraq during their war of 1980–88. The arms-selling countries expected to gain both money and influence, but in retrospect it appears that the United States grossly exaggerated its influence with Iranian and Iraqi leaders. After the Iran-Iraq War ended, the United States continued to sell Iraq various high-technology products. Iraq put many of these products to use in its nuclear and chemical warfare programs.

In the aftermath of the Gulf War, U.S. leaders spoke of the need to

Table **1**

THE SIX LEADING EXPORTERS OF CONVENTIONAL WEAPONS, 1986–90

	1986	1988	1990	Total*
To the Third World				
Soviet Union	10,440	8,658	4,273	43,169
United States	4,981	3,939	3,048	21,761
France	3,446	1,413	1,330	10,490
China	1,463	1,810	926	7,569
Great Britain	1,091	1,281	971	6,211
West Germany	661	367	496	1,946
To the Industrialized World				
United States	5,323	6,564	5,690	32,049
Soviet Union	4,291	3,901	2,099	17,631
France	650	888	469	3,295
West Germany	458	903	468	2,799
Czechoslovakia	373	373	297	1,675
Great Britain	409	120	249	1,542
Total				
Soviet Union	14,731	12,559	6,372	60,800
United States	10,304	10,503	8,738	53,810
France	4,096	2,301	1,799	13,785
Great Britain	1,500	1,401	1,220	7,753
China	1,463	1,868	926	7,684
West Germany	1,119	1,270	964	4,745

* Totals include exports from 1987 and 1989, not shown in this table.
Source: SIPRI, 1991.

Figures are in millions of constant (1985) dollars. They represent deliveries of major conventional weapons. All numbers are rounded.

restrict arms transfers, but U.S. policy changed only slightly. President Bush declared in March 1991 that "it would be tragic if the nations of the Middle East and Persian Gulf were now, in the wake of war, to embark on a new arms race." In July 1991 the United States and the other four permanent powers from the UN Security Council agreed to seek "rules of restraint" for conventional arms transfers. Meanwhile, in the same month, the United States announced a $2.8 billion sale of jet fighters to Turkey and a major sale to Saudi Arabia. Skeptics asked whether the U.S. government was serious about restrictions on the arms trade. Defenders of U.S. policy said that workable restraints would take time to negotiate. In the meantime, they said, if the United States did not sell these weapons, other states such as China would simply take its place.

Table 2

THE SIX LEADING IMPORTERS OF CONVENTIONAL WEAPONS, 1986–90

	1986	1988	1990	Total*
Third World				
India	3,729	3,382	1,541	16,988
Saudi Arabia	2,413	2,046	2,553	10,839
Iraq	2,484	2,155	59	10,315
Afghanistan	692	1,009	1,091	5,743
North Korea	1,019	1,458	516	4,900
Egypt	1,645	348	206	4,717
Industrialized World				
Japan	1,780	2,176	2,083	10,970
Spain	1,039	1,580	639	5,565
Poland	1,057	1,147	330	4,720
Czechoslovakia	1,077	1,054	422	4,572
Turkey	465	1,219	623	4,372
Greece	156	783	613	3,012
All Countries				
India	3,729	3,382	1,541	16,988
Japan	1,780	2,176	2,083	10,970
Saudi Arabia	2,413	2,046	2,553	10,839
Iraq	2,484	2,155	59	10,315
Afghanistan	692	1,009	1,091	5,743
Spain	1,039	1,580	639	5,565

*Totals include imports from 1987 and 1989, not shown in this table.
Source: SIPRI, 1991.

Figures are in millions of constant (1985) dollars. They represent deliveries of major conventional weapons. All numbers are rounded.

Questions to Consider

1. How important are the threats posed by regional powers like Iraq? What kind of military forces does the United States need to counter them?

2. Is the United States too quick to resort to force, or is it too often a "paper tiger"?

3. What are the advantages and disadvantages of offering strong support to a regional power (like Israel) that can pursue an independent policy, or of trying to "balance" U.S. commitments in a region?

4. Should the United States do more to lessen its dependence on imports, or to guarantee its access to them?

5. Should the United States try to stop terrorism? Should it work to prevent nuclear proliferation?

International Problems, International Solutions?

Most of the discussion so far has focused on threats posed by specific nations or groups, aggressors bent on increasing their own power at other countries' expense. Still, this picture of international relations is incomplete. First, it neglects the broad conditions that can provoke war and disorder, and pays too little attention to economic interdependence and economic conflict, both of which play a huge role in foreign affairs. It also disregards universal threats, such as environmental damage, that are neither caused nor solvable by single nations. For some observers, these considerations prove the need for much greater international cooperation. For others, skeptical that international cooperation can work, they simply show the complicated and imperfect world in which the United States must live.

Sources of Conflict: Power Struggles, Aggression, and the Security Dilemma

How do wars begin? The most obvious answer is: wars begin because one country attacks another, generally to gain—or to avoid losing—wealth, land, or power. If this is true, one should take a look at likely aggressors, as we have done in much of this chapter. But examining the cause of wars reveals intriguing differences in how wars begin. Our view of how wars begin can have a subtle but important effect on how we try to prevent war.

In U.S. history, several images of the causes of war have prevailed. In one image, the European powers were competing for supremacy, so naturally they periodically went to war with each other. Early U.S. leaders believed that the United States could avoid war by shunning military rivalries and alliances while emphasizing economic strength. The United States' policy was to defend itself and remain neutral. Later, some U.S. thinkers modified this view. They decided that the United States could not act as an economic great power without taking on a comparable, competitive political role. At times the United States would even have to undertake a war to protect or advance its position. In either case, war was seen as caused by the struggle for power among all leading states.

Currently, there are two important versions of this argument. In one, a state's military strength ultimately determines its power and prestige—including its economic health. In the other, economic strength predominates, although of course a country must be able to defend itself. The two versions overlap, since military and economic strength often go hand in hand. But the economic version offers greater hope—its critics say false hope—of avoiding war in the midst of the struggle for power. In either case, unavoidable competition among states poses the greatest threat to peace.

In a contrasting image, which prevailed in World War II and throughout the Cold War, a few aggressive nations create the threat to peace. In accordance with this view, a guiding principle of U.S. foreign policy has been that democracies are much less likely to go to war with each other than dictatorships are to attack them. In the 1930s and 1940s the democracies were threatened by the fascist Axis governments (Nazi Germany and its allies). Later, the Soviet Union and other communist states emerged as the greatest threats to peace. This "aggressor states" argument does not hold that all dictatorships are equally threatening. The United States found it practical to cooperate with some dictatorships that shared its interest in preventing the spread of Soviet power. The United States even worked with some communist states, such as Yugoslavia and Romania, that opposed Soviet foreign policy. Now some believe that "outlaw states," such as Iraq, pose the greatest threat to peace.

A third image of the cause of war has been important in U.S. policy-making, and indeed in the study of international relations. It suggests that sometimes wars are caused neither by power struggles nor by stark aggression, but by countries' mutual fears of each other. Analysts point to what they call the security dilemma: every country must protect itself—since no one else can guarantee its security—but each state's efforts to secure itself can be interpreted as a threat to another country. If a nation builds up its military forces, it may risk being caught up in a rapid arms race that could lead to war. But if it does not build up, it may risk being left at the mercy of other nations, and few countries are willing to accept that risk. Some observers believe that World War I broke out because the major European powers took increasingly assertive actions, each afraid to fall behind the war preparations of its adversaries. Many saw the U.S.-Soviet rivalry after World War II as caught up in the same potentially tragic dynamic. The two countries' nuclear capability, and the inevitable misunderstandings caused by their different ideologies, seemed to increase the risk of war far beyond the aggressive intentions of either nation. As one observer put it, the United States and the Soviet Union were like a scorpion and a tarantula trapped in a bottle, and therefore doomed to desperate competition.

Ingram Pinn

Ironically, as the U.S.–Soviet nuclear arms race appears to be ending, U.S. observers still debate which of these images best explains the arms race. The first image suggests that the United States and the Soviet Union were competing head-to-head for world dominance. That may imply that the United States and Soviet Union were morally equal in their struggle for global power—a view that most Americans would reject. However, even if the United States' ultimate goals were profoundly different from those of the Soviet Union, it is quite possible that each state believed it needed superiority over the other. Whatever their motives, both countries have used nuclear weapons to influence other states, as well as each other. Their nuclear arsenals have been employed as an instrument of power, not simply in self-defense. For instance, late in the Korean War, President Eisenhower threatened a nuclear attack against North Korea to help win concessions in the peace talks.

The second image, from the U.S. perspective, suggests that the Soviet Union sought nuclear superiority as a means of aggression. In this argument, while the United States had a nuclear monopoly, and later overwhelming nuclear superiority, it could have attacked or blackmailed

Ingram Pinn

the Soviet Union, but it did not. Instead, by the late 1960s the United States pursued various treaties designed to provide rough equality between the two nations' nuclear forces. The Soviet Union, for its part, undertook a massive nuclear buildup that by 1980 gave it superiority in many categories, and it repeatedly violated nuclear arms control treaties.

The third image suggests that the two states repeatedly exaggerated each other's strength and mutual threat. For instance, during his 1960 presidential campaign, John F. Kennedy argued that the Soviet Union had gained a huge lead in nuclear missiles. Kennedy accelerated U.S. weapons production to "close the gap." Soon U.S. intelligence discovered that the United States still had a much larger nuclear arsenal than did the Soviet Union. There are many examples of such misperceptions, some of which took many years to be corrected. Military leaders on each side consider it prudent to take a "worst-case" view of each other's strength. Also, given their mutual suspicion, each country tends to see the other's "defensive" innovations as a threat. Even an entirely defensive system can sometimes be used to make an attack more effective.

None of these images is easily refuted, but most observers end up giving greater weight to one or another of them. The images imply rather different focuses of U.S. policy in the 1990s and beyond. If the United States emphasizes a struggle for power, then it should try to put itself in as strong a position as possible, while steering away from dangerous conflicts. Even then, two different interpretations of the struggle for power are available. One view holds that the United States should stay out of political and military competition whenever possible, while improving and applying its economic power. The other assumes that the United States must compete politically and preserve a powerful military in order to defend its interests. The "aggressor state" image has very different implications. If a handful of undemocratic states pose the main threat to peace, then the United States should act forcefully (with its allies, if possible) to counter or even remove these rogue governments. Finally, if the security dilemma poses the greatest threat to peace, then the United States should negotiate with its rivals—and help other countries negotiate—political and military settlements that guarantee each state's interests.

Remember that these images are not mutually exclusive or completely contradictory: we cannot simply choose the right one. Moreover, even if we settle on the basic nature of the threat, there is still plenty of room for disagreement on policy. If economic strength is most important, for example, the United States may not be able to regain its position as the world's leading industrial power or avoid unpleasant military conflicts. If the United States' goal is to maximize its political power, neither its allies nor its emerging rivals will readily accept its dominance. Even if aggressor states are the main threat to peace, the United States may not be able to remove them all. Finally, if the security dilemma is at the root of war, that certainly does not guarantee that anyone can solve it. (Will any settlement seem fair to the Arabs and safe to the Israelis?) Nevertheless, although the images are simplifications of reality, they are worth thinking about. Most people tend to be influenced very heavily by one or two of them, often without realizing it. By considering the models, at the very least you can better understand how and why people disagree on issues of war and peace. Political scientists also believe that careful research can clarify when each cause of war applies. Such research thus helps us to choose among conflicting policy recommendations.

Economic Interdependence

Trade has always been important to the U.S. economy, but the United States' ties to the world economy have become closer than ever in the past 25 years. The United States has increased both its imports and its exports in manufactured goods, especially high technology. At the same time, U.S. companies have expanded their operations overseas, and foreign companies have invested in the United States, to such an extent that these ventures defy categorization as "American" or "foreign." The United States' exports account for roughly 12 percent of its economic output (GNP), and its imports equal about 15 percent of GNP. These trade figures tell only part of the story. U.S. investments in other countries, and other countries' investments in the United States, each amount to about 10 percent of the GNP. (These figures get harder to calculate every year, as genuinely multinational corporations grow in power.) The value of U.S. currency is largely sustained and determined by events in European and Japanese financial markets. The United States depends on trade with its allies (as well as with other countries). At the same time, the financial successes of those allies raise new questions for U.S. policy.

Policymakers in the United States have long espoused free trade: the freedom of countries to import and export products without quotas, excessive tariffs (import taxes), or other barriers. After World War II, the United States led in the formation of the General Agreement on Tariffs and Trade (GATT). Over 100 states now participate in GATT, and over 90 percent of world trade takes place between GATT members. Under the GATT regime, tariffs have been reduced from an average of over 40 percent in 1947 to under 5 percent by the late 1980s. During the 1950s and 1960s the United States unquestionably benefited from a strong free trade regime, since it was the world's foremost producer of industrial goods and a major agricultural exporter as well. Still, the point of free trade was not simply to promote U.S. exports. A relatively free trade market would—and did—enable Western Europe and Japan to revitalize their economies by focusing on certain products to export, while importing others. This revitalization served U.S. interests, by enabling these countries to resist possible Soviet expansion as well as by rebuilding valuable markets for U.S. goods. Free trade and healthy competition thus helped all these countries.

But international trade was never truly free, and it became less free over time. The European countries, to varying degrees, adopted complicated tariffs, quotas, and import standards designed to protect their respective industries and agricultural producers. Japan adopted one of the most protectionist policies of all, and achieved staggering successes—at what many felt was the expense of the United States. Other East Asian countries, including Taiwan and South Korea, also built strong electronics export markets while limiting imports. Not only did these countries restrict imports, but they provided economic subsidies to certain industries to help them develop and export products at low prices. As all these countries began to cut into U.S. producers' market share, U.S. citizens were thrown out of work, and pressure grew for retaliatory tariffs and quotas. Opponents of such retaliation argued that economic warfare would end up hurting everyone involved. They added that the main problem with U.S. industry was not overseas quotas, but U.S.

mediocrity: a loss of innovation, lack of strategic vision, and/or complacent work force. At the same time, the remarkable success of many protectionist nations suggested that trade restrictions need not always lead to economic disaster. Many believed that even the U.S. economy might benefit from certain protectionist policies, such as government aid for industrial research programs in key technologies.

Meanwhile, another dimension of interdependence had emerged along the North-South axis. After World War II, the United States, Canada, European states, the Soviet Union, and Japan clearly dominated the world economy. (A handful of Southern countries, such as New Zealand, were tied, economically and culturally, to the North.) In most of Asia, Africa, and Latin America, much lower standards of living prevailed. Many of the nations in these regions did not gain independence from European colonial control until after World War II. The European powers had not consistently encouraged the growth of independent industry or democratic institutions in these countries.

After the war, leaders in Third World countries worked with industrial countries and financial institutions to create vibrant industrial economies. At least, that was the avowed intent. What happened instead in many of these countries was some combination of the following: well-armed militaries sprang up, at the beck and call of wealthy landowners or ambitious dictators. The countries took out huge loans that were often embezzled by corrupt officials or squandered on inappropriate "super-projects." (For instance: a $2 billion nuclear power plant built in the Philippines under President Ferdinand Marcos had to be closed because it had been built on an earthquake fault.) Or the countries invested in the production of various commodities whose price soon fell through the floor.

Third World leaders bear a large responsibility for the poverty of their countries, but developed nations are also responsible. The Southern states had little financial clout, and many analysts believe that Northern countries were able to drive down the prices they paid for commodities purchased from the South, well below what they would have paid equal trading partners. In the 1970s, as Middle Eastern oil money (petrodollars) gorged Northern banks, many banks were eager to find profitable investments. The banks sent their most persuasive employees to sell Southern leaders on big loans for big projects, with little concern for whether the projects could actually work. International lending institutions like the World Bank had their own ideas about the right path to Third World development; many of those ideas were expensive mistakes.

Even successful projects sometimes led to trouble: people moved to cities in numbers that were much larger than the available jobs, overtaxing already poor sanitation and transportation systems. The rural poor might have benefited from health care and education, or they might have been better off simply being left alone. Instead, they often were driven off their land by governments or wealthy owners, forced to plant export crops (many of whose prices soon collapsed) instead of food they could eat, and taxed beyond endurance to make interest payments on the wasted loans.

These debts grew astronomically after 1970, as the petrodollars flowed. In that year, four major Latin American debtors—Argentina, Brazil, Mexico, and Venezuela—owed about $22 billion among them; by 1987 their combined debt had reached $300 billion. In Africa over the same time period, the debt of three major borrowers—Ivory Coast, Morocco and Nigeria—ballooned from about $1.5 billion to over $48 billion. Several East European countries, asserting their independence from the Soviet Union, also ran up enormous tabs. These massive debts imposed huge burdens on the borrowing governments, especially those governments that were trying to improve social services and other programs at the same time. They also posed a problem for the lenders: several U.S. banks, such as Citibank and Manufacturers Hanover, found themselves overextended with huge Third World loans.

Ironically, by the late 1980s the United States found itself with the largest trade deficit of all. After dominating automobile manufacturing and other technological industries in the decades following World War II, the United States ceded superiority in high-technology exports to its rivals in the Pacific Rim and Western Europe. The U.S. trade deficit with Japan alone exceeded $50 billion in 1987, before declining to around $40 billion in 1990. In 1990 Japan exported almost $25 billion in motor vehicles and parts to the United States, while importing less than $1 billion worth of goods from the United States. Private firms in Japan and other countries invested part of their earnings in U.S. factories, companies, and real estate. Americans began to worry that the United States was being "bought out." At the same time, U.S. budget deficits soared and the U.S. national debt (the total of its budget deficits) reached the astounding level of $3 trillion. Although there was no direct connection between the budget deficits and the trade deficits, the relative weakness of U.S. exports limited the funds that could be drawn on to close the budget gap. A growing percentage of the U.S. national debt was held by foreign banks, who thus gained leverage in the U.S. economy.

How important are trade and monetary issues to U.S. foreign policy? No one questions that the United States has some stake in preserving healthy trade relations and salvaging the worst of the bad loans. Beyond that, there is plenty of disagreement. Consider three issues:

1. *Protectionism and "fair trade"*: Some people believe that the United States should take urgent steps to narrow the trade deficit with Japan and other trading partners. Specifically, they argue that the United States should require other countries to remove certain trade restrictions and to accept specific, increased amounts of U.S. goods. If these countries refuse, in this argument, they should have quotas and tariffs imposed upon their exports to the United States. Most advocates of a

Bruce Beattie, reprinted by permission of Copley News Service.

"The Auto Import Quotas Gave Me Time to Get Ready to Compete Against You Again . . ."

tougher trade policy prefer to call it not protectionism, but "fair trade." If the Japanese want to sell us cars, for instance, they should be willing to buy more American cars. Skeptics point out that the United States has extensive trade restrictions of its own. If these restrictions have failed to preserve the trade balance, these analysts argue, it is primarily because U.S. products simply are not good enough or cheap enough to compete in the present world market. In this view, trade limits will only delay the needed economic reforms.

2. *Economic aid:* Some people believe the United States should offer considerable aid to promote democracy and economic development in the Third World. (Now that the Soviet bloc has collapsed, many of its constituent states have conditions that are similar to those in Third World countries.) Economic aid, it is argued, can help create a more peaceful, prosperous, democratic world in which the United States can continue to thrive. Others believe that such a policy can only fail, as past aid has often failed. Many also argue that now the United States should take care of its own problems. The actual amount of U.S. development aid is surprisingly small—$3.7 billion in fiscal year 1991, less than one-tenth of one percent of its GNP. Security aid comprised another $8.7 billion, with Israel receiving $3 billion and Egypt $2 billion.

3. *A North American Free Trade Agreement:* In 1989 the United States signed a free trade agreement with Canada, its largest trading partner. The agreement included substantial freedom for U.S. and Canadian companies to do business in each other's territory, as well as the virtual elimination of trade restrictions. The United States has negotiated to extend the agreement to Mexico as well, creating a free

Table **3**

FOREIGN AID EFFORT OF 18 WESTERN DEVELOPED COUNTRIES ANALYZED BY AMOUNT GIVEN AND BY AID AS A PERCENTAGE OF GNP, 1988

Country	Total Amount Given ($ billions)	Rank	Amount Given as a Percentage of GNP	Rank
Austria	$ 0.3	16	0.24%	17
Australia	1.1	10	0.46	8
Belgium	0.6	13	0.39	9
Canada	2.3	7	0.50	7
Denmark	0.9	12	0.89	3
Finland	0.6	13	0.59	6
France	7.0	3	0.73	5
Great Britain	2.6	6	0.32	12
Ireland	0.06	18	0.20	18
Italy	2.7	5	0.35	11
Japan	8.5	2	0.31	14
Netherlands	2.2	8	0.98	2
New Zealand	0.1	17	0.27	15
Norway	1.0	11	1.12	1
Sweden	1.5	9	0.87	4
Switzerland	0.6	13	0.32	12
United States	12.1	1	0.25	16
West Germany	4.7	4	0.39	9

Source: John Rourke, *International Politics on the World Stage*, 3rd ed. (Guilford, CT: The Dushkin Publishing Group, 1991), p. 419.

Aid can be analyzed from different perspectives. In total dollars, the United States ranks 1st. But in percentage of GNP it ranks 16th. Norway is 11th in dollars, but 1st in percentage of GNP giving.

trade zone throughout North America. Supporters of a North American Free Trade Agreement (NAFTA) argue that it will benefit the United States by giving it trade access to 85 million Mexican consumers. They also point out that a NAFTA would rival the European Community in size and potential power.

But NAFTA's critics say that NAFTA highlights the least desirable effects of free trade. First, jobs are displaced to countries with lower wages. Many Canadian firms have moved their factories to the United States because lower wages prevail here; by some estimates almost half a million Canadian jobs have been lost as a result. Likewise, under a 1965 U.S.–Mexican agreement, U.S. businesses have built over 1,500 *maquiladora* factories employing about 500,000 Mexican workers, each earning a fraction of what a comparably skilled U.S. worker would be paid. A free trade agreement would probably lead even more U.S. businesses to move their factories south of the border. Supporters of NAFTA argue that such moves promote economic efficiency and help to develop the Mexican market for future U.S. exports. Critics reply that much of Mexico's competitive advantage stems from the poor wages, working conditions, and environmental standards prevailing there. Thus, in their view, unrestricted free trade leads to the firing of American workers and the degradation—not the economic advancement—of Mexicans. Supporters of NAFTA consider this critique shortsighted. They compare it with the fear of many, during the Industrial Revolution of the eighteenth and nineteenth centuries, that automation would lead to massive unemployment and grinding poverty. In fact, industrialization opened up new opportunities for most people. Likewise, these observers say, NAFTA will confer its own economic benefits. Nevertheless, critics call for safeguards to limit the social disruptions in both the United States and Mexico.

These issues evidently extend far beyond economics. The aid issue raises fundamental and haunting questions: In a narrowly pragmatic sense, does suffering in other countries really affect the United States? How much can the United States afford to help, and how much good can it do? Can the United States find new forms of aid that better meet human needs in the Third World? Trade issues raise other troubling questions. Can the great industrial powers manage to live in peaceful, friendly competition? Or is the world, sooner or later, headed for another global trade war? Is it possible to integrate less-developed countries around the world into the Western economy? If not, how can the rich and poor countries coexist peacefully in the long run?

Ecological Threats: Hanging Together or Hanging Separately?

For many observers, the most disturbing question of all is posed by ecological dangers that may endanger life on the planet. Ecological threats are less obvious, and more controversial, than the destruction that would be caused by a nuclear war. The realization that using nuclear weapons would have dire, widespread consequences helped prevent a nuclear confrontation between the United States and the Soviet Union despite decades of rivalry. Leaders acted cautiously when their actions could make a nuclear war more likely. They have acted, naturally, to protect their own people. Ecological threats such as global warming, in contrast, pose a thornier question for policymakers. These dangers exist in theory, but scientists cannot conclusively verify them. How far should the United States, and all countries, go to counter an unproven risk?

Scientists agree that carbon dioxide (CO_2) and other gases in the atmosphere trap the sun's warmth as it rebounds from the earth. This "greenhouse effect" warms the earth; without it, most life could not survive. Using sophisticated techniques, scientists have estimated atmospheric CO_2 concentrations and average temperatures over 150,000 years into the past. The two values rise and fall together with striking regularity. No one can entirely explain past changes in CO_2 concentration, but human activities, such as burning gasoline and coal, are now raising CO_2 levels. Since the beginning of the industrial age, CO_2 in the atmosphere has increased from 280 parts per million (ppm) to 348 ppm, an increase of 24 percent. At present rates, it will increase by another 50 percent over the next century. Other greenhouse gases, such as methane, are also becoming more prevalent in the atmosphere. Methane is primarily produced by the cattle that satisfy the developed world's demand for beef, and—in lesser amounts—by the rice paddies that provide a staple crop in many Asian countries.

These facts raise the concern that world temperatures will rise in an enhanced, or uncontrolled, greenhouse effect. Some computer climate models measuring the impact of greenhouse gases have predicted increases of 1.5 to 4.5 degrees Celsius (up to 8 degrees Fahrenheit) by the year 2050. Such increases may have many unpleasant consequences. Agricultural patterns may shift around the world as crops no longer grow successfully in their former ranges. Some regions may become more productive, but the disruption may wreck many farmers and threaten fragile economies. Wildlife that may not readily adapt to the shift might become extinct. Melting of the polar ice caps could submerge low-lying islands and flood much of the U.S. seaboard and other coastal areas.

If policymakers accept global warming as a clear and present danger, they must consider drastic economic changes to prevent it. Currently, the world releases nearly six billion tons of carbon into the atmosphere annually by burning fossil fuels. The wealthy industrial countries, with about one-eighth of the world's population, produce roughly half of these emissions. To hold CO_2 levels constant, the global figure would have to be reduced to around two billion tons as quickly as possible. To achieve these reductions, the United States may adopt some or all of the following policies. Most of these are domestic policies, but they have important international implications.

- To reduce gasoline use: In the short term, impose a large gasoline tax, on the order of 50 cents to $1.50 per gallon, to force drivers to conserve. (Most industrialized countries already have such a tax.) Over time, phase out the existing fleet of low-efficiency automobiles, the backbone of U.S. transportation. Replace these with a mix of higher-efficiency gasoline-fueled autos, hydrogen- or battery-powered autos suitable for short trips, and mass transit both within and between cities. Redesign city streets to encourage walking and bicycling, and discourage driving.

- To reduce other energy use: Replace inefficient lights and appliances with initially more expensive, but more efficient, new models. Create large tax incentives for energy-efficient building techniques such as installing heat-trapping windows and built-in solar panels. Increase electricity costs to encourage conservation.

- To reduce industrial carbon emissions: Either impose legal limits on industrial carbon emissions or create "pollution taxes" and/or "pollution licenses" that force companies to pay when they pollute. Such policies encourage companies to invest in new, cleaner technologies that, according to many analysts, will lead to higher profits in the long run.

- To promote cleaner energy sources: Invest heavily in renewable sources of energy, particularly solar, geothermal, and hydroelectric (and perhaps nuclear). Put a stop to subsidies and tax breaks for oil exploration.

- To limit carbon emissions around the world: Pledge to reduce U.S. carbon emissions by 50 to 75 percent through these and other means, and encourage other countries to do the same. Offer extensive technical support to developing countries to improve their standard of living without heavy carbon emissions. Negotiate "debt-for-nature swaps," writing off the debts of poor countries as they adopt ecologically sound policies (such as preservation of forests).

No one knows just what all these changes would cost: in the worst case, perhaps hundreds of billions of dollars over the next decade or two. To those who endorse the changes, the cost of not making them is potentially much greater. These advocates also argue that moderate reductions in military spending can fund the response to this more urgent threat. In the long term, according to many projections, reducing fossil fuel use should lead to greater economic efficiency and thus pay for itself.

Skeptics reply that the claim that global warning is taking place remains unproven. Some studies do suggest that average temperatures have risen by about half a degree in this century. However, random changes and differences between regions—some warming, some actually cooling—make it difficult to isolate an overall trend, if one exists. Some critics believe that the extra heat produced in urban areas has skewed the records, since most weather stations are near cities. (Studies have attempted to compensate for this effect, but scientists debate how accurately they have done so.)

The climate models that predict future temperature increases are similarly unproven. By their nature, such models must leave out many aspects of the real world. Some believe that the ocean may absorb much of the additional carbon, preventing global warming. Also, increased CO_2 levels would tend to stimulate plant growth, again absorbing much of the carbon. Or an initial temperature rise may evaporate some ocean waters, increasing the global cloud cover and forestalling any further increase in temperature. Such possible feedback loops are difficult to predict. Some may actually exacerbate global warming. For instance, an initial thaw could release huge amounts of methane trapped in the Arctic permafrost, driving temperatures even higher. To critics, too much seems uncertain to justify major expenditures on reducing CO_2 emissions.

Critics of massive policy change also emphasize that if moderate warming does occur, some regions (such as Siberia) will benefit as others suffer. Even without warming, some regions will always succeed better than others, just as the United States' Pacific Northwest presently is booming while the Northeast stagnates. In the view of some observers, a policy that attempts to prevent such changes cannot succeed, but can only compound the disruption. And some say that if the long-term economic benefits of avoiding fossil fuels are real, free markets can eventually generate them, perhaps more efficiently than can government programs.

Advocates of policy change reply that to delay action, on the grounds that change may be small or beneficial or unavoidable, amounts to a huge and irresponsible gamble. At least, they say, the United States and other countries should act to slow the likely pace of climatic change, so that any social disruptions will be less painful when they come. Critics point out that the proposed policies themselves constitute a real social disruption, including an increase in government power and meddling with fragile economies overseas.

Other ecological threats have gained world leaders' attention, and some have already led to international agreements.

- The burning of high-sulfur coal releases sulfur dioxide (SO_2) into the air; SO_2 then combines with rainwater to produce the dilute solution of sulfuric acid called acid rain. In North America and in Eastern Europe, some rivers and lakes no longer have fish: acid rain has rendered them unlivable. Canada has long complained about acid rain "spillover" from the United States. A recent accord between the two countries is intended to limit the problem. For instance, it restricts the United States' use of high-sulfur coal.

- Chlorofluorocarbons (CFCs), a key chemical ingredient in aerosol sprays and air-conditioning systems, have been proven to destroy the ozone layer in the upper atmosphere that protects the earth from the sun's ultraviolet rays. In 1987 scientists discovered with some shock that a massive hole in the ozone had formed over Antarctica. In 1987 the United States and 23 other countries signed the Montreal Accords, pledging to reduce their CFC production by 50 percent by 1999. Confronted with evidence that the threat to the ozone layer was worse than anyone had imagined, these states renegotiated and strengthened the agreement.

- The rapid destruction of tropical rain forests for lumber, agriculture, and cattle grazing has also jeopardized tens of thousands of species. In some countries, while wealthy farmers let much of their land lie unplanted, poorer farmers regularly clear forest land, plant crops for a few years until the newly uncovered soil is ruined, then move on to cut down more of the forests. Timber export industries also take a huge toll; many trees are cut not for export, but only to gain access to the rarest, most valuable trees. The United States, the World Bank, and others have offered economic incentives to rain forest countries to halt the destruction.

- Social disruptions in many countries feed into ecological issues. Civil wars sometimes provoke "scorched earth" tactics against defenseless populations; wars often spark massive movements of refugees to other countries, wrecking local agriculture and taxing the resources of whatever countries receive the refugees. As seen in the destruction of the rain forests, economic and political inequities can exact their own environmental toll. Many observers call for a greater UN role in keeping the peace and promoting social reforms as a way of protecting the environment.

- Many poor countries argue that they need help if they are to develop economically without wreaking further environmental havoc. In the North, countries polluted freely in the early stages of industrial development, then gradually learned how to limit ecological damage. If the countries of the South followed the same path, they could do tremendous damage to the environment (as well as themselves).

Some developing countries insist that at the moment they cannot afford "green consciousness." Others solicit Northern aid to promote sustainable development, a development model that seeks to avoid the waste, inequities, and environmental harm of past programs. The ideal of sustainable development is to use Northern (and Southern) technology and resources to meet human needs while protecting the environment.

Each of these initiatives has critics. For instance, some believe that acid rain's effects have been exaggerated and can be countered by applying lime to affected waters, rather than abandoning high-sulfur coal or using expensive cleaning techniques. Others believe that the countries of the world must act much more vigorously to protect the environment. Social policies are especially controversial. The idea of a constructive Northern role in social and economic development draws fire from two directions. Some fear it will mean a massive financial handout to Southern countries that fails to solve their problems. Others are afraid that Northern countries will twist any new agreements for their own purposes.

The United States has a mixed record on ecological issues. For instance, it lags behind other industrialized countries in agreeing to, and attaining, significant reductions in CO_2. The United States has the poorest mass transit in the industrialized world, the heaviest dependence on automobiles, a gasoline tax far below the average, and the greatest use of coal. In June 1992, the members of the European Community pledged to reduce their CO_2 emissions to 1990 levels by the year 2000, and Germany promised to reduce emissions by at least 25 percent by 2005. The United States refused to match either commitment. Some observers believe that the United States will meet at least the EC standard anyway because of federal, state, and local efforts to improve energy efficiency. At the international Earth Summit of June 1992, the United States supported a set of principles to protect world forests and pledged financial support for environmental protection in developing countries, but it shied away from specific, binding obligations. It rejected a treaty to protect species diversity, stating that while the United States would meet or exceed most of the treaty's requirements, some were unfair to U.S. companies. Critics assailed the United States' failure to put its weight into backing strong agreements. Defenders of U.S. policy replied that the United States had a strong domestic record on environmental protection, and had no reason to accept flawed treaty proposals.

The United States' "go slow" position on CO_2 illustrates the difficulty of achieving cooperation on ecological threats. The ecological benefits, to any one country, of changing its policies are uncertain and impossible to measure; the economic costs are obvious and immediate. This problem parallels the security dilemma. No country wants to pursue an "ecologically responsible" policy if other countries gain a significant advantage by not adopting a similar policy. Whatever the ecological

GREENHOUSE EFFECT:

CHANGING THE WORLD'S CLIMATE

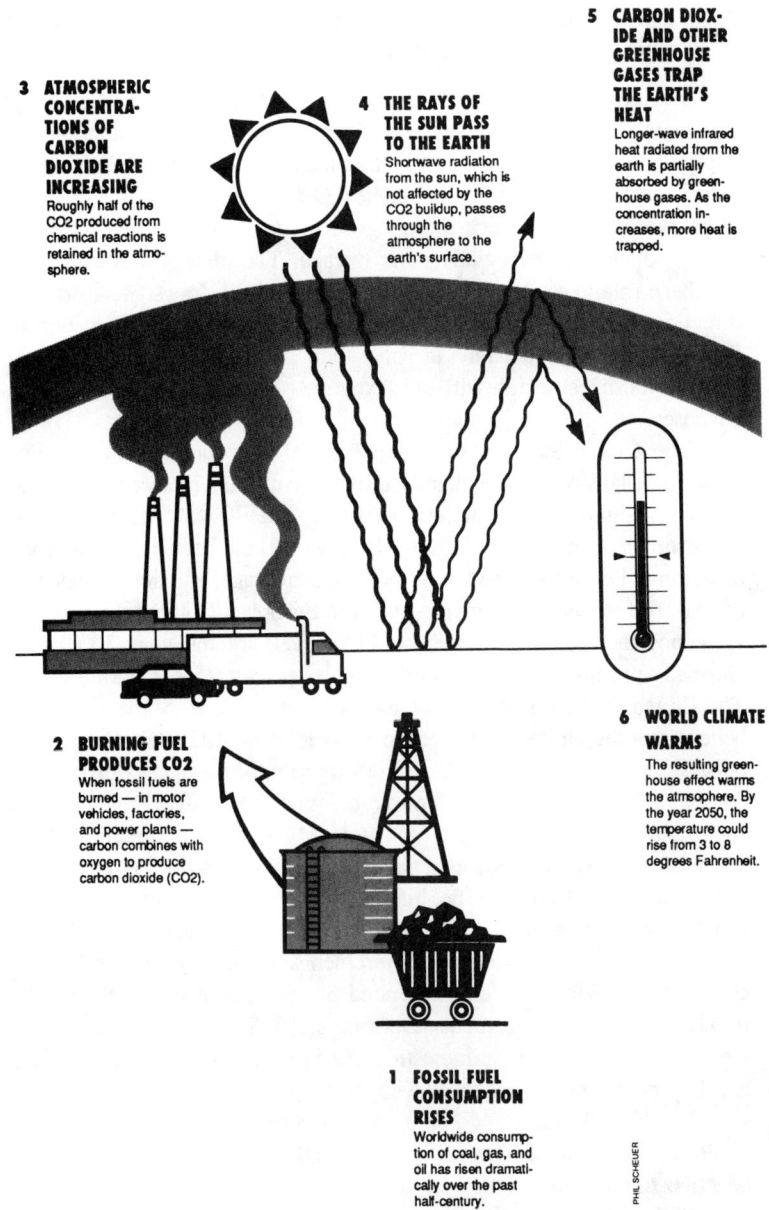

5 CARBON DIOXIDE AND OTHER GREENHOUSE GASES TRAP THE EARTH'S HEAT
Longer-wave infrared heat radiated from the earth is partially absorbed by greenhouse gases. As the concentration increases, more heat is trapped.

3 ATMOSPHERIC CONCENTRATIONS OF CARBON DIOXIDE ARE INCREASING
Roughly half of the CO_2 produced from chemical reactions is retained in the atmosphere.

4 THE RAYS OF THE SUN PASS TO THE EARTH
Shortwave radiation from the sun, which is not affected by the CO_2 buildup, passes through the atmosphere to the earth's surface.

2 BURNING FUEL PRODUCES CO2
When fossil fuels are burned — in motor vehicles, factories, and power plants — carbon combines with oxygen to produce carbon dioxide (CO_2).

6 WORLD CLIMATE WARMS
The resulting greenhouse effect warms the atmosphere. By the year 2050, the temperature could rise from 3 to 8 degrees Fahrenheit.

1 FOSSIL FUEL CONSUMPTION RISES
Worldwide consumption of coal, gas, and oil has risen dramatically over the past half-century.

PHIL SCHEUER

proposal, or package of proposals, some countries will believe that they carry too heavy a share of its burden. Some will be tempted to pay lip service to the proposal, then ignore it in practice—as "free riders" who benefit from the behavior of others. Yet if states cannot agree to joint action, the entire world may pay the price. Conversely, if ecological threats have been exaggerated, then the entire world may pay the price of flawed policies intended to counter those threats.

Questions to Consider

1. Which image of the cause of war—struggles for power, aggressor states, security dilemmas—seems to offer the most useful insight into today's conflicts?

2. How important is "interdependence" as a policy guide? How can the United States reconcile its competitive economic interests with the need for economic cooperation?

3. Will the economic gap between the North and South become a central feature of international relations, and how will it affect the United States?

4. Do environmental threats require fundamental policy changes? What kind of economic aid, if any, would most likely benefit Southern countries?

Conclusion

Obviously the various challenges facing the United States cannot be resolved easily, even by experts. The issues are often muddled, and the problems are sometimes beyond the United States' ability to solve. Thus the United States must establish its priorities, sometimes accepting painful costs, risks, or compromises. The next chapter focuses on the difficult questions of how values and value trade-offs enter into U.S. foreign policy, and how well we can predict the likely consequences of certain policies.

CHAPTER 4

Values, Interests, and Policy: A Tangled Web

How should the United States make decisions on complex foreign policy issues? Chapters 4 and 5 focus on ways to reach sound policy judgments. This chapter examines the contrasting roles played by the public and experts in making policy choices, then explores the complicated relationship between values and interests. The next chapter presents analytical tools used to test ideas and judge the likely success of policies. Together these chapters offer guidance on how to integrate your values and your intellectual judgments.

Values and the Public Role in Policy-Making

Some people believe that foreign policy decisions should be left to our elected leaders and experts, because the public is not sufficiently knowledgeable or sophisticated to understand the issues. They argue that the public tends to be caught up in emotional rhetoric, while experts can be more objective. Certainly most people have large gaps in their knowledge of foreign affairs. Certainly, also, public debates can become bitter and polarized. However, the ideal of the "objective expert" is unrealistic—and dangerous, if it is used to exclude the public from policy-making.

Most important foreign policy issues depend heavily on value judgments and difficult trade-offs. The experts are no more impartial about these issues than the public is. Even when most experts agree, moreover, they can be flatly wrong. Very few experts predicted the 1979 Iranian Revolution or the rapid collapse of the Soviet Union. Some powerful biases, as well as simple human fallibility, led experts to underestimate the forces for change in these cases. On the other hand, experts have often overstated the potential for "modernization" in Third World countries. The economic, political, and social changes desired by

U.S. policy—and tacitly endorsed by many scholars—have met with huge obstacles around the world.

The Choices for the 21st Century Education Project assumes that experts and the public both should play important roles in U.S. foreign policy. Democratic values demand that basic priorities, like those featured in the Futures debate, be determined by the people: these are public choices. Putting these priorities into practice requires expertise that the public at large cannot provide: these narrower policy decisions can be considered expert choices. Of course, experts and the public should work together. Experts can help the public determine what choices are available, and assess some of the likely consequences. Thus they can act as a counter to wishful thinking. On the other hand, the public can criticize policies that seem contrary to public priorities: the people can oppose any tendency toward "tyranny of the experts."

As you examine the relationship between values and interests, you will see some reasons why public choices are difficult to arrive at. You may want to ask yourself: can the United States attain a workable public consensus on its foreign policy priorities? Or are the issues too complicated, and the debate too unclear? What do your answers imply about how foreign policy should be determined in the future?

Values vs. Interests: How Real a Distinction?

The previous chapter showed that the line between values and interests can be hard to draw. Democracy is a value upheld by many Americans, something U.S. citizens support and would like to see around the world. But it is also an interest to the extent that democratic governments are less likely to go to war with the United States. (To further complicate matters, sometimes the United States chooses to support anti-democratic governments.) Similarly, U.S. influence around the world is certainly considered to further the country's interests, but it also reflects the widespread value that the United States should play a special, leading role in world affairs.

Here is one way of drawing the line between values and interests. A country's core interests are physical security, prosperity, and freedom of self-determination. Many other interests pertain to these core interests. For instance, the United States has an interest in access to Gulf oil because it helps to sustain the U.S. economy, although the United States does not depend on this oil for physical survival. Interests, then, are (in theory) objective judgments about what benefits the country and its citizens. Some critics argue that, in practice, "national interests" are determined by a small group of political and business leaders who can favor their own interests at the public's expense. Most Americans would reject this critique in its most extreme form. While they are somewhat suspicious of these leaders, most Americans do not feel basically at odds with them.

However, even if everyone agrees on the interests themselves, there is room for argument about which interests are most important. For individuals, physical survival is often the most basic interest, yet many people would be willing to risk their own lives to defend another person or their country. Many also would be willing, in some cases, to risk national survival to protect another country or oppose some evil. If such a basic interest can be called into question, no wonder we must make difficult, controversial, anything but objective judgments about how to balance all the interests confronting us and our country.

We make such judgments based on our values: our beliefs about how we should conduct ourselves individually and as a nation, and about how others should behave. Values can be rooted in religious beliefs, ethical precepts, or an intuitive sense of what is good or appropriate. Values are not always moral judgments; for example, many of us value privacy without any particular moral argument for doing so. Nevertheless, values are inevitably caught up with moral issues. Because value judgments are both unavoidable and morally charged, political opponents often attack each other's morality. During the Cold War, a perennial foreign policy debate pitted the "hawks" against the "doves." The doves (who favored compromise and negotiation with the Soviet Union) tended to portray the hawks as narrow-minded, short-sighted warmongers. The hawks (who felt the Soviet Union could only be dealt with from a position of strength) often portrayed the doves as cowardly, naive, or unpatriotic. In reality, people were never neatly divided into these two categories. Yet the loudest debaters emphasized the differences, presenting their own position as the right one and the opposing position as wrong—not simply mistaken but evil, at least in its consequences.

Some observers say that a country has "no values, only interests." They argue that a country cannot afford to act on the basis of abstract ideals like "peace and justice for all"; it must act first to preserve its core interests, even if this means compromising its values. Reasonable people may disagree on just how true or false this is, but a few points are clear. First, while the United States may not have to abandon its values, in specific cases it must often accept that its values are unreachable or point in different directions: some compromise is unavoidable. Second, it is impossible to talk about interests without also discussing values. Each Future has some powerful practical arguments in its favor, but in the end, different values influence each Future's view of "reality."

Actually, the debate is not so much over different values, but over different priorities. Most of the values evoked in foreign policy debates are fairly uncontroversial. Almost everyone in the United States wants the country to be strong and prosperous. Also, most people agree that "liberty and justice for all" is a worthy goal, even outside of U.S.

borders. The trouble begins when we need to decide how much emphasis to give to these diverse goals. Can the United States remain at peace while also defending its own freedom and the freedom of others? Can it promote prosperity around the world without undermining its own well-being? How do we reconcile our desire to further our ideals and our reluctance to meddle in other countries' affairs?

Despite the overlap between values and interests, at times U.S. interests do seem at odds with other U.S. values. Americans themselves have often obscured this conflict. Americans sometimes believe that the most moral policy is also the most practical policy, and that the United States can advance its own interests while simultaneously promoting the best interests of all peoples. Many believe, for example, that the United States should support democracies around the world because democracy is morally preferable to dictatorship, and because democracies are more peace-loving than dictatorships. (The latter claim is not always true.) But sometimes pragmatic and moral judgments clash. For instance, the United States has often worked closely with undemocratic governments, sometimes governments guilty of egregious human rights abuses, in order to strengthen U.S. influence overseas. There are moral arguments on both sides of this policy. Alliances with and aid to dubious governments may be necessary to prevent greater evils, such as threats posed by Soviet expansion during the Cold War. If so, such alliances may be moral as well as practical. Critics like to reverse the argument. They say that to support undemocratic governments is both immoral and ultimately impractical, because it creates hostility toward the U.S. and undermines its credibility as a democratic world leader. Both arguments have force, but it is possible that there is an inescapable conflict here between U.S. interests and U.S. values.

An Overview of Key American Values

Many policy debates seem to pit values against interests, morality against expediency. Yet some of the most important debates involve basic values, good in themselves, that come into conflict. Consider the nine values briefly discussed below. Most Americans would agree with each value as it is initially stated. However, as the discussion shows, hard questions emerge when we try to apply these values. Unfortunately, most public debates (and public opinion polls) avoid the challenges posed by the collision of worthy values. Serious answers to the questions below take time to develop—more time than most public arenas provide. You may want to write down some of your immediate thoughts on these questions.

1. The United States should be safe from external attack, prosperous, and free. Therefore, it should defend itself and its interests.

   How strong must the United States be (militarily, politically, economically) to be safe? What kind of foreign policy makes it most prosperous? Can freedom be threatened by concentrating too much on military security?

2. The United States holds, and largely represents, worthy political values. It supports (among other things) democratic elections, the rule of law, freedom of speech, and recognition of human rights.

   Are some of these values more important than others? Should the United States require them of its allies? Try to impose them on other countries? When, if ever, should the United States support undemocratic regimes?

3. The United States should promote peace around the world, because peace is good in its own right.

   How far should this country go in defending the peace? When is the United States itself justified in going to war? When should it stay out?

4. The United States should be loyal to its friends. Whatever additional countries it does or does not defend, it should stand by long-time allies.

   What should the United States do if its allies violate human rights, or adopt policies that threaten the peace?

5. The United States should be generous. It should do what it can to lessen the problems of people around the world.

   How much emphasis should we put on other countries' problems? Does U.S. aid help the right people? What kind of U.S. aid is appropriate?

6. The United States must take care of its problems at home.

   Should this mean reducing the U.S. role overseas, or not? Should the United States have a protectionist trade policy, or not? Should it increase government social spending, or try to reduce the government's size and power?

7. The United States supports and depends on world trade. It is entitled to use whatever resources it can pay for—and, under some circumstances, to fight for whatever resources it needs.

   Should the U.S. accept any limits on its use of raw materials?

8. The United States wants a healthy environment.

   How should the United States reconcile environmental needs with its citizens' generally affluent life-styles?

9. The United States is a world leader.

   A leader in what—in moral values, military power, economic productivity, and/or creativity? Should its leadership take the form of setting a good example, active cooperation with other countries, or superior strength and willingness to act independently?

Some Crucial Trade-offs

The preceding discussion should caution us against making simplistic either/or judgments when key values are involved. But choices must be made, and the tensions and trade-offs among values are real and unavoidable.

Avoiding War vs. Defending Freedom

In the 40 years since World War II and the beginning of the Cold War, most Americans have agreed that the United States should strive both to maintain peace with the Soviet Union and to prevent Soviet aggression against other countries. However, most observers put more emphasis on one goal or the other. One camp believed that the Soviet Union was so evil in intent and dangerous in power that it had to be contained by superior strength, even at the risk of war. A competing camp believed that an arms race increased the risk of a nuclear war that would ravage many millions of innocent people, and this was the greatest evil of all. Therefore the United States should avoid confrontation with the Soviet Union, and reach arms agreements and other accommodations with it if possible. (Of course, the policy debate had other dimensions, but this one attracted much attention.)

Even after the Cold War, the tension remains between avoiding war and defending freedom. Should the United States take a major role in resisting aggression around the world, or should it try to stay out of conflicts whenever possible? (Keep in mind that the defense of freedom can take many forms, some of which will be considered later.) In favor of a major role in defending freedom is the argument that a world free from aggression is one with less human misery and more security for everyone. Unchecked aggressors may ultimately threaten the United States itself. An argument against such a role is that the United States could spend billions of dollars and sacrifice many lives without furthering world peace and freedom. Both the Vietnam War and the 1983 killing of several hundred Marines in Lebanon exemplify failure of U.S. power to further these goals.

When, then, should the United States intervene in foreign conflicts? The simple answer is: only when its interests are directly threatened. However, that criterion is more ambiguous than it may seem. Does civil war in Yugoslavia, or a war between Serbia and Croatia or Bosnia-Herzegovina, "directly" threaten U.S. interests—and if so, what should the United States do about it? Would a war between South Africa and Mozambique, or a Libyan attack on Morocco, directly threaten U.S.

interests? Did the Iraqi invasion of Kuwait directly affect U.S. interests? (Some experts say no: the United States could have gotten plenty of oil no matter what the Iraqis did.) For that matter, did Adolf Hitler really threaten the United States, or would Nazi Germany have been content to control Europe? Were the benefits of fighting World War II demonstrably worth the costs?

Human Rights vs. Realpolitik (balance of power)

One perennial issue is whether the United States should work with or give aid to undemocratic countries. The other side of this issue is whether the United States should actively oppose or work to overthrow undemocratic countries. Like most such questions, these do not lend themselves to simple yes-or-no answers. Consider some narrower questions: Was the United States right in sending aid to the Soviet Union under Stalin during World War II, on the argument that Nazi Germany posed a greater threat? Was it right in assisting the Philippines' dictatorial leader Ferdinand Marcos during the 1960s and 1970s, on the argument that U.S. bases there were essential and Marcos was a relatively humane leader? Was it right in sending aid to El Salvador through most of the 1980s, despite thousands of murders carried out by paramilitary death squads, on the argument that the pro-communist rebellion there threatened all of Central America? Was it right when it opposed sanctions against South Africa, arguing that they would only increase the risk of a civil war and a Marxist triumph, or when it imposed sanctions to hasten the end of the racist apartheid system?

Was the United States right to offer moral support to the Gorbachev regime in the Soviet Union because Gorbachev's reforms offered the best hope for peaceful change, or should it have given no help at all to the central Soviet government? Was it right to end the war against Iraq once Kuwait was free and Iraq had surrendered, or should it have fought to assure the freedom of the Kurdish minority in Iraq? Should the United States now pressure African regimes to become more democratic, and if so, how far should it go in its pressure? Why did the United States stand by while the Ethiopian government deliberately starved some of its people, and what choice did it have? Should it be putting more pressure on Israel to concede some land to the Palestinians?

Some of these questions may seem fairly simple to answer—and, unavoidably, they have been simplified in the asking. But taken together, and with many others beyond them, they raise troubling issues. Because U.S. power is limited and the consequences of many of our actions are unpredictable, sometimes it simply is not clear which policy best serves human rights. Still, some distinctions may be made. There is a real difference between tolerating a country's existence and sending it aid.

negotiated the Panama Canal Treaty and won its ratification by the U.S. Senate despite heavy opposition.

Carter never did achieve consistency on human rights issues. His greatest aberration came in Iran, where he supported the dictatorial shah, until the shah was deposed in the Iranian Revolution. Ironically, this vestige of realpolitik, rather than any idealistic tendency, may have been Carter's most disastrous policy. Iranian resentment of U.S. support for the shah fueled the hostage crisis that irreparably damaged Carter's presidency. In any case, Carter's "human rights policy" had few unambiguous successes. No U.S. ally made dramatic strides toward respect for human rights, nor did the Soviet Union. Carter's defenders believe that, in the long run, his policy initiatives could have enhanced both human rights and U.S. prestige around the world.

Independence vs. Interdependence

At times the United States has offered strong support for efforts to encourage global cooperation; at other times it has protected its own freedom of action. It invaded Grenada in 1983 despite the opposition of many of its own allies, on the grounds that vital U.S. interests were at stake. When the United States has supported United Nations initiatives, it has generally been as a first among equals. For instance, the United States played the dominant military role in the 1950 UN intervention in Korea, and in the recent Gulf crisis.

All countries have reason to resist giving power to international organizations. The United States fears that it may lose its freedom to react quickly and forcefully against obvious threats to its interests if it is required to seek the approval of other nations. Other countries may be actively hostile to the United States, or simply unwilling to endorse strong action. This fear of "having its hands tied" is not unique to the United States. However, the United States has less chance than most countries of being destroyed if international peacekeeping proves ineffective. The United States also fears that it may be called on to finance projects that it considers useless or even harmful to its own interests. As one of the richest countries, it has a great deal to lose. Yet international cooperation may allow real peacekeeping. Cooperation also could enable the global community to grapple with environmental and human welfare issues that it cannot address effectively as a patchwork of independent states.

In the past, schemes for international cooperation have foundered on the lack of responsible power to back them up. Consider the 1928 Kellogg-Briand Pact, in which 62 nations agreed to settle all disputes by peaceful means. The United States worked for the pact as an alternative to the League of Nations, in which the country had refused to participate.

Security Council
15 members
5 permanent, 10 serve
  2-year terms
Veto power for permanent
  members

General Assembly
All UN members
One vote per member

Secretariat
Headed by
  secretary-general,
  5-year term

**Economic and
Social Council**
54 members
  serve 3-year
  terms
One vote per member

UNITED NATIONS

Trusteeship Council
5 members
One vote per
  member

Associated Agencies
20 intergovernmental
  organizations
Includes: World Health
  Organization, World Bank,
  Food and Agricultural
  Organization

**International
Court of Justice**
15 judges
  serve 9-year
  terms

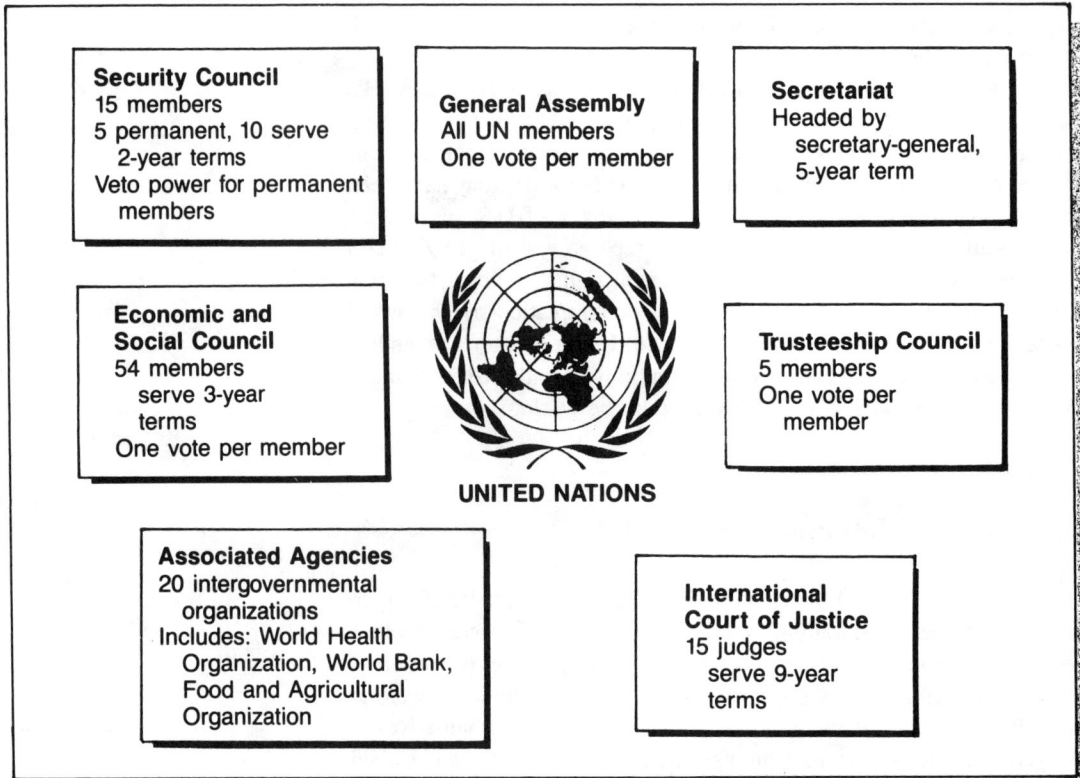

THE STRUCTURE OF THE UNITED NATIONS

The United Nations is a complex organization. It has 6 major organs and 20 associated agencies.

Within a decade Japan, Italy, and Germany betrayed this pledge, respectively attacking China, Ethiopia, and (with little bloodshed) the Rhineland and Austria. They did so with relative impunity: no single country could afford the luxury of punishing them for their violations, and no group of states could agree to do so.

The United Nations' peacekeeping mandate is limited by the veto power given to the five permanent members of the Security Council. Any of these countries, or an ally of one of them, can act with little fear of UN intervention. Many advocates of international cooperation believe that the veto should be abolished because it weakens the United Nations' credibility. If the United Nations abolishes veto power, what should replace it? Will a bare majority of the more than 160 UN states be able to impose terms on other countries? Will countries end up trading favors to get favorite programs adopted by the United Nations? Or will the United Nations end up with even less practical power than it has now? In a democratic country like the United States, political institutions function despite their imperfections because the participants generally accept the rule of law even as they work to change the law. In an anarchic world, the stakes are higher. If the United Nations adopts a hostile policy, or simply fails to act in a timely fashion, a country's very survival may hang in the balance.

The 1990–91 Persian Gulf Crisis: A Case Study in Value Trade-offs

The Persian Gulf crisis offered an unusually clear view of value trade-offs and the complicating factor of uncertain consequences. Iraq's invasion of Kuwait in August 1990 provoked the crisis. Up until the invasion, the United States had sought friendly relations with Iraq. Iraq's leader, Saddam Hussein, evidently aspired to be a regional force, and the United States wanted to be on good terms with as many Gulf powers as possible. The United States had favored Iraq in its long war with Iran, which lasted from 1980 to 1988. Even after the war, the United States offered trade and some military aid to Iraq, despite some congressional opposition.

There were warning signs of an invasion of Kuwait. Iraq's claim to a piece of Kuwait's coastline went back to 1922, when Great Britain dictated boundaries for the new states being carved out of the Ottoman (Turkish) Empire. Iraq was the wealthiest of the new Arab states, but the British carefully denied Iraq access to the sea. Over the years, Iraq had protested the border, and some Iraqi leaders argued that Kuwait itself should have been part of Iraq. In the months before the invasion, Iraq complained that Kuwait was committing "economic warfare" by over-selling its oil quota, which had been established by agreement with other oil-producing states. In May 1990 Saddam Hussein argued that overselling by Kuwait and other Gulf states had driven down the price of oil, in some cases by over 50 percent, thus robbing Iraq of income—an act that he declared "not less than an act of war." There was some truth to the claims, yet they reminded some observers of Hitler's disingenuous insistence that he was surrounded by hostile powers. The U.S. government responded cautiously. In a meeting with Hussein, U.S. ambassador April Glaspie called for a peaceful settlement but told the Iraqi leader that the United States had "no position on the Arab-Arab conflicts, like [Iraq's] border disagreement with Kuwait."[1] Apparently Saddam Hussein interpreted Glaspie's diplomatic statement as an assurance that the United States would not offer practical resistance to an invasion.

---

1. Micah L. Sifry and Christopher Cerf, eds., *The Gulf War Reader: History, Documents, Opinions* (New York: Random House, 1991), 130.

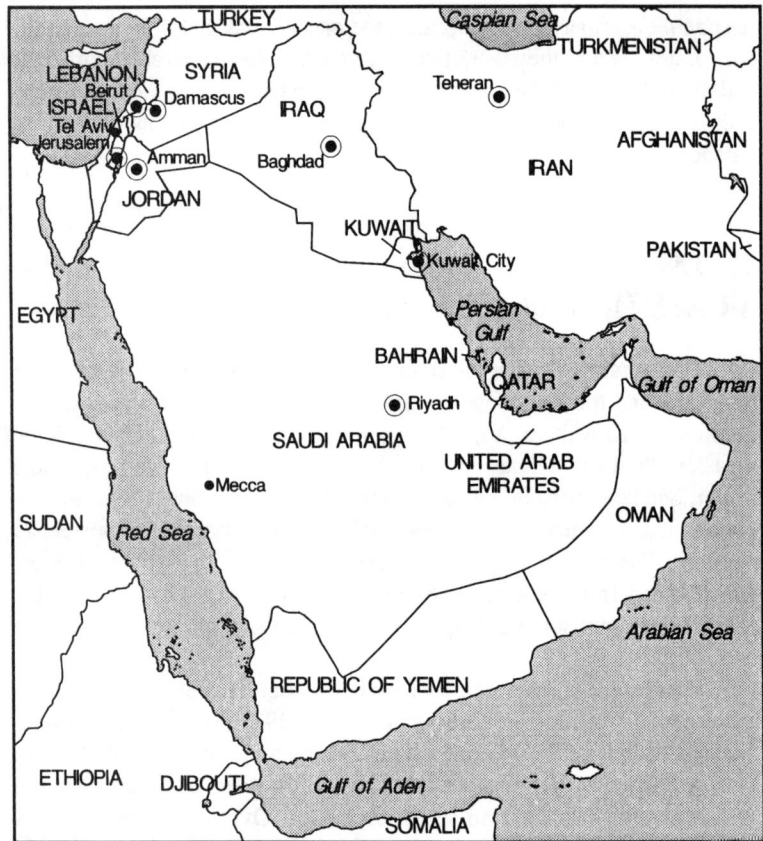

The Persian Gulf Region

On August 2, 1990, Iraqi forces poured across the Kuwaiti border, smashing token opposition and quickly seizing the capital city. Suddenly Iraq controlled Kuwait's huge oil supply, roughly 10 percent of the world's total known reserves. U.S. policymakers feared that Iraq would next invade or intimidate Saudi Arabia, which had considerably larger reserves. Friendly relations with a regional power were one matter; tolerating an expansionist state with a stranglehold on the world's oil supply was quite another. U.S. president George Bush harshly condemned the invasion, and the United States quickly requested and obtained a series of United Nations resolutions calling for immediate Iraqi withdrawal.

In themselves, the resolutions meant little without the power and will to back them up. The United States led the multinational effort to protect neighboring countries and to eject Iraqi troops from Kuwait, although its strategy did not crystallize all at once. Initially, the United States focused on "Operation Desert Shield." In Desert Shield, the

In this session, the UN debated whether or not it would impose economic sanctions on Iraq to force Iraq to withdraw from Kuwait.

United States first deployed about 100,000 troops to the Iraqi-Saudi border to prevent an invasion of Saudi Arabia. This force soon grew to around 200,000 troops, joined by smaller forces from other countries. The United States also helped bring about stringent economic sanctions against the Iraqi regime, intended to pressure Iraq to leave Kuwait. A theoretically complete, and remarkably comprehensive, trade embargo quickly weakened Iraq's economy. But Saddam Hussein seemed uncowed. Publicly, U.S. policymakers stated that sanctions should be given adequate time to work. Privately, they speculated that Saddam Hussein would never give in no matter how much economic hardship his people had to undergo.

Beginning in November, with little fanfare, the United States increased its armed forces in Saudi Arabia to about 425,000. Then it pushed the United Nations to set a deadline—January 15, 1991—for an unconditional Iraqi withdrawal. The Soviet Union and France officially backed the U.S. position, but made large efforts to broker a peace settlement before the deadline. The United States openly discouraged such efforts, on the grounds that Hussein would offer the appearance of "flexibility" without surrendering all the fruits of conquest. Critics suspected that the U.S. government had another reason for opposing

"All the News That's Fit to Print"

The New York Times

VOL.CXL....No. 48,483   Copyright © 1991 The New York Times   NEW YORK, THURSDAY, JANUARY 17, 1991   36 cents beyond 75 miles from New York City, except on Long Island   **40 CENTS**

New York: Today, partly cloudy, windy. High 49. Tonight, clear, cold winds. Low 32. Tomorrow, variable clouds. High 46. Yesterday, high 55, low 38. Details are on page D22.

U.S. AND ALLIES OPEN AIR WAR ON IRAQ, BOMB BAGHDAD AND KUWAITI TARGETS; 'NO CHOICE' BUT FORCE, BUSH DECLARES

RELIEF AND ANGER

News of Attack Sweeps the Country, Stirring Profound Feelings

By JAMES BARRON

In one long moment yesterday evening, word that the United States had attacked Baghdad swept the country. In split-level suburban homes on the East Coast where dinner was in the oven, in big-city restaurants where bars were jammed with the happy-hour crowd and in skyscraper offices on the West Coast where people were still at work, there was an odd mixture of apprehension, sadness and relief.

In malls, shoppers emptied out of stores and cried. Some rushed to call relatives and share the news that after five months of waiting and wondering, America was at war. Some stood silently in front of television sets, stunned that the Bush Administration had decided to act so soon after the United Nations deadline for Iraq to withdraw from Kuwait. Some worried how close to home the conflict might come.

"You don't know what to expect and then you think, 'Am I really going to be affected by this?'" said Carla Houston, 28 years old, of Cupertino, Calif.

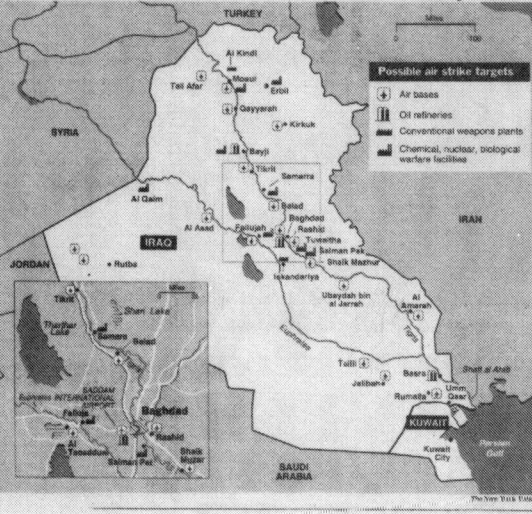

Possible air strike targets
- Air bases
- Oil refineries
- Conventional weapons plants
- Chemical, nuclear, biological warfare facilities

No Ground Fighting Yet, President Tells the Nation

By ANDREW ROSENTHAL
Special to The New York Times

WASHINGTON, Jan. 16 — The United States and allied forces attacked Iraq today, striking Baghdad and other targets in Iraq and Kuwait with waves of air attacks at the start of the long-threatened war to force President Saddam Hussein's army from Kuwait.

"The liberation of Kuwait has begun," President Bush said in confirming the start of the attack with three-sentence statement that was read by his spokesman, Marlin Fitzwater, shortly after the raids began.

Later, in a televised address to the nation, Mr. Bush said, "We have no choice but to force Saddam from Kuwait by force. We will not fail."

Chemical Weapons Targeted

But he also said, "We are determined to knock out Saddam Hussein's nuclear bomb potential. We will also destroy his chemical weapons facilities."

Assuring Americans that ground forces were not yet engaged in the battle, the President added: "Five months ago, Saddam Hussein started this cruel war against Kuwait. Tonight, the battle has been joined."

He said initial reports indicated that "our operations are proceeding according to plan."

"Our objectives are clear," he said. "Saddam Hussein's forces will leave Kuwait, the legitimate Government of Kuwait will be restored to its rightful place and Kuwait will once again be free."

In the written statement issued earlier, Mr. Fitzwater said, "In conjunction with the forces of our coalition partners, the United States has moved under the code name Operation Desert Storm to enforce the mandates of the United Nations Security Council. As of 7 o'clock P.M., Operation Desert Storm forces were engaging targets in Iraq and Kuwait."

The nighttime attack, which began at about 6:30 P.M. Washington time, (2:30 A.M. Iraqi time Thursday) was first revealed in television reports by American correspondents in Baghdad that the skies over the Iraqi capital were alight with anti-aircraft and tracer fire. Initial reports were that multiple waves of warplanes bombed central Baghdad, hitting oil refineries and the airport.

British and Saudis Attack

White House officials said an undisclosed number of British warplanes

---

peace efforts: they believed it wanted to drive Saddam Hussein out of power.

U.S. leaders offered a variety of reasons for their war preparations, both before and after the January counterattack. Some of the reasons were narrowly pragmatic: access to oil was at stake, and Iraq seemed close to gaining a dangerous nuclear capability. Others were more idealistic: an aggressor should not be allowed to enjoy the prizes of conquest, and the Iraqi government's repression of Kuwaiti citizens and its own Kurdish minority marked it as an outlaw state. Observers had no way of knowing which arguments U.S. leaders believed most strongly, and which were considered primarily matters of public relations.

Many observers believed the Bush administration was itself most concerned with access to oil and economic stability. In this view, the moral arguments were necessary because the U.S. public has always been reluctant to go to war, regardless of the objective interests at stake, without a decisive moral rationale. Once presented with such a rationale, the public would strongly support a U.S. counterattack. Other observers were convinced that Bush's outrage at the invasion was quite sincere and at least colored his view of the objective reasons for fighting. According to this view, prior to the war most Americans were never persuaded by the moral arguments or convinced that vital U.S. interests hung in the balance. But the administration was convinced by some combination of the arguments, and managed to launch a war effort that the public supported once it was under way. Still, many observers wondered: if George Bush was so sincerely affronted by the Iraqi invasion, why had he offered only a muted critique of the 1989 Chinese massacre in Tiananmen Square? Did Bush hold regional upstarts to higher standards than great powers? (Bush's defenders replied that, after all, it was hardly possible to launch an attack against China no matter how offensive its actions. Moreover, opposition to external aggression is more easily justified than interference in domestic matters.)

Probably both pragmatic and moral goals entered into the administration's decision, backed by the U.S. Congress, to go to war against Iraq. But in the end, pragmatic goals seemed to call for a narrower policy than moral goals would have. The United States did compel Iraq to withdraw from Kuwait. However, it did not force Saddam Hussein from power, and it refused to support the Kurdish rebellion against his ruling party. Many critics concluded that the United States had sold out its values at a crucial moment. They were especially bitter about U.S. radio broadcasts during the war, which had called on the Iraqi people to rebel. When the Kurds did so, not only did the United States withhold aid, but it took no effective action to stop Iraq when it used helicopter gunships against the rebels. Defenders of U.S. policy argued that it simply was not in the United States' power to impose a democratic regime in Iraq. They say that U.S. support for the rebels could only have created a larger bloodbath—hardly a "moral" outcome.

In the aftermath of the war, many Americans still wondered whether the fighting had been necessary. Some observers were convinced that, sooner or later, economic sanctions would have forced Saddam Hussein out of Kuwait without imposing the full cost of war. While Americans were delighted that few U.S. soldiers died, many were horrified by the toll on Iraqi civilians. By various estimates, up to 70,000 civilians died because of the damage caused by the war. Many also believed that the United Nations would have greater credibility as an impartial peacekeeping force if it had resisted the U.S. call to attack Iraq. Supporters of the administration policy countered that sanctions imposed their own huge human costs, and that they were likely to fail eventually as countries lost patience with the restrictions or, in the case of Arab states, lost their nerve to oppose Hussein. Moreover, they argued, the United Nations' credibility was far better served by military force than it would have been by inaction.

Questions to Consider

1. Among the nine values listed on page 110, which ones do you feel present the hardest questions about priorities? Why?

2. What key values and interests were cited by the Bush administration to justify its policy during the Gulf crisis of 1990–91? Which do you think were most important in determining U.S. policy? Would you have acted differently at some point? If so, why?

3. How important are the conflicts between U.S. values and interests? Do U.S. values and interests generally coincide? Are there policy areas where the United States seems to have followed its values at the expense of its interests, or vice versa?

CHAPTER 5

Beliefs, Evidence, and Policy Implications

etermining preferences among competing values and interests, and coming to grips with inevitable trade-offs, are at the heart of the debate over the U.S. role in the world. The United States' democratic values demand that the general public make such decisions. Making "public choices" among these questions of value is only part of the task, however. Questions of fact also arise, in which people hold competing beliefs about how the world works and so draw conflicting conclusions about the ends or means of U.S. foreign policy. To complicate matters, evidence is often cited in seemingly contradictory ways to bolster competing arguments. To aid you in sorting out these latter, "expert issues," this chapter offers some analytical tools to examine the consequences of different foreign policy ends and means.

To illustrate the difference between questions of value and fact, consider that some people call for the United States to promote democracy abroad on both moral and practical grounds. Ethically, they believe the United States has a responsibility to advance the cause of liberty and freedom. They also believe that the spread of democracies will make the international system more peaceful. The latter belief, unlike the former value judgment, raises a factual question: are democratic governments inherently peaceful? Many doubt that they are. People on both sides of the argument can present evidence for their position. On one hand, there are many examples of dictatorships that started wars and democracies that have behaved peacefully. Future 1 cites an example: Germany, Japan, and Italy were aggressive dictatorships before World War II, but became peaceful democracies after the war. On the other hand, democracies undeniably do sometimes start wars. Democratic Britain, France, and Israel attacked Egypt in 1956; in the previous century, the United States began wars with Mexico and Spain.

For questions like this, when conflicting evidence is available, the question may need to be reframed. One way that may accommodate the seemingly contradictory evidence is to ask: are democracies *more* peaceful than non-democratic states? But even this question may be too broad to be entirely helpful. Perhaps democracies do tend to be more peaceful than dictatorships. This finding, in itself, does not necessarily aid decision-making. After all, in many cities there are more dry days than rainy ones, but no one would advocate doing away with umbrellas because it tends not to rain. Ultimately, a more useful question would be: under what conditions are democracies peaceful? This question will be explored in the first section below.

If the United States is to foster democracy abroad, for whatever reasons, it must decide on means to achieve that end. How can democracy be promoted, when do such efforts succeed, and what are the costs and risks? What can be learned from the mixed record of past attempts to promote democracy? The second section examines these questions. The third section explores one particular policy instrument, economic sanctions. The purpose is to learn the conditions under which sanctions tend to work, and then show how supporters of all four Futures may apply this knowledge to advance their policy goals. The final section offers a few ideas about how the same research methods can help explore the utility of other policy objectives and instruments.

Democracies and Peace

Several studies have attempted to answer whether—and when—democracies are more peaceful than dictatorships. (These studies have varied but roughly similar definitions of democracy.) One analysis of 118 international wars fought between 1816 and 1980 reveals that democratic states almost never fight each other.[1] The exceptions have occurred when a democratic regime was new and fragile, or when one of the governments could not control forces fighting on or launching attacks from its territory. This finding suggests that the fledgling democracies of Eastern Europe now face their greatest risk of war. Nevertheless, during the last two centuries, democratic states have never fought each other in a war involving most of the great powers.

Other scholars have found that democracies are roughly as likely as dictatorships to be involved in wars, but they are somewhat less likely to start the wars.[2] When a democracy starts a war, moreover, it almost

---

1. Michael W. Doyle, "Kant, Liberal Legacies, and Foreign Affairs, Part I," *Philosophy & Public Affairs* (Summer 1983).

2. See Zeev Moaz and Nasrin Abdolai, "Regimes Types and International Conflict, 1816-1976," *Journal of Conflict Resolution* (1989); Rudolph J. Rummel, "The Freedom Factor," *Reason* (July 1983); Randall L. Schweller, "Domestic Structures and Preventive War: Are Democracies More Pacific?" *World Politics* (January 1992); Melvin Small and J. David Singer, "The War-Proneness of Democratic Regimes, 1816-1965," *Jerusalem Journal of International Relations* (Summer 1976); and Erich Weede, "Democracy and War Involvement," *Journal of Conflict Resolution* (December 1984).

always is against a non-democratic state. Democracies have attacked non-democracies for various reasons: for instance, to overthrow morally unsavory regimes, to bring an end to hostile acts, or even to forestall a feared attack. These findings suggest a "democratic zone of peace": no fighting takes place between democratic states. Thus Jack Levy concludes that "the absence of war between democracies comes as close as anything we have to an empirical law in international relations."[3]

Some scholars suspect that these findings are tied to a specific set of historical circumstances, or to the relatively small set of democracies available to study. Thus another scholar contends: "The 'democratic zone of peace' argument is valid as far as it goes, but it may not go very far."[4] In addition, most of the new democratic regimes in Latin America and Eastern Europe have little tradition of democratic rule, and therefore have never been part of the "zone of peace." If these states lack some key trait that Doyle's democracies have in common, then they may not be peaceful at all.

Thus, other conditions that make democracies more peaceful should be considered. Randall Schweller's useful study focuses only on preventive wars among great powers. A preventive war can occur during a shift in the balance of power between two states. The leading—but declining—power may attack the rising power to avoid falling behind and becoming vulnerable. Schweller found that "every preventive war launched by a Great Power—from Sparta's response to its fear of the growth of Athenian power to Nazi Germany's attack against the Soviet Union—has been initiated by a nondemocratic state."[5] No democratic great power has ever launched a preventive war against another great power. Instead, democratic leaders strike compromises with rising democratic challengers, and attempt to counter rising non-democratic challengers by forming defensive alliances.

Schweller's explanation focuses on domestic factors, and it also suggests limits to his findings. He argues that the strength of public opinion in democratic states lessens the incentives for preventive wars in several ways. Unlike their dictatorial counterparts, democratic states lack the large conscript armies, flexibility, decisiveness, and cold logic required to act solely out of considerations of power politics. This peacekeeping effect of public opinion partly depends, however, on the expectation that the war will cost the declining democracy too many lives and too much money. Consequently, the argument presented here holds only for power shifts between states of roughly equal strength. It would

---

3. Jack S. Levy, "Domestic Politics and War," *Journal of Interdisciplinary History* (Spring 1988), 662.
4. Samuel P. Huntington, "No Exits: The Error of Endism," *The National Interest* (Fall 1989), 7.
5. Schweller, "Domestic Structures and Preventive War: Are Democracies More Pacific?" 249.

not pertain, for instance, to the relative decline of a large state vis-à-vis a much smaller state.

Schweller's research offers strong results within the boundaries he sets: power shifts among great powers. Under these conditions democracies have been peaceful. It suggests, moreover, that as democracy spreads, preventive wars will be less common. Thus, if West Germany had sought to acquire nuclear weapons during the Cold War, an autocratic Soviet Union might have been tempted to launch a preventive attack. Now, as long as Russia remains democratic, it is unlikely to attack a unified Germany that seeks nuclear arms.

But what about situations other than power shifts among great powers? Democracies start wars almost as frequently as dictatorships do, and wars launched by democracies have typically been against autocratic countries. Why did these wars occur? How do democracies and dictatorships compare when encountering other causes of war, such as conflicting ideologies, alliance commitments, misperceptions, and miscalculations?

One way to answer these questions would be to examine closely how often, against whom, and when democracies start wars. Unfortunately, a series of case studies could easily fill a large book. It may be helpful to begin by exploring the definition of democracy. Future 1 has a useful definition: democracy is a form of government that represents the will of the entire population of a country. It is based on the principle of majority rule with respect for the rights of minorities. Institutionalized checks and balances further serve to protect citizen rights at home, and they help ensure that the country acts abroad in ways consistent with basic citizen values and interests. More peace is one of the consequences, because in a society with free elections and majority rule, leaders have less power to pursue their own selfish interests through war. Respect for minority rights also helps to preserve the peace. Consider, for example, a multinational state with free elections and majority rule, in which the government represses the language, religion, free speech, or other rights of a minority nationality. A neighboring state with ethnic ties to the oppressed minority may be impelled to support national self-determination for that minority. That confrontation with the multinational state could readily lead to war.

The former Soviet bloc offers many examples of this danger. For instance, Romania's treatment of its Hungarian minority harms relations with Hungary, and Bulgaria's restrictions on its Turkish minority have in the past created tensions with neighboring Turkey. If a former Soviet republic abridges the rights of its Russian citizens, Russia may be tempted to intervene on their behalf. It already did during the summer of 1992, when Russian army units engaged Moldovan forces that were trying to suppress an independence movement by Russians and Ukrainians living in the eastern part of Moldova. The list of flash points goes on.

There are other questions about the supposed peacefulness of democracies. What if a democracy's citizens share an ideology that encourages them to change the international status quo through military means? Some would argue that the United States itself has exemplified this. During the Cold War, the United States several times sent troops to overthrow hostile governments (for instance, in the Dominican Republic in 1965, and in Grenada in 1983). The public supported these interventions in large part as anti-communist measures. Germany under Adolf Hitler provides another case. Hitler was initially elected to power, and then persuaded the legislature to vote him emergency powers. Hitler attained these successes in part because his national socialist ideology— especially his call to unify German-speaking lands and reassert German leadership—was popular. Thus, democratic currents helped bring about the eventual German aggression. Finally, if public values of tolerance and cooperation make democracies more peaceful, then what about countries whose governments are legally democratic, but whose people have not been raised to respect these values? Perhaps these countries are no more peaceful than dictatorships.

Promoting Democracy Abroad

Many times, U.S. initiatives have helped to bring about democratic change abroad. U.S. political pressures helped remove Ferdinand Marcos from power in the Philippines, paving the way for a democratic government. Economic sanctions help compel South Africa to move away from apartheid and toward democracy. Covert military aid to the Nicaraguan Contras, combined with a regional peace conference, pressured the Sandinista government to permit the elections that knocked it out of power. Allied military efforts during World War II brought democracy to Japan, Germany, and Italy; more recently, U.S. military interventions removed tyrants in Grenada and Panama. The United States has also helped to strengthen democratic regimes. The classic example is the Marshall Plan of 1948–52. The plan's economic aid was used to stabilize West European economies, increasing popular support for the region's democratic governments, and reducing the appeal of radical political forces.

Yet there are many cases in which the same means failed to create thriving democracies. For decades political and economic pressures failed to liberalize Marxist regimes in Vietnam, North Korea, and Cuba. Covert U.S. operations in Angola and Afghanistan helped bring about the removal of Cuban and Soviet troops, respectively, but democracy has not become ingrained in either country. Likewise, although the invasions of Grenada and Panama led to the establishment of democratic regimes, critics of the interventions argue that despite subsequent U.S. aid neither country has a thriving democracy.

What Works?

The conditions that create or sustain democracy will be examined here. When does political pressure help to compel compliance with democratic or other human rights values? When do economic sanctions help? Under what conditions is military force effective in defending or imposing these ends? When does success require a combination of political, economic, and military means?

An important, related question concerns domestic objectives: to support the goal of democracy within a country, what should the United States seek to change or support, and what means should it use to achieve these objectives? Will overthrowing a tyrant or bringing about free elections assure that democracy will flourish? Are there additional aspects of a thriving democratic society that require development or support? In general, given the variety of internal conditions in countries in which democracy may thrive, when does the United States have effective leverage?

A recent study of past U.S. efforts to promote democracy in Latin America contributes to an understanding of these issues. Abraham Lowenthal reports that "past U.S. attempts to promote Latin American democracy have met with little enduring success" and that "none of the instruments employed by the United States to promote democracy has ever succeeded in an enduring fashion unless local conditions were propitious."[6] After examining likely explanations for the few successes and the more numerous failures, the study proposes a series of conditions that support the promotion of democracy. A full elaboration of these conditions would require lengthy references to numerous case studies. To simply illustrate some of the points here, however, references will be made to what Lowenthal calls "the best example of a successful U.S. effort to foster democratic politics in Latin America"—U.S. policy toward Chile beginning in 1985.[7] Although this case does not perfectly meet all of the favorable conditions, it shows how many of them operate.

Compared to most post–World War II U.S. efforts to influence Chilean politics, this recent involvement gave priority to supporting the democratic process instead of ensuring that leftists would not gain or

---

6. Abraham F. Lowenthal, ed., *Exporting Democracy: The United States and Latin America—Themes and Issues* (Baltimore, MD: Johns Hopkins University Press, 1991), x, 261.
    7. Lowenthal, *Exporting Democracy—Themes and Issues*, 256.

retain office.[8] In the middle to late 1960s, by contrast, the United States supported a particular candidate, the reformist Eduardo Frei. The U.S. government hoped Frei would reduce the influence of conservatives who wanted no change, and thus prevent the rise of more radical elements who wanted revolutionary change. In the early 1970s the U.S. focus was to prevent the election of the left-leaning Salvador Allende and, when this failed, to encourage his overthrow—which General Augusto Pinochet accomplished in a 1973 coup. Pinochet established authoritarian rule for 15 years. U.S. policy changed in 1985, playing a part in the restoration of democracy several years later.

According to Lowenthal, the various case studies of previous U.S. efforts to promote democracy in Latin America suggest that success is favored when U.S. policy:

- consistently emphasizes concern with the protection of fundamental human rights. Beginning in 1985, the Reagan administration's policy toward Chile changed, subordinating the goal of fighting communism to humanitarian goals of promoting democracy and respect for human rights. Some hard-line members of the administration opposed various U.S. pressures on the Pinochet regime, but their influence had been reduced.

- includes cooperation with other countries to add legitimacy to U.S. efforts. This policy was not followed in the case of Chile: since the U.S. attempt to promote democracy in Chile was part of a larger, quiet process to advance democracy in Argentina, Brazil, and Chile, the United States did not openly seek the help of other countries. Additional countries may have supported the U.S. efforts to promote democracy, but the U.S. efforts were the most obvious to Chileans.

- helps to strengthen the governmental institutions and practices that make up the fiber of democracy (instead of supporting a particular candidate or party). U.S. pressures helped nudge Pinochet toward conducting, in 1988, a fair national plebiscite on whether he should continue to lead. Pinochet lost the vote, and that led to democratic elections the next year.

- supports, both through government actions and activities of private groups, the network of nongovernmental organizations—economic, social, educational, and civic—that express and mediate public demands and build the pluralism needed to keep democracy vital. The United States provided funding and technical help to the democratic opposition in Chile. It also required that the Pinochet

---

8. Thomas Carothers, "The Reagan Years: The 1980s," in *Exporting Democracy— Themes and Issues*, edited by Abraham F. Lowenthal (Baltimore, MD: Johns Hopkins University Press, 1991), 109–110. Heraldo Muñoz, "Chile: The Limit of 'Success,' " in *Exporting Democracy—Case Studies*, edited by Abraham F. Lowenthal (Baltimore, MD: Johns Hopkins University Press, 1991).

regime give television access to the opposition in order to win U.S. recognition of the plebiscite's validity.

- provides clear and consistent signals that the establishment and maintenance of democratic politics is a high-priority goal of the United States. In 1985 the United States appointed a new ambassador to Chile, Harry Barnes. Unlike the previous ambassador, James Theberge, Barnes openly and consistently backed the democratic process, and he was willing to work closely with the democratic opposition.

- helps democratic governments make their economies more productive and equitable, thus strengthening popular support for democracy. When Pinochet was voted out, Chile was already prosperous and hence needed little assistance from the United States.

Lowenthal concludes with a warning against overstating U.S. influence in Chile and other countries:

> External influence, including that of the United States, helped at the margin to restore democracy, but this was in an already fundamentally democratic nation, under conditions of stability and prosperity, with a strong moderate opposition movement and a weak left mostly committed to peaceful and incremental change. Circumstances as favorable as those in Chile for the nurturing of democracy do not often arise.[9]

Knowledge of when and how democracy can be promoted may be advanced by similar research projects covering other regions, such as Africa, Eastern Europe, and the former Soviet Union. Likewise, since countries other than the United States have attempted to support democracy, examining their efforts would also add to our understanding.

Costs and Risks

Besides considering whether and how the United States can effectively promote democracy abroad, we must assess the costs and risks of promoting it—and of failing to promote it.

Sometimes efforts to create democracies are very costly. For instance, converting the autocratic great powers of Germany and Japan to democracies in 1945 required a full-scale war to defeat them. After the war, the United States provided generous economic aid and trade terms to help rebuild these new democracies, in part to foster strength and unity against the perceived communist threat.

In today's world, using military means to convert strong countries to democracy may be even more difficult. China, the least democratic of

---

9. Lowenthal, *Exporting Democracy—Themes and Issues*, 257.

the great powers, has a nuclear arsenal that effectively deters any attempt to impose democracy by force. Less drastic measures have difficulties of their own. Many Western policymakers support economic aid to the new states of the former Soviet Union to help them build democratic governments. But sluggish Western economies and a lack of an obvious common enemy work against large infusions of economic support. Furthermore, many aspects of these new countries, such as their tradition of centrally controlled economies, make it difficult for democracy and capitalism to take root and thrive. Deciding what sort of aid will best promote democratic values in these countries is a thorny question.

In the assessment of costs and risks, the disadvantages of failing to support democracy must also be considered. A classic example is Germany between the two world wars. Germany emerged from World War I as a democracy, the Weimar Republic. Its economy was burdened, however, by wartime casualties, irresponsible borrowing policies to finance the war, and reparations imposed by the victors. The democratic government was seriously challenged by radical elements until the mid-1920s, when U.S. loans and investments helped to bring prosperity. After the 1929 crash of the U.S. stock market, these loans and investments dried up. This lack of capital, along with the worldwide Great Depression, led to severe economic distress. In this climate of misery and anxiety, radical political movements flourished on both the left and the right. This process culminated in the 1933 election of Adolf Hitler, who soon established a totalitarian government. In retrospect, the failure of the victors to support Germany economically contributed to the downfall of the Weimar Republic. These countries' bitterness toward Germany following World War I goes far to explain this failure. The Great Depression also hindered outside support for German democracy. Yet the victorious allies probably suffered much more at Hitler's hands than they would have if they had succeeded in creating a thriving democracy in Germany.

Economic Sanctions

States have often used economic sanctions to achieve foreign policy goals, and promoting democracy is just one possible goal. The country implementing the sanctions seeks to influence the domestic or international behavior of the target state, by raising the economic costs to the target state of continuing an undesirable policy. Sanctions are a controversial tactic, however.

When Do Economic Sanctions Work?

Opinions vary widely about the utility of sanctions. Supporters of sanctions can point to successes. Economic pressures contributed to

A nation that is boycotted is a nation that is in sight of surrender. Apply this economic, peaceful, silent, deadly remedy and there will be no need for force. It is a terrible remedy. It does not cost a life outside the nation boycotted, but it brings a pressure upon the nation which, in my judgment, no modern nation could resist.

—Woodrow Wilson,
speech in Indianapolis (1919)

[A] superpower has claws and it has teeth. The superpower, as against this Third World power, doesn't have to be impatient or impetuous. A superpower doesn't have to feel rushed. We can afford to be patient and let sanctions work.

—Robert Byrd, debate in
Congress (January 12, 1991) on
President Bush's request for
support of military action against
Iraq in the Persian Gulf

[W]e're asked, what's the hurry? Well, after five months of rebuffed diplomacy, every day that this Congress procrastinates Saddam's factories are producing more chemical and biological weapons; more anthrax, more botulism, more sarin, which is a lethal nerve gas, and yes, more progress on nuclear weapons. And make no mistake about it, my colleagues, if we must resort to military force, those factories of death and destruction and terrorism will surely be targets. So today, not next week, not next month, but today, we must give the President the authority to remove this scourge or the face of history will pass judgment upon us as the Congress that failed to do its duty.

—Bud Shuster, in the debate
described above

South Africa's recent move away from apartheid; they also helped bring down Uganda's Idi Amin, and Nicaragua's Anastasio Somoza, in 1979. Supporters also argue that sanctions are better than the alternatives of no action or using military force. Skeptics cite past failures, such as the League of Nations' effort in 1935–36 to compel Italy to withdraw from Ethiopia, the U.S. attempt before World War II to compel Japan to cease aggression in Asia, and U.S. efforts in 1987–89 to oust Panama's dictator Manuel Noriega. Skeptics also highlight the painful impact of sanctions on the populations of target countries, as well as the risks to the country imposing sanctions—for instance, Japan's resentments of U.S. sanctions contributed to its decision to attack Pearl Harbor.

The simplistic question "do sanctions work?" should be set aside in favor of a more useful question: "under what conditions do sanctions succeed?" When assessing their effectiveness, sanctions should be compared to alternative policies—bearing in mind that every policy carries costs and risks.

The most thorough research to date on the effectiveness of sanctions was based on 103 cases in which sanctions were used in the twentieth century.[10] The study found that sanctions succeeded in 36 percent of the cases. Success was defined as making at least a modest contribution to a stated goal that was at least partially realized. By contrasting cases of success and failure, the researchers learned the conditions under which sanctions tend to succeed. These conditions are listed below. Not all of the conditions must always be met for success to occur, but the more that are met, the greater the likelihood of success.

- The policy goals of sanctions are moderate. Sanctions are most often successful when they are intended to weaken a government or to achieve modest policy goals. Such goals are relatively limited and specific in scope: for instance, to deter human rights abuses, nuclear proliferation, or state-sponsored terrorism. Sanctions are seldom effective in impairing the military strength of an important power, disrupting military adventures, or effecting major domestic changes in the target country. Yet these latter, more ambitious policy goals are sometimes achieved, especially when the remaining conditions solidly support success.

- Sanctions impose high economic costs on the target. In the successful cases, the average cost of sanctions to target countries was about 2 percent of the countries' gross national product (GNP). When the sanctions achieved a cost of 4 percent of GNP, they had an 80 percent success rate. For ambitious policy goals against a country with a strong government, even greater economic costs may be

---

10. Gary Hufbauer, Jeffrey Scott, and Kimberly Elliot, *Economic Sanctions Reconsidered: History and Current Policy* (Washington, DC: Institute for International Studies, 1985).

required. Economic pressures are greatest when (a) the target country's economy is already weak; (b) the country imposing the sanctions is able to implement costly sanctions either unilaterally or with the ready cooperation of other countries; (c) the sanctions are applied quickly and completely so that the target country has insufficient time to adjust; and (d) if necessary, the sanctions can be sustained over a long period of time—which may require designing a sanctions policy that presents few costs to the countries implementing them.

- Sanctions are used against allies and close trading partners. These countries are more likely to bend on specific issues in deference to the overall relationship.

- The target country experiences significant domestic political pressures to change its policy. Ruining the country's economy does not constitute success; the government must agree to comply, or be overthrown and replaced with a government that will comply. Weak governments are most vulnerable to sanctions. Strong ones isolated from the economic costs of sanctions and from political pressures are more difficult to compel.

The study concludes with a caution:

Forecasting the outcome of statecraft, like forecasting the stock market, is hazardous business. Idiosyncratic influences are often at play. Human personalities and plain luck may well determine the outcome of a sanctions episode. . . . As one might expect from a diverse collection of 103 cases, the statistical results are not always clearcut. Much depends on . . . factors which are not captured by our variables. Hence our summary assessments . . . must be read as general indicators, not infallible guideposts, in the fine art of statecraft.[11]

How Can Sanctions Be Used to Achieve Goals?

The basic knowledge of when economic sanctions work has practical applications for all four Futures. A Future 1 supporter may want to use sanctions to advance human rights and democracy. To achieve these goals, sanctions would probably be more successful against a small state like Haiti, for example, than when directed against a huge country like China. Furthermore, calling for the restoration of democracy in an unstable country would more likely succeed than trying to impose democracy on a stable country with a long tradition of authoritarian rule. Even where a transition to democracy may be unlikely, it may be feasible to promote certain human rights that the ruling government will not

11. Hufbauer, Scott, and Elliot, *Economic Sanctions Reconsidered*, 79.

consider subversive—especially if the rights are widely appreciated, such as freedom from genocide or torture.

Future 2 supporters seek regional balances and stability, goals that can be advanced by agreements to ban nuclear weapons and to limit conventional weapons useful for large offensive operations. Sanctions can be used against countries that thwart these agreements, including countries that transfer prohibited weapons. The policy objectives would be moderate. Since the United States would be working in cooperation with its allies, moreover, the offending country would experience sanctions from several countries, and the burdens of implementing sanctions would be shared among the allies. If the country transferring banned weapons is also a U.S. ally, its desire to stay on the good side of the United States is another factor favoring success. Of course such sanctions may not always work, but a careful analysis of a particular situation should suggest if they will work and how to implement them to maximize their prospects for success.

Future 3 supporters want to help maintain and restore international peace, the observation of universal human rights, and other goals in keeping with international charters and declarations. When the UN Security Council agrees on a goal, for instance, several factors offer hope that universally employed economic sanctions might work. First, the sanctions would probably be applied by all or nearly all states that trade with the offending country, which would contribute to the latter's economic isolation. Second, since the costs of implementing sanctions would be shared among many UN members instead of just the United States and perhaps its allies, the sanctions could be sustained over a long period of time. Third, a country complying with UN demands would lose less prestige than it would if it bowed to the demands of only one country. These factors do not guarantee that the sanctions will work, however. Also, this approach requires Security Council agreement. On some issues important to the United States, the Security Council may not approve sanctions, or over time members of the Council may lose their commitment to keep up the pressures.

Future 4 supporters believe that enhancing U.S. economic strength is crucial, both to give Americans a high standard of living and to increase U.S. foreign policy leverage as economic instruments become more important than military ones. Until the United States rebuilds its economy, it is unlikely to engage in costly international endeavors—including sanctions that pose significant costs to the United States. The purposes of some sanctions, such as to promote human rights or regional stability, are also not very important to many Future 4 supporters. Yet some who give priority to rebuilding U.S. economic strength may also care about these goals. For those who do, the only plausible sanctions campaigns would be ones that posed few costs to the United States in the short term. Thus, sanctions could be considered if the target country is particularly vulnerable to U.S. economic pressures, or if the burdens are shared among many countries. Once the United States becomes strong economically, however, it will use its economic leverage more freely. Most of the time, U.S. economic power will be used to further U.S. interests in international negotiations. At other times, when U.S. interests are not directly at stake but more universal concerns are involved—such as human rights violations or other suffering in a faraway region—the United States may use economic sanctions, as long as doing so does not threaten important U.S. commercial or other interests.

Different Issues, Similar Research Methods

Most of the research reported in this chapter used the comparative case study method. This method could easily be applied to other foreign policy objectives and means. For example, advocates of the various Futures disagree on the value of alliances for promoting peace and security. To shed light on this issue, an analyst may contrast cases in which alliances helped to prevent war with cases in which alliances actually contributed to war. To guide the research, the analyst must first use relevant theories, arguments, and other sources to develop a set of questions about potentially important conditions. These questions would then be asked in all of the case studies. This research method of "structured, focused comparison" can generate findings that may help guide U.S. policy toward alliances.[12] Similar analyses may be conducted to help learn when other policies might serve U.S. interests, such as working with the United Nations or other international organizations, engaging in arms transfers or efforts to control arms transfers, and establishing bilateral or regional arms control regimes.

Questions to Consider

1. Under what international conditions do democracies tend to be peaceful? What domestic characteristics lead democracies to avoid starting wars (or at least certain kinds of wars)? How conclusive is the evidence on this topic? If the number of democracies increases, will U.S. security be enhanced?

2. What conditions are conducive to imposing or supporting democracy? What are the costs and risks of such efforts, as well as the

---

12. Alexander L. George, "Case Studies and Theory Development: The Method of Structured, Focused Comparison," in *Diplomatic History: New Approaches in History, Theory and Policy*, edited by Paul Lauren (New York: Free Press, 1979).

disadvantages of failing to promote democracy? If the United States and other countries act to promote democracy in Eastern Europe and the states of the former Soviet Union, where do you expect success to be easiest? Why? If the patterns of success for this region are similar to the patterns in Latin America, how could U.S. policy be designed to increase the prospect of success? What sort of research would help to refine your answers?

3. How are economic sanctions supposed to work? What is an ideal set of circumstances for using economic sanctions? When a particular instance fulfills only some of the conditions favoring success, what questions should you ask about costs and risks? How may sanctions be used to advance a foreign policy goal such as respect for human rights or democracy, or regional balances of power and stability? When are cooperative efforts most important?

Conclusions

This analysis of the peacefulness of democracies and the feasibility of various ways to promote democracy largely concerns empirical research and facts. Yet no matter how carefully the likely consequences of a state's actions are analyzed, the country usually still confronts a difficult policy decision. Two important values may be in unavoidable conflict, such as when the desire to promote democracy competes with the principle of nonintervention. And some people care about such value choices more than they do empirical findings. Thus, some will prefer to promote democracy and human rights for value-based reasons even if there is little hope of success, while others will refrain from even potentially successful policies because they oppose interfering in the affairs of other countries. Nevertheless, asking productive questions and conducting careful research can be useful. The process can offer insights about the desirability and feasibility of a foreign policy Future, or about how the knowledge could be used to refine the ideas and prescriptions associated with various Futures.

In some cases the United States must accept large risks no matter what policy is chosen. In circumstances like these, it may be possible to "hedge our bets" by adopting a policy that preserves the greatest possible freedom and seems to provide protection from the greatest dangers. But even determining the "greatest dangers" ultimately depends on a values framework. As a result, expert analysis can clarify choices, risks, and trade-offs, but the public should ultimately determine national priorities.

CHAPTER 6

Back to the Futures: Implications and Limits

The four Futures are intended to raise important questions about the nature of international relations, about values and their impact on foreign policy, and about analytical methods to clarify crucial debates. Before you state your opinions in a questionnaire, and then develop your own preferred Future, it is helpful to examine how the four Futures speak to certain short-term policy issues. This task will highlight both the utility and limits of the four Futures. It will also help you consider policy issues and approaches that you may want to incorporate into your own Future 5 (see chapter 8).

Policy debates can often be better understood by viewing them from the competing perspectives of the four Futures. To illustrate this, we will examine a hypothetical crisis on the Korean peninsula. The scenario presented is imaginary, not based on real knowledge of North Korean actions or intentions. The purpose of the exercise is not to predict the future, but rather to highlight the Futures' contrasting policy directions, as well as areas of debate within each Future. The Futures framework does not, however, fully address all policy debates that you may find important. Two such concerns will be explored later in this chapter: international trade and the environment.

Before proceeding, you may want to review the contents of the four Futures. A quick way to do this is to read *The Four Futures Compared,* a matrix that follows this chapter (pages 156–157).

Crisis on the Korean Peninsula

Imagine the following scenario taking place in the year 1995: U.S. intelligence agencies learn that the South Korean government is under pressure by its military chiefs to launch an air strike on North Korea's clandestine nuclear weapons production facilities. The United States must decide how to respond.

The South Korean military, always suspicious of North Korean intentions and capabilities, finds its worst fears confirmed in 1995. Many members of the government feel deceived by earlier North Korean

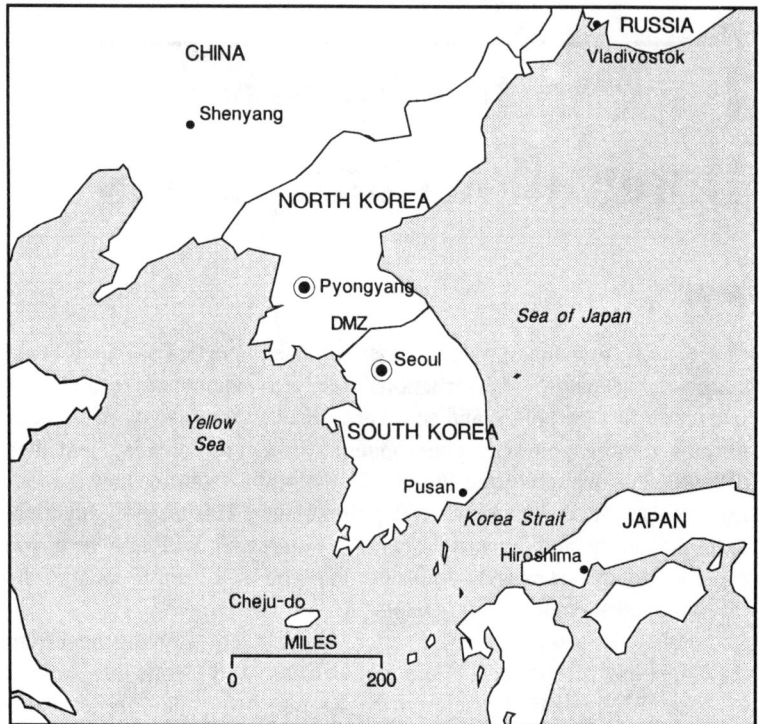

North and South Korea

pledges to reduce tensions, to move toward peaceful unification, and to forgo production of nuclear weapons. In the early 1990s, for example, North Korea had finally concluded a safeguards agreement with the International Atomic Energy Agency (IAEA). This agreement permitted the IAEA to inspect North Korea's nuclear reactors to ensure compliance with the Non-Proliferation Treaty, which North Korea had signed in 1985.

But in late 1994 a Russian physicist defected to South Korea, warning that North Korea—like Iraq—had evaded the IAEA safeguards. The physicist had worked for North Korea after losing his job in Russia at the end of the Cold War. He and other experts had helped the North Koreans to produce nuclear weapons fuel in an underground complex. He also reported that North Korea was seeking to modify the SCUD missiles it obtained from China, so that the missiles could carry the nuclear warheads that he had helped to develop.

Then, in 1995, two chilling discoveries intensified South Korean fears. First, U.S. satellite reconnaissance showed that North Korea had begun massive modifications of its SCUD and FROG missile sites. (Both SCUDs and FROGs are short-range surface-to-surface missiles.) U.S. and South Korean intelligence analysts believe that the North Koreans may be preparing the missiles to carry nuclear weapons. Second, a routine geological survey of the Demilitarized Zone (DMZ) separating the two Koreas revealed five new tunnels, each sufficiently large for columns of troops and their equipment to invade the South. Previously, in the more than 40 years since the end of the Korean War, only four tunnels had been discovered. The South Korean military concludes that North Korea is preparing to invade the South, awaiting only completion of its nuclear weapons capability. Moreover, South Korean analysts predict that within a few months North Korea will have produced enough enriched uranium to fabricate its first atomic bomb. The South Korean military wants to destroy the uranium production facilities before this point is reached, just as Israel had responded to Iraqi uranium production in 1981.

U.S. intelligence analysts have surveyed the situation, but it is unclear what the South Korean government will do. The United States knows that an attack on the underground facilities will risk full-scale war on the peninsula. This war would not only devastate the two Koreas but it could escalate and engage neighboring countries, such as China, Russia, and Japan. Particularly catastrophic would be a North Korean counterattack on South Korean civilian reactors. These reactors, located on the periphery of highly populated areas, provide electricity for major urban centers. Civilian reactors, unlike reactors geared toward weapons production, contain large amounts of radioactive material. The fallout damage from an attack on South Korea's reactors would exceed the 1986 Chernobyl disaster in Ukraine. On the other hand, the 1981 Israeli attack on Iraq's nuclear reactor did not lead to widespread damage, in large part because Iraq did not dare launch a counterattack. Will North Korea be as restrained? If the United States backs a South Korean attack, even diplomatically, it risks condemnation by many countries that do not support the attack. More importantly, it risks getting involved in a major war on the Korean Peninsula. China may also enter the war, as it did in the Korean War of 1950–53, possibly leading to a U.S.–Chinese confrontation. And, China now has nuclear weapons.

Not attacking, and thereby permitting North Korea to continue building nuclear weapons, carries risks too. North Korea may use the weapons either to attack or to coerce concessions from the South. Further nuclear proliferation may also result, if South Korea and Japan acquire nuclear weapons to deter North Korea from using them, or if North Korea sells the technology or complete weapons to countries like Libya or Iran, as it has done in the case of ballistic missiles. These concerns were behind the October 1990 statement by Richard Solomon, assistant secretary of state for East Asian and Pacific Affairs, that the United States viewed "nuclear proliferation on the Korean Peninsula as the number one threat to security in East Asia."[1]

1. Leonard S. Spector and Jacqueline R. Smith, "North Korea: The Next Nuclear Nightmare," *Arms Control Today,* March 1991, p. 9.

Options

Given this situation and its attendant risks, what should the United States do? The president must decide at least three questions. First, should the United States convince the South Koreans to halt or delay their attack, or give them a green light or even assistance? Second, if South Korea does not attack, should the United States work to compel North Korea to stop developing nuclear weapons? If so, how? Third, if North Korea acquires nuclear weapons, should the United States strive to prevent North Korea from using or threatening to use these weapons? Once again, if the answer is yes, how? The Four Futures suggest a range of alternatives.

• **Future 1—Standing Up for Human Rights and Democracy—** would lead the United States to protect democratic Japan and semi-democratic South Korea from the North Korean dictatorship. However, Future 1 supporters may disagree on how to accomplish this goal.

Some will want to ensure that North Korea never acquires a nuclear arsenal. In this scenario, immediate military action may be the only way to prevent North Korea from completing a nuclear weapon. Proponents of military action may recognize its dangers but argue that inaction is far more dangerous. For these people, the United States should either approve a South Korean attack or carry out the attack itself or in coalition with the South Koreans.

Other Future 1 supporters may believe, on the contrary, that the dangers of an attack outweigh the risks of permitting North Korea to gain nuclear weapons. These observers would urge the president to stop the South Korean attack, but to accompany this action with a U.S. commitment to defend both South Korea and Japan against a North Korean nuclear attack. This defense would have to involve more than attempting to shoot down North Korean missiles, because the South Korean capital is only a 20-second missile flight away from North Korean mobile launchers—hardly enough time for an anti-missile system to respond effectively. More practical would be a U.S. commitment to retaliate with its own nuclear weapons. This threat of nuclear retaliation is so grave that it may effectively deter a North Korean attack.

Finally, some Future 1 supporters will not be satisfied until North Korea adopts a democratic government, or until it agrees to peaceful unification with the South under a democratic government. To achieve this goal in the short term, the United States could adopt two forceful policies. First, the United States may launch or support an immediate attack on North Korean nuclear facilities. Second, it may participate in a broader war, invading North Korea to overthrow its government. Advocates of invading the North may likely assume that China will stay neutral, despite China's protective alliance with North Korea.

Another approach to advancing democracy is more cautious, based on greater concern about U.S. losses in such a war and the risk that

China—with its substantial nuclear arsenal—may come to North Korea's aid. This approach could combine economic sanctions against North Korea with commitments to protect South Korea and Japan. Complete economic isolation of North Korea would require the cooperation of many countries, including China, which borders it on the north. An economic embargo of North Korea would obviously be less risky than a war, but possibly much less effective.

• **Future 2—Charting a Stable Course**—would lead the United States to seek a regional balance of power by affirming its defensive alliances with South Korea and Japan. Probably the United States would also encourage South Korea and Japan to make a commitment to each other's defense. These policies are designed to convince North Korea that its attempts at conquest or nuclear coercion cannot succeed. The policies would also help to maintain stability and a balance of power. Since neither South Korea nor Japan has nuclear weapons, the United States would protect them with its "nuclear umbrella." South Korea and Japan would pay their fair share of any U.S. personnel and equipment required, and they would commit their own military forces to back the alliance. Alliance decision-making would also be shared. If Japan does not agree to protect South Korea, the United States would continue to act as South Korea's primary ally, and the two countries would share the burdens and risks of countering North Korea.

Future 2 supporters may disagree on attacking the North Korean nuclear facilities. Those who desire the attack would want a joint allied strike. Yet in the absence of actual North Korean aggression, the operation would be a surprise blow during peacetime to prevent a shift in the balance of power. Such a preventive war is consistent with keeping a regional balance, but it clashes with the traditional defensive nature of the U.S.-Japanese alliance. Also, Japan has been reluctant to engage in military operations, and may not support a joint attack. Perhaps other U.S. allies, such as Great Britain or France, would participate in a multilateral operation, as they did in the 1991 Gulf War against Iraq. Unlike in the 1991 Gulf War, however, Great Britain and France have few interests at stake in East Asia.

Other Future 2 supporters who want North Korea to give up its nuclear program may feel that any attack is undesirable or unfeasible. An approach consistent with their desire for regional stability is to follow the Japanese strategy, using economic incentives to coax North Korea out of its isolationist and paranoid shell. This policy assumes that with the dissolution of communism throughout most of the world, North Korean leaders believe that their way of life is threatened by Western hegemony. With severe reductions in economic and military aid from the former Soviet Union, the North Koreans feel even more isolated and are pursuing a policy of self-reliance in most matters. Nuclear weapons are a way to maintain a military presence and dissuade others from interfering in their affairs. Yet North Korean leaders also want economic support from Japan and elsewhere, in order to strengthen their economy. This desire for economic aid, trade, and investment may be a useful lever to convince them to completely give up building nuclear weapons. In 1992, for example, when North Korea agreed to permit IAEA inspections of its nuclear facilities, a major incentive was Japan's promise to restore diplomatic relations and build trade ties. The United States may use this approach, making additional economic support conditional on immediate and more extensive IAEA inspections. This policy, or a strategy of using economic sanctions to compel compliance with the Non-Proliferation Treaty, would have fewer immediate risks than an attack, but neither path is certain to succeed.

The question of interfering in North Korea's domestic affairs would also spark debate. Some Future 2 supporters may advocate covert operations to sabotage the nuclear facilities or to change North Korea's foreign policy. Others may prefer a U.S. commitment not to meddle in North Korea's domestic affairs if it forgoes nuclear weapons.

• **Future 3—Cooperating Globally**—would involve UN leadership to cope with this crisis, with the United States acting to support the United Nations.

North Korea's clandestine nuclear facilities are in violation of the IAEA safeguards agreement negotiated under the Non-Proliferation Treaty. The UN Security Council, charged with dealing with threats to peace and security, would take up the issue and seek a consensus policy among at least the five permanent members (those with a veto). The question is, a consensus for what? Some agreements are easier to reach than others.

The Security Council may readily support policies with relatively low costs and risks to UN members. One example is an explicit commitment to provide for the collective defense of any victim of North Korean aggression. With about 5,000 UN troops in and around the DMZ, however, the United Nations is already committed to protect South Korea from North Korean attacks. Another possibility is to impose joint economic sanctions on North Korea until it stops violating the safeguard agreement.

It would be much harder to achieve consensus to attack and destroy the illegal facilities. Although the United States, Britain, and France may agree, China—which shares a border and protective alliance with North Korea—may balk from fears of foreign military actions near its border or even future UN intervention in Chinese affairs. Russia's position is hard to predict; it probably depends on the state of its relations with the other permanent members. If the Council does support an attack, however, it could be a joint operation with shared costs and risks.

If South Korea launches an attack on its own, the UN will probably be divided on how to respond. Some states would cheer South Korea's decisiveness while others would condemn its unilateral military action. With these divisions, the UN would be unlikely to engage in forceful actions against South Korea. If South Korea attacks first, however, it will decrease the prospect of unanimous UN support for South Korea if the North then invades the South. The United States should so inform South Korean leaders, so that they do not erroneously count on U.S. or UN support.

• **Future 4—Building U.S. Economic Strength**—would lead the United States to disengage itself from the crisis. According to this view, U.S. vital interests are not endangered, since North Korea is unlikely to attack the United States. Moreover, Japan and South Korea are thought to be sufficiently rich and resourceful to protect themselves from any serious threats. Thus, Future 4 supporters see no reason to risk U.S. lives and wealth in this conflict. U.S. leaders would say that what South Korea does to the North Korean facilities is its business and not ours.

Future 4 calls for bringing all U.S. troops home, but gradually, so that some may still be in South Korea in 1995. Any U.S. troops in South Korea would be at risk if the South Korean strike led to wider war on the peninsula. If they remain, moreover, the U.S.–South Korean alliance will probably still be in force. In this case it would probably be too late for the United States to withdraw its troops, and the U.S. may therefore want to discourage a South Korean attack. The president may inform South Korean leaders that if South Korea provokes a war, the United States will not defend it and will immediately withdraw U.S. troops. Alternatively, the president may decide that U.S. treaty commitments bind it to defend South Korea even after an attack on the North Korean facilities.

If South Korea does not destroy the nuclear facilities, and if North Korea continues its nuclear program, some Future 4 supporters may believe that U.S. interests will not be harmed if South Korea and Japan build nuclear arsenals. North Korea may then prefer a nuclear weapons free zone, rather than an arms race that North Korea would probably lose. Also, Japanese and South Korean nuclear weapons programs would signal prospective nuclear states that their nuclear programs may back-fire by provoking threatened neighbors to acquire matching arsenals. However, if Japan and South Korea abrogate their IAEA commitments in order to develop nuclear arsenals, the Non-Proliferation Treaty will be weakened, perhaps causing more, not less, nuclear proliferation world-wide. Moreover, a nuclear-armed Japan would disturb its neighbors, who have not forgotten Japanese aggression in World War II. A regional arms race may ensue. Nuclear forces in these countries may provoke preemptive attacks, meant to destroy the weapons on the ground. Also, some Future 4 supporters would argue that regional arms races undermine the political stability in which U.S. trade can thrive. These arguments illustrate how hard it can be to tell if some policies will harm or enhance U.S. economic interests.

Conclusions

The Futures framework helps to clarify U.S. policy options in this crisis. It also shows, however, that each Future leaves ample room for debate. Finally, it reminds us that our judgments about values and priorities must be tempered by an understanding of concrete situations, with their dangers and opportunities. At times the policy that seems most desirable may not be feasible. Policymakers must seek the knowledge that will help them to make better decisions; they also must deal with the inevitable uncertainties.

International Trade

U.S. foreign economic policy has sometimes emphasized protecting U.S. industries, promoting U.S. values or interests abroad, and supporting international trade free of tariffs, quotas, and other barriers. The balance among these themes has varied with specific circumstances.

For its first century and a half, the United States selectively shielded various industries from foreign competition while preserving strong trade opportunities. During the 1930s it enacted the Smoot-Hawley tariff and other extreme protectionist measures. During the Cold War, the United States had a differentiated policy. It promoted free trade among noncommunist states, but restricted trade with communist countries, especially the sale of high-technology products. The United States has also occasionally used economic sanctions and concessions to oppose or support other governments.

Even trade among "free world" countries has never been completely open, however, as noted on page 93. All of them, including the United States, have retained some trade barriers in order to protect domestic producers. Recently, domestic political pressures have increased in order to protect U.S. industries from "unfair competition" by countries such as Japan. Skeptics counter that U.S. economic problems are primarily home-grown and cannot be solved by protectionist measures. So in the post–Cold War era, what sort of foreign economic policy should the United States adopt?

The Futures and International Trade

Supporters of Future 1—Standing Up for Human Rights and Democracy—would call upon the United States to use trade (along with other policy instruments) to advance human rights and democracy.

INCREASING WORLD TRADE (in dollars)*

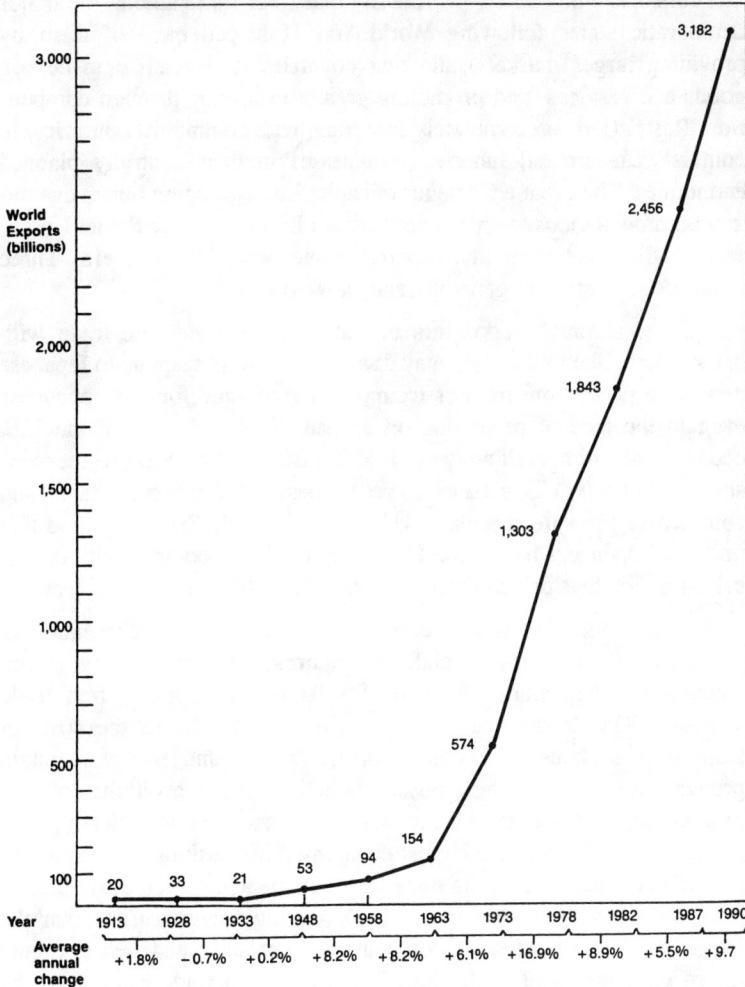

World Exports (billions)

Year	1913	1928	1933	1948	1958	1963	1973	1978	1982	1987	1990
Value	20	33	21	53	94	154	574	1,303	1,843	2,456	3,182
Average annual change	+1.8%	−0.7%	+0.2%	+8.2%	+8.2%	+6.1%	+16.9%	+8.9%	+5.5%	+9.7	

*Figures are rounded.

Data sources: The 1913–58 figures are from Root (1973:24). The 1963–82 figures are from GATT (1983:126). The 1987 figure is from UN (1988:102). The 1990 figure is from UN (1990c) and is projected from figures in the first two quarters.

Source: John Rourke, *International Politics on the World Stage*, 3rd ed. (Guilford, CT: The Dushkin Publishing Group, 1991), p. 355.

This figure shows the rapid expansion of trade measured in exports, especially during the last quarter-century when it grew approximately 1,000 percent to reach $3,182 billion in 1990. Foreign commerce and international economics in general have become more important aspects of international relations and of the domestic economic health of individual countries.

The dominant trend would be selective free trade: free trade among states that respect these values, and restricted (or no) trade with dictatorships. Future 1 supporters say that freer trade among the major democratic states following World War II helped each of them by providing larger markets, allowing countries to specialize in certain goods and services, and promoting greater efficiency through competition. Restrictions on completely free trade with communist countries, in contrast, exacerbated inherent weaknesses in their centrally planned economies. The great advantages of capitalism over communism eventually became obvious to citizens of Eastern Europe and the Soviet Union, feeding the revolutions that ushered in the post–Cold War era. Three issues complicate this general trend, however.

First, although supporters of Future 1 advocate free trade with democracies like Japan, they may disagree on how to respond to Japanese economic protectionism. For example, some argue for U.S. openness even in the face of protectionism abroad. They believe that the U.S. economy would benefit anyway: U.S. industries gain access to inexpensive components, U.S. consumers get the best and cheapest products, and competitive pressure stimulates U.S. firms to excel. Critics respond that unilateral openness harms the U.S. economy by flooding it with underpriced goods that drive comparable U.S. industries out of business.

In a similar but more complex vein, some say that maintaining predominantly free trade relations requires a leader, a very strong country or "hegemon," that benefits from and supports free trade relations. This leader must be strong enough to absorb the costs of leadership, such as the unfair competition of countries that maintain protectionist policies. These observers believe that to avoid the collapse of international trade, the United States must assume this leadership role because it has the world's largest economy. This position would require the United States to open its markets to all countries, even those that do not fully open their own markets. Dissenting analysts argue that the United States is no longer dominant economically and hence cannot afford the burdens of leadership. They say that if trade wars are to be prevented, major trading countries must agree to remove all vestiges of protectionism. This latter position would permit the United States to insist, for instance, that other countries must lower their import barriers in order for the United States to keep its barriers low or to lower new ones. This is the "fair trade" argument.

Although both the free trade and the fair trade positions support the principle of free trade with fellow democracies, the former opposes all U.S. trade restrictions so that the United States will continue to benefit from trade or will exercise leadership by force of example. The latter, by contrast, asserts that in order to enjoy the benefits of free trade, the United States must pressure other countries to respect free trade—even if this means using protectionist policies as a lever.

The second complicating issue is that some who want to support struggling democracies in Eastern Europe and in the former Soviet Union call on the United States to bestow favorable (and not simply equal) trade terms. Their historical analogy is a modification of the one above: U.S. post–World War II trade relations with Japan were very generous, granting Japan more unimpeded access to the U.S. market than the reverse. This was one factor speeding Japan's postwar recovery, and its democratic institutions thrived, helping Japan avoid revolutionary currents that might have aided Soviet or Chinese interests. Since proponents of this view may concede that non-reciprocal market access continued too long after Japan recovered, they would not advocate permanent concessions to the fledgling democracies—only temporary concessions until they become stable politically.

The third complicating issue is that the general prescription, "free trade only with democracies," leads to a conflict between two Future 1 strategies. One is to limit trade with dictatorships as much as possible to weaken their economies, thereby making them less threatening to their neighbors and more vulnerable to domestic discontent. The other is to trade with dictatorships, so that the United States has economic leverage to encourage policy changes. Future 1 supporters who find economic policy important must either find a way to use the two strategies together (such as by prohibiting trade only in goods that have military applications), or choose their own priority on this dilemma. The appropriate approach may depend on answers to questions such as the following: Does the dictatorship present a military threat to the United States or other democracies? How economically advanced is it or can it become? Would economic sanctions work?

Supporters of Future 2—Charting a Stable Course—can hold quite diverse stands on U.S. economic policy, depending on which would best serve this Future's goals of stability and regional balances of power.

Economic strength is a component of national power, and in some regions military power largely depends on economic power. In such regions, the United States may want to preserve a regional balance of power by strengthening a weaker country's economy or undermining a stronger one. The former objective would call for U.S. free trade with, or economic concessions to, the weaker country. The latter objective may lead the United States to impose trade restrictions on the stronger state. These policies follow from the argument that in an anarchic environment, relative gains matter. In other words, even if all countries gain something from free trade (i.e., they gain absolutely), some gain more than others and therefore become more able to get their way in international affairs. Thus, the United States should be attentive to the relative gains that countries in a region achieve from trade, and it may want to adjust its foreign economic policy to facilitate regional balances of power and stability.

Yet such a policy may not be appropriate everywhere. In other regions, the military balance of power may have little to do with economic strength. Punishing a state simply because it has a strong economy may also do more to make enemies than to guarantee peace and stability. And often the United States has only limited economic leverage, even when its allies cooperate. Hence, the United States must tailor its policies to each region, trying to anticipate how various countries will respond to U.S. actions.

Finally, the United States may increase free trade relations with China and other stable dictatorships as long as they agree not to cause trouble in regions vital to U.S. interests. With this added U.S. trade, the dictatorships would have less economic need to sell weapons to dangerous countries and groups.

Supporters of Future 3—Cooperating Globally—would call upon the United States to support free trade and other collaborative arrangements, and to coordinate these efforts through international organizations. If countries of the world are truly interdependent economically, then they will rise or fall together. Protectionist policies adopted by some countries spread to others, so that trade declines and all economies suffer. Economic cooperation, represented by free trade with mutually approved restrictions, benefits all countries.

The world's primary institution promoting free trade is the General Agreement on Trade and Tariffs (GATT). Established in 1947, GATT now has over 100 member countries. GATT sponsors rounds of multilateral negotiations to lower tariff barriers, and it provides rules to encourage free trade and the orderly settlement of trade disputes. Thus if the United States thinks that another country, such as Japan, has unfair trade practices, the United States could take its complaint to GATT and rely on its procedures—instead of taking unilateral actions to push accused countries to change their ways.

Several exceptions to free trade can arise under this Future. First, if a country violates the UN Charter, the Security Council can order economic sanctions against it. This situation would lead the United States to curtail or halt its trade relations with the guilty country, but not for protectionist reasons. Second, members of the UN may decide that poor countries deserve temporary trade concessions from the rich. These concessions would be intended to help the poor countries develop economically, so that they would shift from dependence on the rich states to a relationship of interdependence. Thus, the United States would temporarily help protect and develop the economies of poor countries, so that later they could compete on an equal basis under free trade rules. Finally, certain trade restrictions, such as common environmental standards for imports, may enhance rather than violate the spirit of cooperation that serves the interests of all.

Supporters of Future 4—Building U.S. Economic Strength—give priority to rebuilding the U.S. economy and enhancing U.S. economic competitiveness. To serve these ends, they would use whatever foreign economic policy worked—whether protectionism, "fair trade," or free trade—with only secondary references to other goals, such as promoting human rights, regional stability, or international cooperation. (Some Future 4 supporters may approve, for instance, of economic sanctions against countries that egregiously violate human rights.)

Future 4 advocates may also argue that to revive U.S. economic strength, the United States must protect some industries from foreign competition or subsidize the export of their products until they can rebuild—whether or not other countries grant the United States reciprocal access to their markets.

This protectionist policy has important costs and risks that must be addressed. U.S. consumers would pay more for products, since cheaper (and sometimes better quality) imports would be limited or shut out. It would be hard to choose which industries to protect, without knowing which ones are most likely to succeed. Moreover, this policy may lead to retaliation by other countries. At worst, international trade may collapse, as it did during the 1930s. In the resulting world depression, the term "competitive edge" had no meaning. If this policy is implemented, therefore, the United States should probably protect only a few industries and commodities, in order to minimize the risk of a trade war.

Other Future 4 supporters may argue that the United States should be concerned if other countries overtake the United States in economic power, even if they pose no military threat. With the decline of the Soviet threat, the argument goes, the United States should be even more concerned about its relative economic standing. Therefore it should avoid economic policies that benefit its main economic competitors more than itself. In this view, U.S. free trade in the face of Japanese protectionism would obviously be harmful. However, mutual free trade that benefits Japan more than the United States would also be a mistake. In either case, the United States should adopt some protectionist tactics to ensure that it gains at least as many benefits as its trade partners receive.

Yet some Future 4 supporters may think that as long as the United States remains safe from attack, and trade relations do not give unfair advantages to its trade partners, it need not be concerned about relative gains. These supporters may agree that economic power is becoming more important than in the past, but disagree that the United States must strive to keep an economic balance of power. Thus there would be little reason to worry about "relative advantage" as long as the trade relations are fair.

Finally, some may believe that the U.S. economy benefits from trade regardless of what other countries do. For them, Future 4 can be as supportive of free trade as any other Future.

Conclusions

Future 3 has the clearest preference for free trade (with certain restrictions) over protectionism. It views free trade as desirable, because this approach to trade is consonant with the universalist beliefs and values of Future 3. The remaining Futures see trade as a possible policy instrument, and each would pursue free trade or protectionism selectively depending on which would best further its preferred goals.

Ecological Issues

Ecological threats such as global warming, ozone depletion, and deforestation pose an increasing concern for policymakers. Ecological policy debates hinge to an unusual degree on scientific judgments about long-term consequences. In contrast, while U.S. observers during the Cold War may have disagreed on both Soviet intentions and military strength, almost all agreed that the USSR posed an immediate potential threat.

If ecological issues were simply a matter of unfolding scientific knowledge, they would probably not be discussed in a text that emphasizes fundamental choices. But the debate, while covering scientific ground, is intensely value-laden. Just as there are many uncertainties surrounding this debate, so there is a wide variety of responses to these uncertainties. Some observers argue that it is foolish to risk doing permanent and grave damage to the environment, and that we should act decisively to reduce the threats. Others argue that, on the contrary, it would be more foolish to enact expensive, disruptive policies in response to a merely hypothetical threat.

For instance, some people believe that endangered species should be protected whenever possible. They consider destruction of animal and plant species bad in itself, and argue that it deprives our planet's ecosystem of an irreplaceable resource. A wide diversity of species helps life on Earth to adapt to environmental changes and survive natural disasters. It also provides a biological storehouse for humanity to draw on: for instance, rain forest plant species may be used to develop important new medicines.

On the other side of the debate, critics maintain that the environmental movement places the preservation of wildlife above the interests of humans. In the United States, the Endangered Species Act of 1973 has been used to block dam projects, logging, and other employment sources in cases where just one obscure species was at risk. These critics say it is possible to preserve the environment without going to such extremes. In their view, healthy economic growth depends on making good use of natural resources. Many observers across the spectrum call for a sensible balance between economic and environmental interests. Unfortunately, there is no consensus on the meaning of the word "sensible." Hence, value priorities play a pivotal role in the environmental debate.

Environmental Threats and the Four Futures

Many readers initially assume that Future 3 is the "environmental Future," because environmental hazards are among the global threats addressed by this Future. Actually, each Future can embrace a variety of viewpoints on ecological issues. Simply put, supporters of any Future may consider ecological threats very serious, or unimportant.

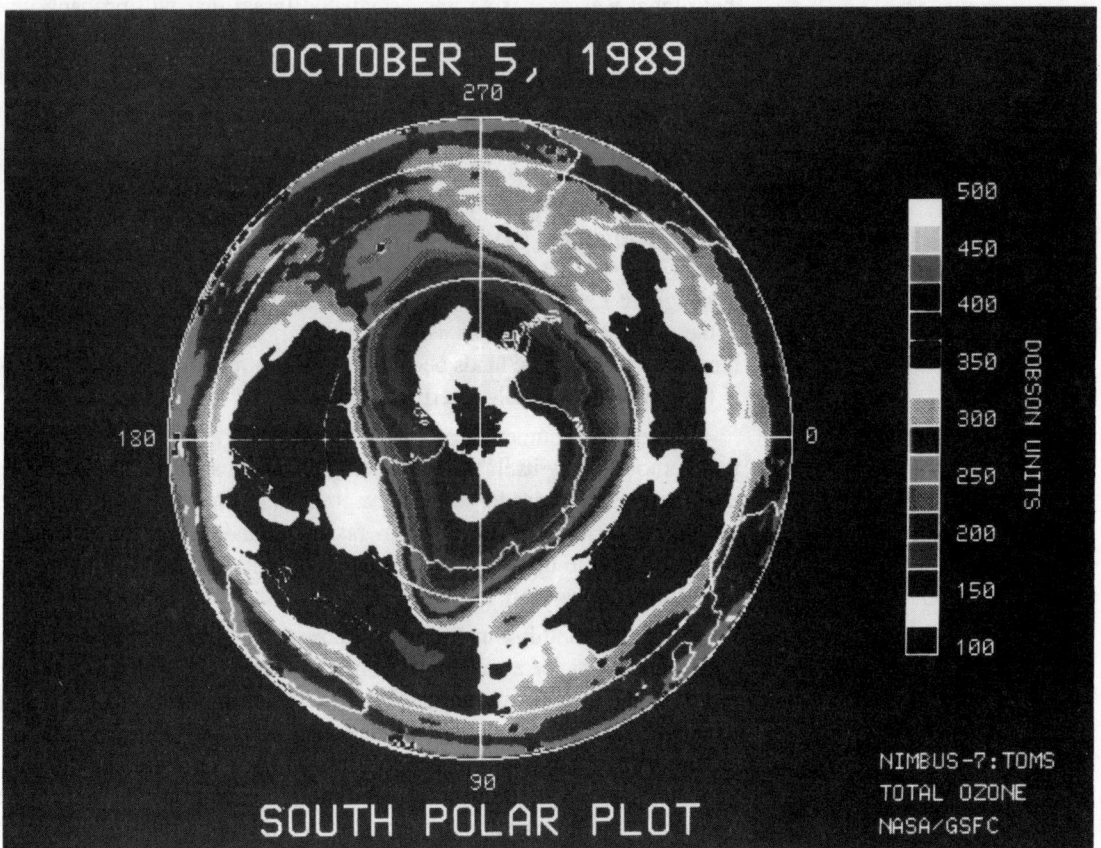

In 1989 it was discovered that a hole in the ozone layer had developed over Antarctica.

Supporters of Future 1—Standing Up for Human Rights and Democracy—may focus on environmental problems that threaten the legitimacy of fragile democratic regimes. For instance, global warming may promote the growth of deserts (desertification) in Africa, droughts and lowland flooding in Asia, and other weather changes that would disrupt agriculture and social structures. Ozone depletion may allow more harmful radiation to reach earth, degrading plant growth both on land and at sea. Such disruptions may create human hardship and contribute to political instability. They may even undermine popular support for democracy and increase the appeal of demagogues with simple answers. Problems in a neighboring country may also lead to an inflow of "environmental refugees" who would further challenge a country's ability to provide adequate services. In this view, the United States should respond to environmental threats both through international cooperation as appropriate, and through special aid to fragile democracies.

However, other Future 1 supporters may doubt that many of these environmental consequences will occur. For example, they may think that global warming is an unsubstantiated threat that will probably not emerge.

Supporters of Future 1 may also argue that ecological threats often stem from authoritarian regimes. In the former Soviet Union and Eastern Europe, entire regions suffer the ill effects of toxic waste dumping and other government-sanctioned pollution. Saddam Hussein's burning of Kuwaiti oil wells during the Gulf War produced horrendous pollution and gave rise to a new term, "ecological terrorism." Elsewhere, environmental abuses are closely linked with privations of human rights. Throughout Latin America and Africa, rain forests are being decimated at the expense of the people who live in them. In many countries wealthy landowners overgraze lands because they can afford to, while the poor—if they have land at all—overuse it because they see no alternative.

Given environmental problems in all countries, no one can claim that democracy by itself leads to ecological responsibility. Nevertheless, democracies do seem to be more responsive to pressures to protect the environment. Also, when governments enact land reform programs that distribute land to the poor, the new owners generally have a larger stake in preserving the land.

Certainly nothing in Future 1 opposes unilateral actions to protect the environment, or even a wide range of international cooperation. Yet Future 1 supporters may balk at close cooperation with (and especially aid to) authoritarian regimes, particularly if this mutes U.S. criticisms of human rights violations. Moreover, if protecting or restoring the environment is costly, these efforts may detract from other expensive economic programs intended to support democratic regimes or to advance human rights. Such trade-offs would be especially significant to those who doubt the seriousness of potential environmental hazards.

Supporters of Future 2—Charting a Stable Course—may also worry about local instabilities caused by environmental degradation, but their focus would be on how instability can harm relations between countries in various regions. For instance, many Middle Eastern countries have bitterly contested the use of rivers that flow between them. In such regions, water is a precious commodity. Desertification, global warming, water pollution, and rapid population growth may all exacerbate this problem and make war more likely. In other regions, droughts and famine may create environmental refugees, increasing tensions between countries. Both sets of problems would be particularly acute if accompanied by the spread of nuclear weapons. While most Future 2 supporters would agree that water shortages are an important source of conflict, especially in the Middle East, not all of them believe that the problem will be exacerbated by "global warming."

Future 2 supporters may emphasize that political instability is likely to exacerbate environmental degradation. Again, Iraq's 1991 burning of Kuwaiti oil wells and creation of a huge oil spill in the Persian Gulf is one example. Civil and regional wars in Africa have also created refugees who tax the ability of their new habitat to sustain them.

For Future 2 supporters who give a high priority to environmental issues, solutions would probably focus on cooperation among U.S. allies—most of which are advanced industrial states and major sources of some pollutants. They would also say that U.S. leadership on environmental issues (such as resolving disputes over water) will improve the prospect of environmental cooperation among its allies, and perhaps by other countries as well.

Other Future 2 advocates may give higher priority to different issues, like supporting the economic and military strength of allies. For them, potential economic costs of restoring the environment would compete with other important uses for funds.

Supporters of Future 3—Cooperating Globally—are most likely to cite ecological threats as an argument for their own position. Environmental degradation anywhere can affect the entire world: acid rain and ozone depletion do not respect borders. Yet Future 3 supporters do not have to consider ecological threats urgent. There are many other plausible rationales for backing Future 3, and other threats may take higher priority.

Consistent with the beliefs underlying Future 3, two sources of environmental problems are likely to receive special attention. One arises from the anarchic structure of the international system: so long as no international authority exists that can compel countries to cooperate, individual countries hesitate to exercise self-restraint if other countries can gain economic advantages by not adopting a similar policy.

To overcome this obstacle to multinational cooperation, regional and international agreements may be necessary. International institutions like the United Nations Environmental Programme can help, by monitoring and publicizing environmental conditions and countries' environmental policies. To ensure significant changes in national policies, agreements should be binding, specific, and enforceable; countries that violate these agreements should be punished, to deter other potential offenders. However, countries often resist such agreements, precisely because they impose definite limits on national freedom of action. Some Future 3 supporters believe that the benefits of binding agreements outweigh the costs; others believe that voluntary compliance is adequate.

The second source of problems is a set of economic, social, and political factors that cause environmental damage (some of which were discussed in Future 1). Cooperation on these issues may serve to reduce environmental damage and to advance other Future 3 objectives, such as improving the standards of living for the world's people and enhancing their social and political rights. Cooperation may not be forthcoming on all of these issues, however, as many governments may feel threatened by proposed reforms.

Yet some supporters might feel differently, considering environmental threats less important, especially when trade-offs are involved. For instance, some solutions to environmental problems are likely to be expensive, at least in the short term. Funds used for this purpose would then be unavailable for other tasks such as international peacekeeping operations. Finally, there is nothing inherent in Future 3 that precludes unilateral actions to help control environmental degradation.

Supporters of Future 4—Building U.S. Economic Strength—are likely to see economic challenges as more threatening to U.S. interests than ecological problems. However, supporters may easily disagree about the seriousness of environmental threats, their cause, and what the United States should do.

Future 4 advocates may be very skeptical of calls for international cooperation on environmental issues, especially collaborative efforts that involve economic costs and the surrender of some sovereignty. Then again, if that is necessary to serve U.S. interests, they may endorse close cooperation.

This Future calls for ending U.S. military commitments to other countries and rebuilding the U.S. economy, but it does not require the United States to ignore problems that are truly global in scope. Some practices, moreover, serve both ecological and economic ends. Recycling and improving insulation on buildings, for instance, increase efficiency and thus promote sustainable economic growth. Because military bases are common sources of toxic wastes, a military cutback may also reduce such environmental threats.

For Future 4 supporters who worry about global warming, this Future's objective of energy self-sufficiency may reduce U.S. production of CO_2—the major "greenhouse gas." CO_2 reductions may occur if the energy strategy reduces reliance on fossil fuels (including oil, coal, and natural gas), and instead concentrates on the development of alternative sources of energy, conservation, and additional measures to improve energy efficiency. Such unilateral steps, if seriously pursued, may also increase the feasibility of cooperative arrangements to reduce CO_2 emissions.

In short, the ecological debate evokes difficult questions of value, but not necessarily the same ones evoked by the Futures. In creating your own Future 5, you will have to decide for yourself whether and where to place this issue.

Sizing Up the Futures

This chapter shows that the Futures framework can illuminate complex policy debates. The four Futures, each of which highlights a distinctive set of assumptions and value priorities, raise important questions that one might not consider without them. The framework can be applied to many other issues besides those considered here.

However, the Futures do not answer every question, or organize all ideas on complex issues. Sometimes supporters of a given Future may disagree on a specific policy, or supporters of different Futures may agree on a policy. Many issues have more complexities, or depend on contrasting assumptions, than the four Futures present. This illustrates a limitation of the framework. Yet it also suggests grounds for agreement on specific policies among people who disagree on broad policy directions. Thus the framework can help us explore key points both of disagreement and of agreement.

Next, you will review key points of disagreement among the Futures. Then you will complete a questionnaire assessing your considered beliefs and value priorities as well as the four Futures themselves. Because every Future has evident strengths and weaknesses, you may question the value of choosing any one of them. However, choosing among imperfect alternatives is not just an intellectual exercise, but a common necessity in the real world. If being forced to choose from just four broad directions seems artificial, consider that in most policy discussions only two or three options are actively considered. Moreover, policies presented as moderate positions or as compromise positions sometimes contain contradictory elements, or fail to address the most difficult policy questions. Later, when you formulate your own preferred Future, you will probably have to accept some costs and risks that you would rather avoid, just as the four Futures do. Nevertheless, your Future can present reasoned, attainable goals that serve U.S. interests and values, and policies that advance these goals at minimal costs and risks.

THE FOUR FUTURES COMPARED

	FUTURE 1 Standing Up for Human Rights and Democracy	FUTURE 2 Charting a Stable Course	FUTURE 3 Cooperating Globally	FUTURE 4 Building U.S. Economic Strength
The Nature of International Relations	A struggle for power between democratic and despotic states dominates international relations.	Anarchy and power politics dominate international relations. Every state must defend itself, even if this means endangering others.	Interdependence dominates international relations. States share mutual interests and face common threats that outweigh their rivalries.	Economic rivalries dominate the post–Cold War era. In this environment, economic strength is much more important than military strength.
Greatest Threats	Dictatorships pose a military threat to democratic states (as well as to each other). This threat to peace will endure as long as despotic governments exist. The United States must lead a powerful coalition of democratic states committed to each other's defense. To ensure long-term peace, it must work to spread democracy around the world.	Power imbalances, especially in times of political uncertainty and instability, are a major cause of war. These wars can threaten U.S. interests even if the United States is not attacked directly. The United States must play a balancing role around the globe. This means opposing states bent on regional dominance, and promoting political and military agreements to keep the peace.	The preeminent threats—wars and violent ethnic conflicts, famine and poverty, refugees, disease, environmental damage, terrorism, and drug trafficking—transcend state borders. To counter these threats, the United States must cooperate extensively with other states through the United Nations and other organizations.	For the United States, the preeminent threats are not military but economic. The country faces a loss of economic competitiveness and a decline in the living standards of its people. Also, its policy of establishing defense commitments and intervening militarily around the globe is unnecessary and dangerous. To counter these threats, the United States must sharply reduce its military spending and forces abroad and concentrate on rebuilding its economic strength.
Value Priorities	The United States must consistently promote democracy and human rights for all people. These principles should take precedence over "stability." They should not be diluted by standards reflecting only what the international community can agree upon, nor should the United States ignore its commitments to humanity by turning inward.	The United States pragmatically considers hard realities and the necessary actions they require. U.S. interests demand participation in alliances, even if sometimes the United States' allies are non-democratic or violate U.S. human rights standards. Efforts to impose U.S. values everywhere can backfire, undermining stability and harming U.S. interests.	The United States has no right to impose its values on others unilaterally, and may not always get its way in international organizations. To make effective cooperation possible, the United States must accept some compromises and increase payments and support to international organizations.	For the United States, putting its own house in order must take priority over keeping the peace in distant lands or imposing democracy and human rights abroad. The United States encourages the spread of democracy and respect for human rights, but it has no business imposing these values on others. U.S. leadership comes from the force of example.
Critiques of Past Policy	Sometimes the United States has been too quick to cooperate with dictators and un-democratic forces as the "lesser of two evils." At other times it has been naive and ineffectual in its response to tyrannical, aggressive states and movements.	Sometimes the United States has "taken sides" in a regional conflict when a more neutral, mediating policy would better assure peace and stability. At other times moral qualms or indecision have led the United States to a passive policy in which it abrogates its crucial balancing role.	Sometimes the United States has downplayed emerging transnational concerns such as developing-country debt and global warming. At other times it has played too assertive a "leadership role" in circumstances where greater international cooperation would have been preferable.	Sometimes the United States has allowed its economy to suffer while it built expensive weapons systems with too little regard for how they could be used or even if they would work. At other times the United States has become entangled in regional wars that a more prudent policy could have avoided.

THE FOUR FUTURES COMPARED

	FUTURE 1 Standing Up for Human Rights and Democracy	FUTURE 2 Charting a Stable Course	FUTURE 3 Cooperating Globally	FUTURE 4 Building U.S. Economic Strength
Allies	The United States should maintain strong alliances with other democracies and keep U.S. troops in strategic locations around the world. It should avoid close ties to un-democratic governments and movements.	The United States should maintain or form alliances with any states that share its commitment to stability and regional balance of power. U.S. allies should share the cost and risks of maintaining stability, and the United States should share control over alliance policy.	The United States should work toward broad cooperative coalitions rather than narrow alliance commitments. Working with the United Nations and other international organizations, it should promote peace—and oppose aggression—as part of a multinational group.	The United States should phase out its overseas alliance commitments: they increase the risk of war and strain the U.S. economy.
Military Intervention	The United States should intervene, unilaterally if necessary, on behalf of any democracy attacked by a dictatorship, and fight until the dictator is overthrown. This will allow democratic elements to take over. The United States should also consider intervention to prevent dictators from acquiring weapons of mass destruction, promoting terrorism and drug trafficking, or murdering large numbers of their own people.	The United States should intervene militarily when necessary to defend its allies against attack. It should also consider deploying forces to maintain a military balance in unstable regions.	As global cooperation grows stronger, the United States will no longer need to intervene unilaterally. The United States should support the creation of multinational forces (including U.S. troops) to keep the peace or, if necessary, oppose any aggression.	The United States should redesign its military forces to defend only North America. It should also maintain a small rescue force that could intervene around the world where American lives are at stake, but it should not maintain a larger "Rapid Deployment Force" able to intervene in regional conflicts.
Aid and Trade	The United States should offer military aid to democracies threatened by their neighbors, and economic aid to developing democracies like those in Eastern Europe. It should trade freely with democracies, but trade selectively with—or embargo outright—non-democratic governments. It should sell weapons only to democratic governments.	The United States should provide economic and military aid as appropriate to foster regional power balances. It should trade freely with all states—both democratic and non-democratic—provided that they do not threaten regional stability. It should support agreements to limit armaments and arms transfers, if this will enhance regional military balances.	The United States should support international aid programs for developing countries, as well as other cooperative programs. It should trade freely with all countries, unless they have been placed under international embargo. Mutual trade restrictions that serve common needs, such as environmental protection, would be acceptable. U.S. military aid and trade should be limited by an international treaty binding on all major arms suppliers.	The United States should eliminate military aid and reduce economic aid. The top priority for our economic aid should be programs that directly serve U.S. interests, and what is left over can serve humanitarian and ideological goals. The United States should trade with all countries in whatever manner serves its interests, be it a policy of free trade or some variety of protectionism.

CHAPTER 7

Focusing Your Thoughts

Answering the following questions will help you to focus your thoughts before you express your preference among the Futures or begin to forge your own Future. These questions fall into five categories: threats to U.S. security and prosperity; fundamental assumptions about how the world works; fundamental values and priorities; policy proposals and trade-offs; and, finally, the four Futures. Since every important issue may not be raised and some of the questions defy simple answers, jot down notes for yourself about issues you want to consider and questions you may usefully refine.

Threats to U.S. National Interests

Experts agree that there is a wide range of threats to U.S. national interests. They disagree, however, on which are most important, and on how to counter them. In this section, we ask you to weigh the importance of various threats as policy concerns over the next several decades. In other words, which of these threats should U.S. policy focus on? Keep in mind that the greatest policy concerns may not be the most likely threats; even a relatively unlikely threat may be so dangerous that we must move to address it. Also, some threats may not be policy priorities because they are extremely unlikely, may be easy to prevent, or are impossible to counter at an acceptable cost.

Classify the threats as follows:

URGENT: a threat that seems likely to cause great harm to the United States unless the United States takes immediate and concentrated action to prevent it.

CENTRAL: a threat that can cause great harm, and hence which requires considerable action to counter, but is not sufficiently likely, dangerous, or imminent to be an urgent priority.

MODERATE: a significant threat requiring some policy attention, but a lower priority than the urgent and central threats because it is less likely, less dangerous, or less imminent.

MINOR: a threat that should be paid some, but not very much, attention in U.S. policy-making compared to the others, because it is easily countered or not very dangerous.

NO THREAT: although some analysts may consider this a threat, they are mistaken; no danger is presented, so no policy response is required.

Possible Threats

	Urgent	Central	Moderate	Minor	No Threat
1. Economic weakness in Eastern Europe and the Soviet Union will undermine West European economies and U.S. trade relations.	1	2	3	4	5
2. The United States will be dragged into wars because of its alliances and the presence of its troops around the world.	1	2	3	4	5
3. Political upheaval in the former Soviet Union and Eastern Europe will lead to explosive civil or regional wars that will harm important U.S. allies or other vital U.S. interests.	1	2	3	4	5
4. Terrorist groups and outlaw countries will threaten to use nuclear weapons against the United States.	1	2	3	4	5
5. Nuclear weapons in the former Soviet Union will fall into the hands of irresponsible leaders, threatening the United States or its allies.	1	2	3	4	5
6. Economic disorder in the former Soviet Union will cause nuclear proliferation, because unemployed nuclear and missile scientists are desperate for work anywhere.	1	2	3	4	5
7. The spread of economic protectionism will harm U.S. prosperity by weakening trade relationships.	1	2	3	4	5
8. Japan will gain economic dominance over the United States.	1	2	3	4	5
9. A single country will control the flow of Middle East oil, threatening the world economy and hence U.S. prosperity.	1	2	3	4	5
10. International drug trafficking will further undermine U.S. society.	1	2	3	4	5
11. Dictatorial governments around the world will undermine U.S. security by conquering other countries, and by engaging in terrorism and drug trafficking.	1	2	3	4	5
12. Environmental threats will spiral out of control because the United States and other countries fail to cooperate.	1	2	3	4	5

	Urgent	Central	Moderate	Minor	No Threat
13. The United States' economic weakness will undermine its power and influence in the world.	1	2	3	4	5
14. One country, such as a united Germany or Russia, will conquer or otherwise dominate all of Europe—threatening U.S. security and prosperity.	1	2	3	4	5
15. Domestic problems—such as budget deficits, poverty, crime, drugs, AIDS, and poor education—will ruin the U.S. way of life.	1	2	3	4	5

Fundamental Assumptions

Your views on these issues will greatly influence the direction you think U.S. policy should take. For each of the following statements, indicate whether you agree or disagree, and how strongly.

	Strongly Agree	Somewhat Agree	Somewhat Disagree	Strongly Disagree	Unsure
1. International politics is primarily a struggle between aggressive dictatorships and non-aggressive democracies.	1	2	3	4	5
2. The United States can have a principled foreign policy without sacrificing its major national interests.	1	2	3	4	5
3. The United States will always have to compete with the world's other countries for power.	1	2	3	4	5
4. If all countries on earth were democracies, wars would still occur.	1	2	3	4	5
5. Power imbalances around the globe threaten world peace and U.S. interests.	1	2	3	4	5
6. The United States needs military strength to defend vital interests in Europe and the Middle East.	1	2	3	4	5
7. Because of its nuclear arsenal, the United States can defend its vital interests, no matter what happens in the rest of the world.	1	2	3	4	5

		Strongly Agree	Somewhat Agree	Somewhat Disagree	Strongly Disagree	Unsure
8.	Since the world's major economic, military, and environmental problems transcend borders, to solve these problems the international community must create strong organizations to reach—and enforce—agreements.	1	2	3	4	5
9.	U.S. economic strength depends on an international environment that encourages free trade and investment.	1	2	3	4	5
10.	States, not transnational and subnational organizations and groups, will continue to be the world's most important actors.	1	2	3	4	5
11.	The United States will be more secure if it strives to establish mutual security arrangements that make all countries safer.	1	2	3	4	5
12.	Major countries will never surrender any real power to international organizations.	1	2	3	4	5
13.	In the long run, helping other countries to solve their economic problems makes the United States safer and gives it better trade and investment opportunities.	1	2	3	4	5
14.	U.S. military and economic aid to other countries is rarely worth its cost to the United States.	1	2	3	4	5
15.	It is possible to prevent or abolish war around the world by building a sense of global community and by strengthening international legal and peacekeeping institutions.	1	2	3	4	5
16.	It is better for the United States to have the world's strongest economy with a military capable only of protecting its homeland, than a military with decisive global reach but an economy less dynamic than Japan's or Germany's.	1	2	3	4	5
17.	A policy of political and military isolationism is more dangerous to the United States than one of alliance commitments.	1	2	3	4	5

	Strongly Agree	Somewhat Agree	Somewhat Disagree	Strongly Disagree	Unsure
18. Since nuclear weapons provide the United States with security at an affordable cost, complete nuclear disarmament is not in its national interest.	1	2	3	4	5
19. In foreign policy, economic power is becoming—or has become—more important than military strength.	1	2	3	4	5
20. The United States can effectively promote democracy and human rights abroad.	1	2	3	4	5
21. If the United States acts as the dominant country in the world, and especially if it tries to impose its values on repressive or dictatorial governments, other countries will join together to oppose U.S. power.	1	2	3	4	5

Fundamental Values

Your values and the priorities you assign them will also influence the direction you think U.S. policy should take. For each of the following questions, indicate whether you agree or disagree, and how strongly.

	Strongly Agree	Somewhat Agree	Somewhat Disagree	Strongly Disagree	Unsure
1. It is wrong for the United States to trade with governments that have poor human rights records, even if that trade benefits the U.S. economy.	1	2	3	4	5
2. Human rights, like the right to vote and freedom from governmental abuse, are universal values that the United States should strongly support everywhere.	1	2	3	4	5
3. The United States has a special obligation to help spread democracy around the world—even if that means interfering in the domestic affairs of other states.	1	2	3	4	5
4. Although the United States should support democracy where people have chosen it, the United States has no right to tell others how to live; it should not try to impose democratic values on dictatorships.	1	2	3	4	5

		Strongly Agree	Somewhat Agree	Somewhat Disagree	Strongly Disagree	Unsure
5.	Intervening on behalf of human rights and democracy is appropriate as long as the policy instruments are non-violent—such as moral suasion, political pressure, and economic sanctions. Military intervention and aid to armed rebels are not appropriate.	1	2	3	4	5
6.	Although the United States can offer economic incentives to countries that begin to adopt democratic practices, it has no right to coerce countries to reform using economic sanctions or any other means.	1	2	3	4	5
7.	The only justification for the United States interfering in the domestic affairs of another country is a UN call to action.	1	2	3	4	5
8.	Since all of humanity should be valued, not just Americans, the United States has responsibilities toward people in other countries as well as its own citizens.	1	2	3	4	5
9.	Fairness requires that the United States' share of international humanitarian and other collaborative projects be proportionate to its wealth (about a quarter of the world's GNP), rather than to its 5 percent share of the world's population. Other countries, including Japan and Germany, should follow the same principle.	1	2	3	4	5
10.	Fairness in trade relations means that no country, including the United States, should grant any of its producers unfair advantages in the international marketplace through mechanisms such as price subsidies, tariffs and quotas on competitors' products, or more subtle barriers to free trade.	1	2	3	4	5
11.	Americans should take the greatest pride in what the United States does to promote opportunity at home and to serve as a model of democracy to the world, not in its military power and global reach.	1	2	3	4	5
12.	The United States should not let citizens who served in the military and worked in defense industries suffer as a result of reduced military spending.	1	2	3	4	5

Policy Proposals and Trade-offs

Almost any policy will have advantages and disadvantages, risks and trade-offs. For each of the policies listed below, do you support or oppose the policy, considering both its long-term goals and immediate trade-offs?

	Strongly Support	Somewhat Support	Somewhat Oppose	Strongly Oppose	Unsure
1. The United States should actively promote human rights and democracy around the world, even if that requires expensive programs.	1	2	3	4	5
2. The United States should defend and advance both human rights and democracy abroad, even if it occasionally means going to war.	1	2	3	4	5
3. The United States should intervene on behalf of human rights and democracy abroad only as part of UN efforts, even if that means the UN will sometimes fail to act.	1	2	3	4	5
4. The United States should station troops on the territory of its allies to add credibility to its commitments, even if that keeps its military budget high.	1	2	3	4	5
5. The United States should require its allies to accept more of the costs and risks of maintaining alliances, even if that means the U.S. must share policy-making responsibilities and operational command.	1	2	3	4	5
6. The United States should focus on making the world a more stable place and keeping itself powerful, even if this means the United States must sometimes support governments that are undemocratic or that have poor human rights records.	1	2	3	4	5
7. The United States should strive to maintain an open international economic order, even if free trade policies cause unemployment in some U.S. industries.	1	2	3	4	5
8. The United States should protect American jobs by putting tariffs and quotas on imports, even if that means paying more for lower-quality U.S. goods.	1	2	3	4	5

	Strongly Support	Somewhat Support	Somewhat Oppose	Strongly Oppose	Unsure
9. If the UN takes a leadership role in opposing aggression, the United States should back its efforts, even if this means accepting costs and risks without total control over the policy.	1	2	3	4	5
10. If the UN fails to lead the response to international aggression, the United States should take the lead itself, even if it has to shoulder most of the responsibility and cost.	1	2	3	4	5
11. The United States should avoid taking world leadership positions, even if that means a coalition will not be built to deal with global and regional problems.	1	2	3	4	5
12. The United States should avoid interfering in the domestic affairs of other countries, even if their governments engage in flagrant human rights violations.	1	2	3	4	5
13. The United States should greatly reduce its military budget and channel the savings to strengthen its economy, even if that means it will no longer be able to use massive military strength around the world.	1	2	3	4	5
14. Part of any money saved through U.S. military budget reductions should be spent on retraining soldiers and defense plant workers who lose their jobs, even if this means less money is available for other purposes.	1	2	3	4	5
15. The United States should strive for energy self-sufficiency, even if that means enacting a large tax on gasoline to encourage energy conservation and to make non-polluting sources of energy more competitive economically.	1	2	3	4	5
16. The United States should strive for energy self-sufficiency, even if that means relying more on coal, nuclear energy, and oil drilled offshore and in wilderness areas.	1	2	3	4	5

	Strongly Support	Somewhat Support	Somewhat Oppose	Strongly Oppose	Unsure
17. The United States should lead international efforts to stop weapons sales to unstable regions, even if that means U.S. arms manufacturers will have to lay off workers.	1	2	3	4	5

The Four Futures

Now, consider each of the Futures:

FUTURE 1—Standing Up for Human Rights and Democracy   By 2005 the United States is following a principled foreign policy, defending and advancing human rights and democracy around the world. It is successfully using political pressures, economic incentives and sanctions, and occasionally military means to achieve these ends. The era of the dictator is ending, and the world is becoming a safer and more humane place for all.

	Very	Fairly	Not Very	Not At All
How desirable is this Future, if it is possible?	1	2	3	4
How likely is it that the United States can attain this Future?	1	2	3	4
How safe is it to attempt to reach this Future?	1	2	3	4

	Strongly Favor	Somewhat Favor	Somewhat Oppose	Strongly Oppose
OVERALL, do you favor or oppose adopting Future 1 as a U.S. policy goal?	1	2	3	4

FUTURE 2—Charting a Stable Course   By 2005 the United States is a major source of international stability and security. Its participation in alliances preserves regional balances of power and makes our competitive world a safer place. The United States' allies (not all of which are democratic) share the risks and costs of this task, and the United States shares control over alliance decisions. Aggressive countries are deterred from attacking their neighbors and upsetting the world economy, and other states feel no need to acquire nuclear weapons for protection.

	Very	Fairly	Not Very	Not At All
How desirable is this Future, if it is possible?	1	2	3	4
How likely is it that the United States can attain this Future?	1	2	3	4
How safe is it to attempt to reach this Future?	1	2	3	4

	Strongly Favor	Somewhat Favor	Somewhat Oppose	Strongly Oppose
OVERALL, do you favor or oppose adopting Future 2 as a U.S. policy goal?	1	2	3	4

FUTURE 3—Cooperating Globally By 2005 the United States is cooperating extensively with other countries to solve the many economic, military, and environmental problems that affect us all in an interdependent world. Instead of trying to police the world single-handedly, for example, the United States relies upon and assists the UN in its efforts to maintain peace. The United States increased its financial contributions to support peacekeeping and other international efforts. In working together to address common concerns, all states are becoming more secure and prosperous.

	Very	Fairly	Not Very	Not At All
How desirable is this Future, if it is possible?	1	2	3	4
How likely is it that the United States can attain this Future?	1	2	3	4
How safe is it to attempt to reach this Future?	1	2	3	4

	Strongly Favor	Somewhat Favor	Somewhat Oppose	Strongly Oppose
OVERALL, do you favor or oppose adopting Future 3 as a U.S. policy goal?	1	2	3	4

FUTURE 4—Building U.S. Economic Strength By 2005 the United States is much more competitive economically, having addressed its many domestic problems. It financed these efforts by cutting its military budget by two-thirds. The United States phased out all alliances except for those with Canada and Mexico and brought its troops home—thus ending unnecessary, costly, and dangerous commitments to other countries' security. Although it is no longer a military giant, the United States can still defend North America and citizens overseas. With renewed economic strength, it serves as an example of a vibrant, prosperous democracy.

	Very	Fairly	Not Very	Not At All
How desirable is this Future, if it is possible?	1	2	3	4
How likely is it that the United States can attain this Future?	1	2	3	4
How safe is it to attempt to reach this Future?	1	2	3	4

	Strongly Favor	Somewhat Favor	Somewhat Oppose	Strongly Oppose
OVERALL, do you favor or oppose adopting Future 4 as a U.S. policy goal?	1	2	3	4

Please Rank the Futures in Your Order of Preference as Actual Policy Goals (entailing specific policies, costs, and risks): "1" being your first choice, "4" being your last.

FUTURE 1—Standing Up for Human Rights and Democracy   _____

FUTURE 2—Charting a Stable Course   _____

FUTURE 3—Cooperating Globally   _____

FUTURE 4—Building U.S. Economic Strength   _____

CHAPTER 8

Crafting a Future Five

What Role Should the United States Play in the World?

You have considered four alternative Futures for the United States' role in the world. These Futures span a wide range of beliefs, values, and priorities. The chances are good that you did not entirely support any of the Futures, but rather saw important advantages, and important disadvantages, in all of them. Now it is your turn to construct your own Future 5, to reflect your personal beliefs and values—including any that you feel were not considered by the four Futures. Your job is to explain what direction you think the United States should take in the future.

Your preferred direction for U.S. foreign policy may resemble one of the four Futures, or it may combine elements from several of them—as well as your own new ideas. You are not limited to presenting a single sketch of the world in the year 2005. You may want to suggest a series of goals to be accomplished in sequence, or to propose some alternative strategies depending on future events. Unfortunately, no matter how sophisticated your Future is, it will not be foolproof. Any Future must inevitably accept some trade-offs, uncertainties, and risks. It is your responsibility to think critically about how feasible your Future is, how much risk it entails, and what options will be available to the United States if the Future does not proceed as planned.

The Structure of a Future

Your Future should contain four essential parts, though you may present each section in any manner you choose.

1. State the Future's goals for the year 2005 and briefly explain why these goals are most important. The year 2005 was selected because it is far enough in the future to permit important gradual changes, yet close enough to the present to allow plausible projections. Also, writing from the perspective of the future encourages you to focus on long-term goals and not be overly

concerned with contemporary issues (such as the recession of the early 1990s). You may prefer to choose some other year, or specify some goals for the year 2005 and others for a later year such as 2010 or 2015. Your time frame should be long enough to formulate long-term goals, but not so long that reasonable assumptions are impossible.

2. Identify the underlying beliefs for your Future. Your analysis should clarify the key threats and opportunities that you think will challenge the United States in 2005. Be sure to state your assumptions about the nature of the international environment. If several threats are likely, state and justify your priority of concerns. Given these assumptions, describe and explain the objectives that will best serve U.S. interests. Being explicit about your assumptions may seem artificial, but it helps you to establish the differences between your views and the ones presented in other Futures.

3. Discuss the values that are reflected in your preferred Future. Clarify and justify your priority of values, and explain how these priorities affect your policy preferences. Keep in mind that you can give preference to one value without totally ignoring another. Focusing on the ideas in Futures 1 and 4, for example, one way to give priority to solving U.S. domestic problems over promoting democracy abroad is to reduce the military budget, reallocate most of the savings to domestic programs, but spend some of the funds to bolster new, fragile democracies. An "either/or" approach, which of course is possible, would involve spending no funds on foreign aid—even in collaboration with other donor countries.

    Don't simply combine sentences and paragraphs from the various Futures and the questionnaire. If you do, the resulting text will be choppy and probably hide contradictions and trade-offs. Instead, after careful consideration of the competing ideas, make informed judgments and use prose that reflects what you really think. Use phrases such as "I believe . . ." or "The United States' top priority should be. . . ." Avoid broad statements like "Americans believe . . . ," although you can refer to public opinion data if it is properly qualified.

4. Summarize your short-term policy recommendations—some of the things the United States should do during the 1990s to help bring about your Future. Expressing opinions on several current foreign policy controversies will also serve to liven up your essay. Since your essay reflects what *you* think, do not use an inappropriate phrase from the Futures such as "supporters do not have to endorse all policies listed."

These four elements form the basic structure of the Future, but other elements are essential to make your argument convincing. For example, give your Future a title that reflects the thrust of the role you prescribe. Somewhere you should also consider the economic consequences of your

Future. In key places you should offer an honest examination of the evidence as you support your views and proposals. This is in contrast to the advocacy thrust of the four Futures, which tend to cite only supportive evidence. Though you are advocating a Future, your case will be stronger if you demonstrate analysis, with systematic as opposed to anecdotal use of evidence. You will be more credible if you show that you recognize not only the trade-offs and risks involved in your Future, but also counterarguments and some conflicting evidence used to support them. Then explain why you disagree with these arguments, how your Future deals with them, or why you believe they are outweighed by the arguments for the Future.

Finally, if you believe some important uncertainties exist, acknowledge them. If appropriate, you may speculate about how one development or another will affect your conclusions. You may also offer suggestions for further research that might help to refine your policy ends and means.

Some Criteria for Feasibility

You will be most convincing if you demonstrate that your Future is not only desirable but also feasible. Two essays may propose the same goals and direction for U.S. foreign policy, for example, but a reader will be more impressed with the one that acknowledges obstacles to change and devises a realistic strategy for overcoming the obstacles. To help you construct a Future that is feasible, the following eight criteria can be applied to any proposal for a fifth Future.

1. The United States cannot change the world overnight. It is unrealistic, for example, to envision a meeting of world leaders that instantly leads to a decision to establish a world government. While it may be true that an attack from outer space would unite the planet's countries, it is not in our power to arrange one. In the same vein, we cannot count on inventing some technical solution that will make us totally immune from all environmental degradation. Even narrower objectives, such as strengthening the economic foundations of new democratic states, will take some time.

2. For some goals, more time may not help. If a desirable goal is not immediately possible, it is tempting to say, "Well, in the long run we can do it." However, time does not solve all problems or even make all problems easier. To return to the example of world government, some observers argue that such a government should be phased in over a number of years, with every country slowly yielding more and more power to a global authority. Skeptics say that no country is likely to concede power to an

international body—even in phases—if that means risking its own interests. Thus, tiny concessions that look like steps in the right direction may actually lead nowhere at all. Of course, many important changes do happen gradually over time, skepticism notwithstanding. Thus, if you propose a step-by-step process for any goal, you should explain how the steps will help achieve the goal.

3. Beware of the argument that "it is necessary, so it is possible." Some people argue that all countries must cooperate intensively now to prevent a global ecological disaster. Even if they are right, there is no guarantee that their recommendations for joint action will win out. As we have seen, environmental cooperation faces serious political obstacles. For instance, no country wants to make economic sacrifices while others refuse or delay, thus gaining a competitive advantage. You are invited, of course, to devise plausible strategies for overcoming such obstacles.

4. Big projects cost big money. The United States has had budget deficits of well over $100 billion every year since 1982, and it has had large trade deficits for even longer. Experts differ on the significance of these deficits, but all agree that the government cannot afford to spend money on everything it would like to. For instance, it would be difficult to fund a massive U.S. foreign aid program to support new democracies or to create regional stability, and to invest massive amounts to strengthen the United States' economic infrastructure. With scarce resources, you must accept limits on some—if not all—of the programs you would otherwise wholeheartedly support. If you believe that some international programs are vital, however, you may think about the benefits and trade-offs of sharing the burdens with other countries.

5. U.S. plans must take other countries into account. Any course of action the United States follows will affect the rest of the world in some way. For example, the security of allies or other countries may increase or decrease, or the amount of aid to countries may be altered. Moreover, the United States cannot automatically count on other countries' cooperation. Other countries may oppose some U.S. policy proposals or goals, or may follow policies contrary to U.S. interests. Although you may decide that the reactions of other countries do not affect your proposals, you should consider their possible reactions carefully before deciding. Somewhere in your paper you may also want to include some fallback positions: what you intend to do if, for example, other countries respond differently than you hope.

6. The United States cannot at the same time threaten a country and cooperate intimately with it. Thus we should not expect a country to become an ally or cooperate closely with our environmental initiatives while at the same time we are pressuring that country, through economic sanctions or military operations, to become democratic. If your Future involves elements of both competition

and cooperation, you should carefully consider which is a higher priority.

7. If you give high priority to some threats, consider possible dangers of dismissing others. For instance, if you believe the threat posed by environmental degradation is central but the threat posed by non-democratic states is also serious, you cannot focus on the environmental challenge and altogether ignore the threat of aggressive actions by despotic regimes. If you believe that both threats are real and important, you must deal in some way with both of them, even if you conclude that you will have to accept some risks in coping with one or the other (or quite possibly with both). The same is true for other threats the United States faces: while you can judge that some threats are unlikely to develop or will pose only moderate costs if they materialize, you cannot simply prioritize them out of existence.

You may find crafting a Future Five more difficult than it seems at first. After all, if it were easy to identify and address emergent threats to the United States, the policymakers would have formulated a foolproof strategy by now. You may enjoy working out plausible solutions to some of the challenges facing the United States in the post–Cold War world. The more difficult the questions you ask yourself about the desirability, feasibility, trade-offs, costs, risks, and uncertainties of your Future, the better and more convincing your product will be, and the more your understanding of the issues will increase.

You do not have to reach a definitive conclusion on the role of the United States in the world. Your consideration of the various Futures, including your own, may raise as many questions as it answers. Even if you are reasonably comfortable with your conclusions, keep an open mind as you learn more and the world itself continues to change.

Resources

T here are many excellent books that cover the main themes of this text, and hundreds more focus on specific issues. The selected bibliography below suggests some well-respected books that can provide background information, varied viewpoints, and further references. Periodicals are also useful, and some key ones are listed. (To avoid duplication, not included here are sources for the sidebars accompanying the four Futures, and the material cited in endnotes.) Finally, several organizations with useful resources are described.

The History of U.S. Foreign Policy

Stephen E. Ambrose. *Rise to Globalism: American Foreign Policy Since 1938*. Sixth Revised Edition. New York: Penguin Books, 1991.

Felix Gilbert. *To The Farewell Address: Ideas of Early American Foreign Policy*. Princeton, NJ: Princeton University Press, 1970.

Robert C. Hilderbrand. *Power and the People: Executive Management of Public Opinion in Foreign Affairs, 1897–1921*. Chapel Hill: University of North Carolina Press, 1981.

George Kennan. *American Diplomacy 1900–1950*. Chicago: University of Chicago Press, 1951.

Thomas G. Paterson, ed. *Cold War Critics: Alternatives to American Foreign Policy in the Truman Years*. Chicago: Quadrangle Books, 1971.

Thomas G. Paterson, ed. *Major Problems in American Foreign Policy: Documents and Essays. Volume I: To 1914; Volume II: Since 1914*. Third Edition. Lexington, MA: D. C. Heath Company, 1989.

John Spanier. *American Foreign Policy Since World War II*. Twelfth Edition, revised. Washington, DC: Congressional Quarterly Press, 1992.

Challenges Facing the United States

Graham Allison and Gregory F. Treverton, eds. *Rethinking America's Security*. New York: Norton, 1992.

Robert J. Art and Robert Jervis, eds. *International Politics: Enduring Concepts and Contemporary Issues.* Third Edition. New York: Harper-Collins Publishers, 1992.

Jeffrey T. Bergner. *The New Superpowers: Germany, Japan, the U.S. and the New World Order.* New York: St. Martin's Press, 1991.

Michael T. Clark and Simon Serfaty, eds. *New Thinking and Old Realities: America, Europe, and Russia.* Washington, DC: Seven Locks Press, 1992.

Helen Fein, ed. *Genocide Watch.* New Haven, CT: Yale University Press, 1992.

David Fischer. *Stopping the Spread of Nuclear Weapons: The Past and the Prospects.* New York: Routledge, 1992.

Graham E. Fuller. *The Democracy Trap: Perils of the Post–Cold War World.* New York: Dutton, 1991.

Senator Al Gore. *Earth in the Balance: Ecology and the Human Spirit.* Boston: Houghton Mifflin, 1992.

Owen Harries, ed. *America's Purpose: Visions of U.S. Foreign Policy.* San Francisco: ICS Press, 1991.

Charles W. Kegley, Jr., ed. *International Terrorism: Characteristics, Causes, Controls.* New York: St. Martin's Press, 1990.

Charles W. Kegley, Jr., and Eugene R. Wittkopf, eds. *The Future of American Foreign Policy.* New York: St. Martin's Press, 1992.

Geoffrey Kemp. *The Control of the Middle East Arms Race.* Washington: Carnegie Endowment for International Peace, 1991.

Robert O. Keohane and Joseph S. Nye. *Power and Interdependence.* Second Edition. Boston: Scott, Foresman and Company, 1989.

Sean M. Lynn-Jones and Steven E. Miller, eds. *America's Strategy in a Changing World.* Cambridge, MA: MIT Press, 1992.

Joshua Muravchik. *Exporting Democracy: Fulfilling America's Destiny* (Washington, DC: American Enterprise Press, 1991).

Kenneth A. Oye, Robert J. Lieber, and Donald Rothchild, eds., *Eagle in a New World: American Grand Strategy in the Post–Cold War Era.* New York: HarperCollins, 1992.

Rene Schwok. *U.S.-EC Relations in the Post–Cold War Era.* Boulder, CO: Westview Press, 1991.

Richard Smoke and Andrei Kortunov, eds. *Mutual Security: A New Approach to Soviet-American Relations.* New York: St. Martin's Press, 1991.

Gregory Treverton. *America, Germany, and the Future of Europe.* Princeton, NJ: Princeton University Press, 1992.

Stephen W. Young, Ronald J. Bee, and Bruce Seymore II. *One Nation Becomes Many: The ACCESS Guide to the Former Soviet Union.* Washington, DC: ACCESS, 1992.

Domestic Sources of U.S. Foreign Policy

Cecil V. Crabb, Jr., and Pat M. Holt. *Invitation to Struggle: Congress, the President, and Foreign Policy.* Fourth Edition. Washington, DC: Congressional Quarterly Press, 1992.

Roger Hilsman. *The Politics of Policy Making in Defense and Foreign Affairs: Conceptual Models and Bureaucratic Politics.* Englewood Cliffs, NJ: Prentice Hall, 1987.

Charles W. Kegley, Jr., and Eugene R. Wittkopf. *American Foreign Policy: Pattern and Process.* Fourth Edition. New York: St. Martin's Press, 1991.

Charles W. Kegley, Jr., and Eugene R. Wittkopf, eds. *The Domestic Sources of American Foreign Policy: Insights and Evidence.* New York: St. Martin's Press, 1988.

John Lehman. *Making War: The 200-Year-Old Battle Between President and Congress Over the Way America Goes to War.* New York: Scribner's, 1992.

James M. McCormick. *American Foreign Policy and Process.* Second Edition. Itasca, IL: F. E. Peacock Publishers, 1992.

James A. Nathan and James K. Oliver. *Foreign Policy Making and the American Political System.* Second Edition. Boston: Little, Brown and Company, 1987.

John Spanier & Eric M. Uslaner. *American Foreign Policy Making and the Democratic Dilemmas.* Fifth Edition. Pacific Grove, CA: Brooks/ Cole Publishing Company, 1989.

Robert A. Strong. *Decisions and Dilemmas: Case Studies in Presidential Foreign Policy Making.* Englewood Cliffs, NJ: Prentice Hall, 1991.

Daniel Yankelovich. *Coming to Public Judgment: Making Democracy Work in a Complex World.* Syracuse, NY: Syracuse University Press, 1991.

Key Periodicals

Useful periodicals on international relations and foreign policy include *Bulletin of the Atomic Scientists, Foreign Affairs, Foreign Policy, International Security, Orbis, The National Interest, World Policy Journal,* and *World Politics.* All of these are excellent sources of current expert thought on challenges facing the United States and the U.S. role in the world. Newsmagazines such as *The Economist, Newsweek, Time,* and *U.S. News & World Report* can give helpful background on U.S. foreign policy debates. *World Press Review* contains excerpts from the international press. It shows what journalists from numerous countries think about world affairs, and it has regular sections on Eastern Europe, the former Soviet Union, the Middle East, and other regions. For the best information on events in other countries, a number of publications focus on specific regions; consult with your instructor, reference librarian, or a specialist in the field.

Other Resources

A Washington-based nonpartisan referral service called ACCESS can help you find information about international topics by putting you in touch with a range of organizations that work in the field of national security and international relations. In addition to providing assistance with individual inquiries, ACCESS publishes timely briefing papers and several useful guides and directories. For further information contact: ACCESS: A Security Information Service, 1730 M Street, NW, Suite 605, Washington, DC 20036. (800) 888-6033.

The nonpartisan Congressional Research Service publishes papers and reports on a wide range of U.S. policy issues, providing a wealth of detail that may be hard to find elsewhere. Often, if given adequate notice, your U.S. representative or senator will gladly obtain relevant reports for you.

Ballot: Policies and Trade-offs

The questions below are designed to gauge your ideas about three key aspects of U.S. foreign policy. By participating in this survey, you will be adding your voice to a nationwide poll of your peers. The results will be sent to interested policymakers and scholars.

Part I: *From the list below, circle what you think are the three most urgent threats facing the United States.*

    a.   Aggressive dictatorships.

    b.   One nation in a vital region getting too much power.

    c.   Conflicts in developing countries.

    d.   Conflicts in the former Soviet bloc.

    e.   Nuclear, biological, and chemical weapons proliferation.

    f.   Loss of U.S. access to oil and other key resources abroad.

    g.   Social and economic problems at home.

    h.   Global problems such as environmental damage and AIDS.

    i.   Loss of economic competitiveness to Japan and other countries.

    j.   Terrorism.

Part II: *Policy decisions depend both on general priorities and on specific circumstances. The following questions explore your priorities. They ask for what purposes, if any, you would support employing U.S. troops, or giving economic assistance. Check the most appropriate category in each case.*

1. Should the United States use military force (either independently or under UN auspices) for the following purposes?	Usually/ Always	Occa- sionally	Rarely/ Never
a. To defend democratic governments.	_____	_____	_____
b. To stop aggression against any state, whether democratic or not.	_____	_____	_____
c. To protect crucial U.S. interests overseas, such as access to oil.	_____	_____	_____
d. To protect civilians from brutality at the hands of their own governments.	_____	_____	_____
e. To defend U.S. territory from military attack.	_____	_____	_____

2. Should the United States give economic aid to foreign countries for the following purposes?

	Usually/ Always	Occa- sionally	Rarely/ Never
a. To improve alliances with countries important to the United States.	_____	_____	_____
b. To help the poorest people in developing countries.	_____	_____	_____
c. To reduce environmental damage in developing countries.	_____	_____	_____
d. To help those countries that are trying to build democratic institutions.	_____	_____	_____

Part III: *Here are four courses of action that the United States could pursue over the next 10 years. Rank the courses of action 1 through 4, assigning 1 to the statement with which you most agree and 4 to the statement with which you least agree.*

_____ 1. The United States should give top priority to promoting and protecting human rights and democracy in all countries, even if this antagonizes governments with which it has friendly relations.

_____ 2. The United States should give top priority to protecting its own interests abroad, even if this means supporting governments that are undemocratic and do not support human rights.

_____ 3. The United States should give top priority to working with other countries through the United Nations, even if the United States has to sacrifice some of its sovereignty (giving up the right, for instance, to use military force abroad without UN approval).

_____ 4. The United States should greatly reduce its military budget and give top priority to domestic issues and improving its economic competitiveness, even if its economic and military withdrawal from weak, unstable countries and regions might set the stage for more wars in those regions.

The following information is requested for analysis purposes.

Freshman/Sophomore _____   Male _____   Female _____

Junior/Senior _____   Zip Code _____

Other _____

Please return this form to: Choices Project Poll, Center for Foreign Policy Development, Box 1948, Brown University, Providence, RI 02912.

Photo Credits